277 7310

# Bullfighting
## ART, TECHNIQUE
## & SPANISH SOCIETY

John McCormick

# Bullfighting
## ART, TECHNIQUE
## & SPANISH SOCIETY

with a new introduction and
postscript by the author

illustrated by Roberto Berdecio

**ta**

Transaction Publishers
New Brunswick (U.S.A.) and London (U.K.)

New material ths edition copyright © 1998 by Transaction Publishers, New Brunswick, New Jersey 08903.
Originally published in 1967 by The World Publishing Company, and by Weidenfeld and Nicolson.

Grateful acknowledgment is given for permission to reprint excerpts from these published works:

From *Love Lies Bleeding* by Peter Viertel. Copyright © 1964 by Peter Viertel. Reprinted by permission of Doubleday & Company, Inc.

From *The Sun Also Rises* by Ernest Hemingway. Copyright © 1954 by Ernest Hemingway. Reprinted by permission of Charles Scribner's Sons, Publishers.

From "The Undefeated," in *The Fifth Column and the First Forty-Nine Stories* by Ernest Hemingway. Copyright © 1938 by Ernest Hemingway. Reprinted by permission of Charles Scribner's Sons, Publishers.

This book is printed on acid-free paper that meets the American National Standard for Permanence of Paper for Printed Library Materials.

Library of Congress Catalog Number: 97–28425
ISBN: 1–56000–345–6
Printed in the United States of America

Library of Congress Cataloging-in-Publication Data

McCormick, John.
    Bullfighting : art, technique, and Spanish society / John McCormick ; with a new introduction and postscript by the author ; illustrated by Roberto Berdecio.
        p.   cm.
    Rev. ed of: The complete aficionado. 1967.
    Includes bibliographical references and index.
    ISBN 1–56000–345–6 (cloth : alk. paper)
    1. Bullfights—Spain. 2. Bullfighters. I. McCormick, John. Complete aficionado. II. Title.
GV1108.5.M42    1997
791.8'2'0946—dc21                                    97–28425
                                                                    CIP

*To the Memory of Paul Feeley: 1910–1966*

STARBUCK WAS NO CRUSADER AFTER PERILS; in him courage was not a sentiment; but a thing simply useful to him, and always at hand upon all mortally practical occasions. . . . For, thought Starbuck, I am here in this critical ocean to kill whales for my living, and not to be killed by them for theirs. . . .

HERMAN MELVILLE, *Moby Dick*

. . . JE SAIS MAINTENANT *qu'un intellectuel n'est pas seulement celui à qui les livres sont nécessaires, mais tout homme dont une idée, si élémentaire soit-elle, engage et ordonne la vie.*

(I know now that an intellectual is not only the man who must have books, but any man whose life is engaged and ordered by an idea, no matter how elementary it may be.)

ANDRÉ MALRAUX, *La Lutte avec l'ange*

# CONTENTS

# INTRODUCTION TO THE TRANSACTION EDITION

T HIRTY-FIVE YEARS AGO I went to Mexico City on the invitation of
the National Autonomous University, an institution so undemanding of a visitor that in fifteen months there, I found time to live
through many of the experiences and to arrive at the theories
incorporated in *Bullfighting: Art, Technique and Spanish Society*. After seeing my first corrida years before, I had wanted to write a
book about bullfighting (henceforth *toreo*: untranslatable). I had
never supposed, however, that I could ever know enough from
what I came to regard as the only appropriate point of view, that
of the active *torero* (bullfighter), as opposed to the usual spectator's
impressions and enthusiasms.

Through a Colombian painter friend, Roberto Berdecio, who
was to draw the illustrations for the eventual book, I met Mario
Sevilla, a retired *matador de toros* who had also wanted to write a
book, but who was not an experienced writer. Sevilla and I agreed
that I would do the writing, but not before he had taught me the
rudiments of toreo in sufficient depth to be competent to face
young bulls in the plaza, not to show what a hell of a fellow I was,
but to learn from the inside some of the emotions and realize
the discipline essential to survival. Mario knew no English; my
Spanish was adequate, for as the Spanish say, "Los toros no hablan
ingles." It will be obvious that Mario is the "Carlos" of the final
Chapter.

I did not want to write about myself, but I did want in all
objectivity to write about the thing itself in order to sort through
its complexities, bewildering even to the experienced observer,
and to suggest to skeptics the aesthetic, social, and moral dimensions of an art that is geographically limited, but universal when
seen in the round. To many people, to try to justify toreo is like
justifying bank robbery or pandering; toreo, like any art, does

not require justification. Toreo does evoke unusual indignation in a large population, not only outside Spanish-speaking countries but in Spain itself. For them, toreo is no more than a peculiar, barbarous spectacle performed by and for brutes.

The public who attend corridas is composed of several groups, and such groups are changing rapidly, as the postscript, "Ice Cream at the Bullfight" indicates. Despite changes, you may see the lifelong, Spanish-speaking *aficionado* (enthusiast) who knows what he knows from family tradition and from personal observation. A larger group are those who attend occasionally to be seen, to booze, and have a good time. Many tourists attend in season, often leaving after or during the death of the first bull. Small in number but of some influence are the foreign afición, made up of a handful of people, well-read in the subject and discriminating about what they see in the plaza. A much larger group of foreigners are the coffee-table aficionados, whose knowledge derives from the numerous coffee-table books published over the years. They tend fanatically to follow a favorite torero, indiscriminately. ("Fanaticism consists in redoubling your effort when you have forgotten your aim."—Santayana).

In English, the aficionado best known to layman and aficionado alike is Ernest Hemingway, who in his fiction gave to many innocents the notion that the fiesta is a cross between romantic risk and a drunken party, and the torero bait to nymphomaniacs. From the non-fiction of *Death in the Afternoon*, readers might conclude that toreo was an elaborate substitute for war, ending in wounds or death. His descriptions of the "beauty" in toreo are lyrical but short on imaginative creation of how such beauty, through technique and discipline, comes about. Hemingway created a mystique of toreo, his own, and why not? But in so doing, he ignored or slighted, in the opinion of some, the full, unique nature of the subject. As the master of American prose he was, Hemingway seduced a large audience, many of whom dropped away when they read the superficial journalism of *The Dangerous Summer*, evidence of a mystique worn thin.

While having felt the attraction of Hemingway's approach, I knew that I was being seduced by elements in his prose that had little to do with toreo. To try to put right for myself if not for others Hemingway's distortions, I named the first edition of this book *The Complete Aficionado*, which later I recognized to appear to be directed only to the spectator, while my object was more comprehensive than that. Upon rereading my own prose after so many years, always an unpleasant experience, I felt an unaccustomed (and inexcusable) brief pride that I had got several things right. My cast of toreros has disappeared from the sands of the plaza, as have some of the *ganaderías* (breeding ranches), but the classical principles that Mario and I enunciated may still be seen, and still be appreciated by a healthier form of criticism than that we saw in Franco's lamentable times. The book had been a pleasure to write; now I must hope that it may be a pleasure for others to read.

# PREFACE

THIS BOOK is addressed to the large public that has already made an acquaintance, however brief, with the art of *toreo,* or as we misleadingly translate it into English, bullfighting. Although interest in toreo is comparatively recent in English-speaking countries, it is widespread, and increasingly proportionate in intensity to the attention which that absorbing art merits. The authors are aware that most literate people have, by now, read Hemingway's *Death in the Afternoon,* or one of the other less adequate primers on the subject. While primers are necessary, they often oversimplify and distort. At their best, primers in English (Hemingway's foremost) are guilty of romanticizing the subject, of substituting rhetoric for technical information, and of surrounding the emergent portrait of the matador with the neon glare of melodrama. At their worst, the primers present toreo as sport, circus, or spectacle, for the good reason that such books are written from the point of view of the spectator, rather than professionally, from the point of view of the *torero* who has suffered through his apprenticeship and faced and killed bulls in the plaza. In Spanish-speaking countries the situation is little better. The last technical treatise of value by a professional torero, the great Domingo Ortega's *El arte del toreo,* was published in Madrid in 1961 and is virtually unobtainable; it has never been translated into English. In any event, Spanish and Latin-American *aficionados* tend to believe that they know all about the fiesta through their mystique of *sangre* (blood) and thus they do not need to read books.

As a result, the fiesta is in the dangerous position of being a great art that lacks criticism. What passes for criticism in Spain or Latin America is little more than review (often paid for by the torero, thus corrupt), biography, anecdote, or gossip. For a comparable situation, we should have to think of drama without Aristotle; of poetry without Horace, Sidney's *Apologie,* Shelley's *Defence,* Baudelaire's *Curiosites esthéiques,* or T. S. Eliot's essays.

The problem of the relationship between art and criticism will always remain agitated, yet one must agree with Walt Whitman when he said that great poetry needs great audiences. The fiesta cannot flourish before ignorant audiences, nor can it survive ignorant or venal criticism.

While I cannot claim to be either the Aristotle or the Horace of the fiesta, I see my work as venturing beyond the mere primer to become an intermediate and advanced reader. I have not described the cape and *muleta* nor told the reader that the picador rides a horse. Vincent Kehoe's excellent *Aficionado!* (New York: Hastings House, 1959) goes into such details with scrupulous accuracy. Neither have I attempted to write a history; rather, I have used history to explain and to illustrate my true subject, modern toreo. I have attempted to treat the reality, not the illusion; to endow the subject with the dignity, the seriousness, and the accuracy of the professional torero. During the period of preparation, the author came to think of the book as a treatise in practical aesthetics. Perhaps that description is the most precise of all.

Both the author and the illustrator, Roberto Berdecio, wish to express their gratitude to Dr. Samuel Baldwin Leyva, Professor of Veterinary Medicine at the National University of Mexico and member of the veterinary staff of the Plaza de Toros México, in Mexico City. Dr. Baldwin Leyva contributed long hours of time and, more important, original material on the visual and skeletal structure of the *toro de lidia* that I have incorporated into this book.

J.M.

# A NOTE ON MECHANICS

Spanish words and phrases used in bullfighting (toreo) are unusually vexing, if not impossible, to translate. To the Spanish mind, the very idea of a bull "fight" is heretical, for it implies that the torero (bullfighter) has in fact lost his bull, has given up with a particular animal and is punishing it through doubling passes rather than accommodating himself to the animal's conditions. The proper term for such a "fight" is *lucha,* a term used of boxing and often derisively of the work of a torero who is unequal to a particular bull.

The usual solution to the problem is a glossary, which by nature is unwieldy for the reader and unsatisfactory to the writer, for the specific term needs to be defined in context while the entire sequence of meaning is alive in the reader's mind. Another solution occasionally found in books on the fiesta is the parenthetical explanation in the text; this is unsatisfactory because it intrudes upon the text and can render a paragraph incoherent. At the same time it is a bore to the reader who knows some, or much, Spanish. Our own solution is to translate or define each Spanish term, for the most part in a footnote, at its first use. From that point on, we use that phrase in Spanish in a missionary effort to encourage the non-Spanish speaker to associate the word with the concept. Difficulties arise in the first place because the Spanish word is more than a mere word: it usually signifies a concept that the aficionado must learn if he is to qualify as complete. All Spanish words and phrases are also listed in the index.

Spanish words that are defined in a note have been designated by an asterisk or dagger, while standard bibliographical footnotes have been designated by arabic numerals. We have furnished such footnotes to indicate borrowings, of course, and to refer the reader to other works of particular interest. Many standard works, so-called, have been omitted because they are without value or are downright harmful.

# CHAPTER 1

# TOREO AS ART

Good art is usually the product of innate talent, intelligence, submission to a discipline, historical study, awareness of the self and of society—of willing apprenticeship, hard work, and most important, of a certain mental and often physical disposition that creates the essential will and energy to excel. Great art always seems to stand in paradoxical relationship to nature and to reality; the artist is in nature yet apart from it. He manipulates reality in order to create the illusion of reality; he dominates his materials, whether paint and canvas, words, physical motions, or cement and steel, recombining them into a new reality. The great artist may be said to add a dimension to reality that did not exist before he completed his task. Sport, on the other hand, differs fundamentally from art. The great athlete too needs innate talent, intelligence, submission to discipline, hard work, and a certain mental and physical disposition that creates the energy and will to excel. Yet, while we may be tempted to call a boxer or a fencer an "artist," we can only use that term metaphorically, because the paradoxical relationship between reality and illusion is lacking in sport. The athlete does not transform reality in any manner; he is rather an ultimate *of* reality, and his finest performance is rooted in his physical strength and his shrewd application of strength to the principles of his sport. He is forever in nature, not apart from it; he is always the craftsman, never the creator. The artist finally creates; the athlete cannot possibly do so, he can only refine.

The *torero** shares with the athlete the need for intelligence, coordination, and a degree of physical fitness, as well as the fact that he performs in public. There all resemblance ceases. An athlete cannot play American football unless he is of a certain weight and build; no such restriction applies to toreros. Although the majority of toreros are young men, many are not. *Banderi-lleros*† of fifty and sixty are not uncommon, and men of eighty have been known to kill bulls.[1] The fact is that the bull is dominated by the torero's intelligence and by his command over his own instinctive reactions, which tell him to flee; but he can no more dominate a bull by strength than he could a tank. One is re-minded of Juan Belmonte's remark in his autobiography that he was literally unable to build up his bodily strength, that exercise depleted him to the point of exhaustion. Toreros tend to be slight and wiry, almost never heavily muscled or large-boned. Certain toreros, such as Carlos Arruza or the Girón brothers, have been athletes, but that has been their limitation. A merely athletic performance is invariably vulgar.

The torero and the athlete seem to share an identical rela-tionship to the public, since by granting or withholding ap-proval the public can influence an individual performance. Doubtless both torero and professional athlete depend upon pub-lic approval for their very survival. Here again, however, the resemblances are more apparent than real. A large proportion of the public reaction to an athlete derives from statistics. X is batting in the .300s, and Y has turned in such a performance for blank years. The result of a specific performance is not necessarily predictable, but the public often gives the impression that it ought to be. An athlete is applauded, left in silence, or hooted, in

---

* *Torero:* Not only the person called in English a "bullfighter," but also banderilleros and picadors—all who have to do with the living bull in the plaza. Generally, however, the term defines the matador.

† *Banderillero:* A member of the matador's *cuadrilla,* or team, who places the *banderillas,* runs (*bregar*) the bull before the matador performs his preliminary cape work, and stands by at all times to assist the matador should he get into trouble. Each matador hires three banderilleros, one of whom, the banderillero *de confianza* (of confidence), will be in his permanent employ. The others may or may not be. Two picadors, hired by the matador, complete the cuadrilla.

[1] See Plate 1 of Domingo Ortega at age fifty, performing beautifully before the Madrid public.

proportion to his ability to keep to his statistical potential. The whole effort of the trainer is to eliminate temperament in the athlete and to produce a performance as close as possible to that of a machine. The known variables in a given sport are simulated repeatedly in practice, so that when the sport is played in competition the player will act out a conditioned response. Alertness and intelligence are required first for the recognition of the known and trained-for situation, and only secondarily for the new situation. Professional athletes who go to pieces when an entirely new situation arises are not uncommon; baseball players in particular are notorious for inexplicable lapses. Stupid players may be kept on and may prove valuable for some particular talent. They may be able to hit but not run, or run but not hit; their value to the team depends upon their willingness to abandon their own intelligence and to perform precisely as the base coach or the manager instructs them. Parallels in other sports are obvious and need not

PLATE 1.    Domingo Ortega, at age fifty, gives his *trincherazo de Ortega* to a toro of Antonio Pérez in Vista Alegre, Madrid, 1956.

3

be stressed here. The public knows of these matters and often is indulgent of a player's poor performance or downright stupidity. North Americans affect a cult of indulgent fondness for stupid athletes, particularly for witless boxers, baseball and football players: consult the fiction of Ring Lardner.

The stupid torero in all probability will promptly be hospitalized or killed, for reasons we shall go into presently. The torero's relationship to the public differs in essence from the athlete's, because very little of his performance is predictable. The torero is a performer, like the athlete, but he is much more than a performer. He might be compared to the actor but for the fact that he writes his own script, in collaboration with the *toro*. Or he might be compared to the dancer, but for the fact that he is his own choreographer and his own composer, again in collaboration with the toro. As is the case with the playwright, composer, or actor, the torero must win his audience anew with each performance, each new play, each new composition. The audience does not have a statistical preconception of his performance, even though the aficionado will know that X has cut so many ears and so many tails during the season. Unlike the athlete's audience, the torero's has rather a preconception of quality that may or may not be appropriate to the capabilities of the individual torero. Where baseball spectators tend to be sentimentally indulgent when favorites have a bad day, week, or even season, the torero's following is short of memory, fickle, cruel, and exigent. A matador may cut ears from his first bull and be whistled out of the ring for what may appear—or be, in fact—a cowardly performance with his second. Vicente Blasco Ibáñez's hero in *Sangre y arena,* Juan Gallardo (modeled upon the historical matador, Frascuelo), is literally killed by the exigence of the mob: hooted in the plaza and approaching the last afternoon of his life, Gallardo reflects, "Ah, the public! A mob of assassins who long for a man's death, as if they alone have families and look forward to long life!"[2]

The fundamental differences between toreo and sport are obvious, yet they must be underlined at the outset because of a basic, long-standing confusion in the minds of writers and aficionados of the bulls concerning what the torero does, who the torero is, and how he got that way. Although honorable exceptions exist, virtually all discussions in English and in Spanish make a cursory nod

---

[2] (Barcelona, 1958), p. 275.

in the direction of toreo as an art, then go on as though it were indeed a sport and the toreros athletes. Toreo, to be sure, is an art form, but one that presents formidable obstacles to criticism, not only for toreo's apparent relationship to sport, but also because of two further complications: the necessary involvement of toreros in the business side of their careers, and the changing nature of the mass audience. These complications are more fully related than might at first appear. Like all the arts, toreo is enduring a crisis in many dimensions. The exact dimensions will occupy most of the pages to follow; for the moment, we refer to the crisis created by the sudden internationalization of what was for generations a local, if not provincial, affair. Before World War II, toreo was confined to Spain and to parts of the Spanish-speaking world. Both the torero and the critic could count on an audience that had an easy, intimate, lifelong familiarity with toros and toreros; there existed a community to which the art belonged. That community had its own language, its own dress, its own manners and mores. The Spanish Civil War shattered the physical existence of the community, while succeeding political and social events in Spain and in the entire Western world made impossible the exclusiveness and provincialism of prewar days. The flood of tourists into Spain after 1955, coupled with comparative prosperity, has acted explosively upon institutions, customs, and most important, of course, upon individual sensibilities. The *apoderado** of the young torero has visions of riches untold; the *empresario*† has visions of riches untellable; and the torero, unless endowed with the character of a saint, is subjected to temptations to cheat and cut corners, to be blind to one abuse and to encourage another to a point where the art of toreo may possibly disappear altogether, to be replaced by fatuous parody.

The apoderado and empresario, mildly or grossly crooked, are encouraged in their ways by the apparent ignorance of the new audience. ("Apparent" because the audience is wonderfully complex, and in rapid process of change.) It is the business of criticism to make certain that the change is in the right direction; that ways are found to convey the true dimensions of toreo to the spectator who has never handled a cape, no matter how awkwardly, or never

---

* *Apoderado:* The matador's manager.

† *Empresario:* In English, impresario. Producer of the fiesta, manager of the plaza.

seen a herd of *toros bravos*\* in nature. The critic, that is, can no longer take such things for granted as he once could, or thought he could. Thus the criticism of toreo, like everything else connected with toreo, is unique and peculiarly demanding. History makes it clear that one may be a superb critic of poetry or painting without ever having written a poem or painted a canvas; poetry and painting are probably more universal arts than toreo, and their materials more apprehensible by critic and public. The materials of toreo are the self, the bull, and the public. The result of one afternoon's work cannot be known generations later in print or on canvas. The result is in the act itself, of which the effect in part depends upon rapidity and evanescence. Toreo is an art unto itself that must be apprehended in its own terms.

The relationship of the torero to the public has always been uneasy. If he reaches the eminence of being a *figura*,† the public is likely to demand risks amounting to his life. He will be dogged and bedeviled by the public, subjected to all the filth of modern publicity, allowed neither privacy nor peace unless he moves incognito, all the while knowing that his idolators can and probably will turn into his enemies in a matter of minutes. Belmonte and Manolete, among modern figuras, both reported their distress at the exigence of the crowd, whom no excellence might satisfy, no risk appease—that same crowd that was stricken at their death, and that will long continue to observe their anniversaries with a quality of sorrow reserved usually for the commemoration of blood relations.[3] As a performer, however, the torero needs the very adulation that flays him. He knows, at least in theory, before he commits himself to his career, that he must suffer the public and risk both its pleasure and displeasure. Joselito Huerta, when asked about his relationship to the public, said, "The toro is the torero's only friend, in the plaza and out of it."

In this respect the art of toreo differs from other arts. T. S. Eliot said that once a poet is accepted, "his reputation is seldom disturbed, for better or worse."[4] There are many obvious reasons for

---

\* *Toros bravos:* Brave bulls, or bulls suitable for toreo, a separate breed native to the Iberian peninsula.

† *Figura:* A star performer.

[3] One observed that the national mourning in Spain was greater at the deaths of Manolete and Belmonte than at that of Pope John XXIII.

[4] *The Sacred Wood* (London, 1928), Introduction, p. xii.

the discrepancy. For one thing, the poet's reputation is established by his peers and by a body of educated, cultivated opinion, rather than by the opinion of a vast, amorphous public. Lacking true criticism, and therefore lacking an entire necessary frame of reference, toreo is subjected to whim, fashion, and variation in a degree unknown in the other arts. The uninstructed public is frequently wrong about the virtues of a torero's performance; an "easy" bull can be made to look dangerous, while a "difficult" bull may not reveal his difficulties to the uninstructed. An honest, brave performance by the matador may be received in silence or worse. If criticism does nothing else, it labels the second-rate and lauds the excellent; it establishes standards and instructs the audience by the application of those standards.

By its adulation and by its exigence, the torero's audience sets him apart from the run of men. The athlete is usually revered for his commonness; the torero never. The torero's conception of himself and of his work is apart from nature; his quality depends upon his ability to suppress his natural fear, or rather to use his fear for the creation not of percentage points but of beauty. The audience knows this, and with one part of its collective consciousness resents it. When the audience has caused a goring or a death through its resentment of the torero's apartness, it attempts to wipe clean the slate of its guilt through excessive emotion, amounting to despair. Such responses are neither abnormal nor unnatural; they are very human. Nor, it must be emphasized, are such responses confined to people of Latin "blood." Northern Europeans in Spain and North Americans attending *corridas**
along the Texas border display the same responses, the same exigence, the same tendency to idolize and to destroy.

The question of the Spanishness of the art of toreo is unfortunately confused with nationalistic sentiment both in Spain and in Mexico, the two countries where toreo is most passionately practiced. Without exception, Spaniards and Latin Americans will assure one another loudly and volubly that without sangre, Spanish blood, one can neither *torear,* nor observe a corrida intelligently, nor have a sane opinion about any aspect of the fiesta. Toreo, according to this cliché, is a unique expression of the

---

* *Corrida:* Literally, a "running" of bulls. "The corrida" may be used to refer to the six bulls of the usual performance, or it may refer to the performance as a whole. *"Encierro"* more precisely defines the string of bulls, for it lacks the ambiguity of "corrida."

Spanish sensibility and is made possible only through the unique Spanish sense of honor, through Spanish valor, and through a religious conception that honors Roman Catholicism and the cult of the toro. The readers of *El Ruedo* (Madrid) are assured that elegance as it is found in toreo is allied to the Spanish sensibility and "presupposes a high popular conception of man's destiny and of his mastery over himself."[5] More alarming but equally typical is the statement, "Such is Spain, in its rural areas and towns, as in its fundamental principles: with a faith and a mythology. A pure faith and an incomparable Catholicism [together with] a mythology of the bull as a totemic animal, racial and mysterious, and the secular pleasure of the Spaniard in the bull's deception."[6] The statement is virtually impossible to translate, for it is not conceived in the logic of prose but as poetic incantation.

Such notions about the Spanishness of toreo are commonplace not only among the Spanish; these clichés are repeated in virtually every book in English on the subject. Behind these notions lies a complex of feelings and ideas that must be explored here, if only to support the writers' basic thesis that toreo is an *art*, not a sport or circus spectacle, and that art, by definition, is not limited by geography or political boundaries. We need to look into the origins of toreo in order to substitute fact or legitimate hypothesis for nationalistic rhetoric and the foreigner's desire to say of the corrida, "How quaint, how colorful, how Spanish."

Histories of toreo abound: Díaz Arquer's *Bibliografía de libros y opúsculos sobre toros* (Madrid: 1931) lists more than two thousand works, dating virtually from the invention of printing. Since 1931, writers have continued to turn out books with regularity—the most notable, of course, being José María de Cossío, the author of *Los toros: Tratado técnico e histórico* (four volumes, Madrid: 1943–1961). Even a passing acquaintance with the historical bibliography indicates that historians of toreo, like political historians, are capable of reproducing the errors of their predecessors, par-

---

[5] José María Bugella, "La Elegancia," *El Ruedo,* September 13, 1962, n.p.

[6] "¡A los Toros!," *El Ruedo,* November 22, 1962, n.p. The Spanish for this hermetic statement must be given: *"Así es España en sus medios rurales, en sus pueblos, en sus entrañables fundamentos. Con una fe y una mitología. Fe limpia y culta de catolicismo impar. Mitología racial y misteriosa del toro como animal totémico y del secular gusto del español por burlarlo."*

ticularly where theories of the origins of toreo are concerned. Cossío, exceptionally reliable in most aspects of his encyclopaedic work, remains cagey about the origins of toreo, maintaining a discreet silence and seeming to promise a separate, later work on the subject.[7] It remained for an historian of religion, the late Angel Alvarez de Miranda (1915–1957) to produce an authoritative work on the origins of toreo, *Ritos y juegos del toro.*[8]

At least six more or less contradictory hypotheses of the origin of toreo have been developed over the centuries. In the order of their conception they are: the Roman hypothesis; the Arabic; the Spanish prehistoric; the Cretan; the folkloric; the totemic. The idea that toreo was simply a Spanish adaptation of the Roman practice of gladiatorial combat between man and various beasts, including bulls, was common in historiography from the sixteenth through the nineteenth centuries. It was particularly current in the sixteenth and seventeenth centuries, when it evoked the displeasure of churchmen who saw corridas as an inheritance of paganism: *"spectaculum daemonom y abominación de los gentiles, rito pagano."*[9] (A demoniac spectacle and an abomination of the heathens; a pagan rite.) This same moral sentiment resulted in Popes Pius V and Gregory XIII forbidding corridas and the participation of the clergy, under pain of excommunication. Evidence for the Roman hypothesis is slight or negligible, certainly insufficient to warrant belief.

The Arabic hypothesis, frequently repeated by later writers, is the work of Nicolás Fernández de Moratín (1737–1780), who published his *Carta histórica sobre el orígen y progresos de las fiestas de toros en España* in 1777. Moratín held that, although combats between bulls and men undoubtedly did take place in Roman amphitheaters in Spain, their character was so different from that of the true corrida that their relevance to the origin of the fiesta was negative. Rather, Moratín said, toreo was native to Spain just as toros bravos were native. The native bull was undoubtedly a source of food, a dangerous quarry before whom it

---

[7] Vol. I, 572, 684, 788.

[8] The authors are indebted to *Ritos y juegos* (Madrid: Taurus Ediciones, 1962) for much of the material that follows in this chapter.

[9] J. Pareda, *Los toros ante la Iglesia y la moral* (Bilbao, 1945). Cited in Alvarez, *Ritos y juegos,* p. 37.

was natural to demonstrate the exceptional man's valor. Corridas de toros were surely practiced in Spain, on foot and on horse, from the earliest of times. Such was Moratín's conjecture. Moving to the historical period, Moratín cites documents regarding corridas of the twelfth century and repeats popular legend about the hero of the re-Conquest, Rodrigo Díaz de Vivar (el Cid Campeador), who in the eleventh century was supposed to have fought a bull from horseback. Reviewing the glories of knightly corridas from the twelfth to the fifteenth century, which reached their apogee in the court of Juan II, Moratín asserts that the Arab occupiers, too, fought corridas, both on foot and on horseback. He explains the origin of the cape pass in the Arab burnoose, and asserts the suitability of Arab horses for the combat with the lance. Moratín's ideas, repeated over the years by López Pelegrín, Bedoya, and others, might have gone unremarked had it not been for his friendship with Goya. Goya's famous and splendid *Tauromaquia* is literally an illustration of Moratín's book; it would appear that Goya's authority as a painter has invested Moratín's words. This is comprehensible, but it does not erase the fact that Moratín invented his Arabic idea without documentation beyond the single record that in 1354 a sultan of Granada organized a corrida to celebrate his son's circumcision. Moratín provides no earlier documentation, nor has subsequent research (including the writers') revealed any.

The Roman and Arabic theses were displaced, if not superseded, by the discoveries of paleolithic and neolithic cave paintings in a multitude of Spanish archaeological sites: Teruel, Alpera, Albarracín, Yecla, Albacete, Vallorta, Altamira, and many more. In 1918 (a significant date in the history of all modern art), an important exhibition took place in Madrid, "El Arte en la Tauromaquia," in which reproductions of the now-famous cave paintings were shown for the first time to a wide public, and emerging from which was the thesis we may call prehistoric. According to the catalogue of the exhibition, it was "proved by the artifacts that the fiesta is extremely ancient, genuinely Iberian and previous to the Roman occupation." Aficionados rather than professional archaeologists proceeded to assert that the caves indicated the existence of a religious cult of the bull in Spain, and of the indubitable origin of the modern *estocada* (see footnote on page 35) in the sacrifice of the bull to various divinities in time of trouble. Such a theory is of course satisfyingly nationalistic and is constantly reiterated in the popular press. It seemed, further, to reinforce a casual statement of Diodorus, writing a few years before the beginning of the Christian era, that bulls "are considered sacred among the Iberians even to our own times." With characteristic common sense, Alvarez remarks that the cave paintings show absolutely no evidence of a religious cult of the bull; they do show evidence of the abundance of the aurochs* in the Iberian peninsula. And as for Diodorus, we must agree with Alvarez that no other evidence exists to substantiate his famous statement. Paleolithic and neolithic man left us no more than evidence of his probable addiction to magic, in which the bull paintings reproduced his feeling for the generative power of the animal, and for the importance of the bull as a source of food, an object of the chase.

Sir Arthur Evans' researches on Crete into the Minoan civilization as presented in *The Palace of Minos* (four volumes, 1921–1935) seemed to support the prehistoric hypothesis. Others before him had tentatively dealt with the subject, but Evans boldly called the frescoes at Cnossus "The Tauredor Frescoes" and proceeded to identify the sport, game, or rite depicted in terms taken from Spanish toreo. In the frescoes, as is well known, young girls and possibly young men are shown seizing the horns of a magnificent bull in full charge, using the force of the bull's toss to do a somersault on his back, then leaping to the ground (a procedure which looks impossible to anyone who has had intimate dealings with bulls). Evans uses such terms as "torero," "corridas de toros," "tauromaquia," and "matador," to describe the frescoes; he also insisted upon the religious character of the Cretan games, carried on before an altar in the arena itself, and he assumed, without proof, that the bull was killed by a "matador." He suggests as a possible antecedent the capture of sacred bulls by the Babylonians, dating from at least the end of the third millennium; and most important of all for the Spanish nationalists he draws parallels between the aristocratic nature of the participants, comparing the young aristocrats of Crete with the young nobles of the Spanish court who fought bulls from horseback at a comparable period in Spanish history. Evans himself did not suggest that any direct connection existed between Crete and the Balearics or Spain;

---

* *Aurochs:* The primitive European bison, from which toros bravos were developed by selective breeding.

Ortiz-Canavate, however, did not hesitate to make just that connection, saying that the Cretans could have brought to Spain their
sport or rite involving toros bravos.[10] Schulten added further
authority to the argument by remarking the similarity between
the magnificent bronze bulls' heads found at Costiç, in the Balearics, and the Cretan bulls of the Minoan period. He deduced
that there must have been some manner of encounter in the third
and second millennium between Crete and the Balearics.[11] Again,
one must agree with Alvarez that no proof for the hypothesis
exists; all is conjecture and intuition.

Ironically, the one hypothesis of origin most capable of proof by
documentation has been ignored by historians of toreo: the hypothesis of folk origin. It is further ironic that Spanish nationalists
have overlooked this most Spanish of all hypotheses. Alvarez, who
was not a nationalist nor setting out to prove anything *a priori,*
presents an argument from comparative religion, folklore, and
traditional social custom the logic of which is powerful.[12] Alvarez'
conclusion is that the modern corrida derives from an association
in the naif or unscientific mind between vegetable and human
fertility, symbolized totemically by the bull in many cultures and
countries, and dramatized in Spain for centuries in a "corrida"
involving a hobbled bull and the bridegroom and his friends for
the benefit of the bride. The emphasis, significantly, is upon
marriage and the hopes for fertility in marriage, not upon toreo;
thus we may understand the lack of interest on the part of the
historian who would emphasize man's valor rather than woman's
hopes for children, danger rather than domesticity. After all, there
is nothing glamorous about a hobbled bull.

For this hypothesis Spanish folklore provides one basis and one
manner of proof. The story of the bull with the golden horns, *La
narración del oricuerno,* is widely diffused, with variants, throughout Spain and Mexico. It is the tale of a young girl, loved by two
young men. Her preferred lover is murdered before her eyes by

---

[10] L. Ortiz-Canavate, *El toreo español,* Vol. I of *Folklore y costumbres
de España* (Barcelona, 1934), pp. 377–378. See discussion of Alvarez,
*Ritos y juegos,* pp. 42–43.

[11] A. Schulten, *Tartesos* (Madrid, 1945), pp. 72ff. No foreign aficionado visiting Madrid should fail to see these bronzes in the
National Archaeological Museum.

[12] *Ritos y juegos,* pp. 59–134.

his rival; seeking revenge, the girl goes out into the streets and kills not only her lover's murderer but a friend of his as well. Frightened of punishment, she dresses as a man, calls herself "Carlos," and goes out into the world, finding work in a shop.

The daughter of the shopkeeper falls in love with "Carlos" and, in her amorous pain, tells her father of her love. The father in turn informs "Carlos" of the situation and suggests that "Carlos" marry his daughter. "Carlos," trapped, has no recourse but to marry. On her wedding night, "Carlos" confesses all to the bride, who reassures her and says that they will carry on just as though "Carlos" were in truth a man.

Years go by, and since the marriage is not blessed with children, the wife's father and the townsfolk decide that "Carlos" is in fact a woman. The father sets various tests that come to nothing, culminating in the proposal of a hunt followed by a swim in the river. "Carlos," invited to swim, asks for a delay; she goes upstream, in despair, where she encounters a magnificent bull with great golden horns. The bull indicates that she is to undress. When she does so, the bull makes a cross on the appropriate part of her anatomy with his golden horn, and Carlos is metamorphosed into a man, to the consternation then delight of all concerned.

The above version is from Cuenca. In a Mexican version, "Carlos," after undressing, plays the bull (black in color) with her clothing in the manner of a modern matador; the bull is then transformed into a cow and "Carlos" into a man. The theme of change of sex is as old as folklore, particularly in the Orient, while that of the transvestite is even more widespread. More than a hundred versions exist in Spanish alone.

Before considering the significance of the bull with the golden horns, two more legends should be examined. The legend of Bishop Ataúlfo occurs in one form or another in six mediaeval chronicles of Spain; the version that follows is from the *Historia compostelana,* recorded in the first half of the twelfth century.

Bishop Ataúlfo, zealous in his pastoral and religious duties, incurred the envy of certain enemies, who denounced him to the king for sodomy. The king, angry, condemned him to trial by exposure to a ferocious bull before the council. The holy bishop celebrated his last mass before his imminent martyrdom, dressed in his episcopal robes, and awaited his fate in the ring. The bull, frenzied by lances and the attacks of dogs, confronted the bishop and was transformed from bravery to tameness. Approaching, he placed his horns in the bishop's hands, thus saving the bishop from a terrible fate.

The third legend—that of "The Golden Bull"—belongs to the oral lore of the region of Trujillo. It was first published in 1944.

There was once a king whose daughter was dishonored and abandoned by a neighboring prince, her lover. The princess asked her father to secure for her a golden bull, life-sized. The king agreed, and while the golden bull was being made, the princess went to the artisans, ordered that the bull should be made hollow, and that they swear silence about her visit.

In due time the hollow bull of gold was delivered to the palace and installed in the princess's chamber. The princess then hid herself inside the bull, remaining there for several days. Missing his daughter, the king ordered a search for her which was carried out without success. Shortly thereafter, items of food were found missing from the palace, yet the king did not suspect that his daughter was the thief. Then the king began to miss not only food, but other items of value. Angered by these events and miserable over the loss of his daughter, the king fell so ill that he called home his son from a distant land.

When the prince arrived and saw the golden bull, he asked the king to give it to him, but the king, weeping, refused, saying that it was a memento of his beloved daughter but that after his death it would of course belong to the prince. At length the king died, and the prince removed to his own quarters the golden bull, not suspecting that it was hollow and that his sister was inside. Presently the prince too began to miss items of food as well as various other objects. Not wishing to lose the golden bull, too, to the unknown thief, the prince had the bull removed to his own chamber. One night when the princess believed her brother to be asleep, she emerged from the bull to continue her thievery. But the prince, who was not asleep, saw her, and said, "Ah, it was you all the while!"

"Yes, it was I," the princess answered. "But do not tell a soul, because I do not want anyone to see me or to know that I am here."

The prince gave his promise, but not long afterward he had to go off to the wars. First he arranged that food should be left for the princess, then he said to her, "Listen my sister, I am sorry that I must leave, but I shall return as soon as I can. When you hear three knocks on the bull's haunch, come out without fear, for it will be me knocking." The two embraced, and the prince left.

One day when the servants were cleaning the prince's room, one of them said, "See what a pretty bull of gold the prince has." And she knocked three times on the bull's haunch. The princess came out, and when they saw her the servants said, "She's the one who has been robbing the household." Then they seized her and flung her through a window into the brambles below.

A woman who lived nearby recognized the princess and took her to her house. In a few days when the prince returned and gave the signal upon the bull's haunch, no one of course emerged, and the prince, in misery, fell ill. His sister the princess, remaining in the neighbor's house, gave birth to a son, and learned that her brother had returned from the wars and was lying upon his sickbed. She then prepared a large hamper of flowers and put her baby among them, placing in the baby's hand a letter telling where she was. She sent a young girl with the basket to the prince's palace, instructing her to offer flowers to the prince and to give the basket to no one but the prince. Faithfully the girl did as she was told. The prince found the letter in the baby's hand, went to find his sister, greeted her happily and asked her how she had come to leave the golden bull before his return. The princess told him the story, and the prince, furious, went to his palace and ordered that the guilty servants be slain. The good woman who had rescued his sister came to the palace together with his sister.

The prince's wife, who knew nothing of her sister-in-law, asked who she was; the prince told her that she was his sister and that from then on she would live with them in the palace. The prince and his wife reared their nephew as though he were their own and, since they were childless, made him their heir. And they all lived many years in happiness, taking particular care of the golden bull.[13]

The three stories recounted have in common antiquity, as witnessed by their combining folk-wisdom with the charming naïveté of the oral tale, and an emphasis upon human sexual sterility in relation to the symbolic fertility of the bull. In the story of "Carlos," the bull's horn of gold is evidently phallic, while the phallic power is transferred magically, not divinely or through

---

[13] Curiel Merchán, *Cuentos extremeños,* (Madrid, 1944), pp. 321–323; and cf. commentary by Alvarez, *Ritos y juegos,* pp. 84–86.

any religious intervention, to the distressed "husband." Doubtless the Mexican version, in which "Carlos" plays the bull with her clothing is a late variant, probably dating from after the development of toreo on foot in Spain or in Mexico. Fertility in the "Carlos" story is more than mere reproduction of the species; in the variants which recount the transfer of fertility from the bull to "Carlos," phallic power goes out of the bull, which becomes a cow, to "Carlos." The stories imply "Carlos' " sexual ability to beget children but do not actually recount that fact. The point of the stories has to do with the awesome regard of the primitive mind for sexuality itself.[14]

The story of the golden bull, recorded late, doubtless contains additions and corruptions, causing the original force of the story to be dispersed in the twentieth-century version. Such an addition would seem to be the prince who dishonored the princess and who plays no real part in the story. Similarly, we do not know why the princess wants the golden bull; beneath the accretions, however, is obviously another fertility story, deriving from magic, not from religion. We do not need Freud to indicate the significance of the hollow bull, and the fact that the golden bull is the agent of fertility, the "father" of the princess's baby, who in turn is given to the prince and princess who are infertile, childless. Gold, in both the story of "Carlos" and that of the princess, represents the substance of fertility, semen, which is equated in the folk mind with the most precious of metals.

In the story of Bishop Ataúlfo, the matter is presented in reverse, and while the story has religious trappings, it is still basically magical. The crime of which the bishop is accused, sodomy, is of course a denial of fertility and therefore a denial of the duty, or instinct, to perpetuate the race. The bull which testifies miraculously to the bishop's innocence also acts inversely, but by analogy identically, to the golden bulls of the other two legends. He deposits his horns or phallic symbols in the bishop's hands, thus testifying to the bishop's own manhood and to his voluntary but honorable renunciation of the flesh in accordance with his vow of chastity. Thus magic and theology join in a legend more superficially sophisticated and probably more recent in ori-

---

[14] One is reminded that in Plato's *Timaeus* the male and female sexual organs are described as having a life of their own, unrelated and even annoying to the mind of the human being.

gin. But the framework remains virtually identical in all three legends, while they serve to remind us of the frequency in Greek myth of erotic connection between bulls and women: Pasiphaë, Ariadne, Europa. The Spanish legends are not erotic in tone or intent, unlike the Greek; one must agree with Alvarez that their tone is more archaic and that typologically they are more original than the Greek.

If legend serves to guide us into the primitive folk mind and preserves for us the primitive (and enviable) ability of that mind to go directly to basic human needs and objectives, ritual may serve to amplify and to clarify the complex origins and the strange attraction that the phenomenon of toreo poses. In her authoritative *Ancient Art and Ritual*, Jane E. Harrison points out that religion, art, and (to a degree) ritual are only possible because man, unlike the lower animals, is capable of an intermediate stage between knowing and doing. For the most part, the animal no sooner perceives than it acts. Man enjoys (or is cursed by?) an interval in which he may consider several choices; in this interval, "Perception is pent up and becomes, helped by emotion, conscious *representation*." Art and religion then arise from the interrupted sequence, from "unsatisfied desire, from perception and emotion that have somehow not found immediate outlet in practical action."[15] Ritual, according to this hypothesis, derives from the primitive, universal impulse to re-enact, to repeat through *representation*, a vivid emotion or successful action. A successful hunt might be re-enacted for the benefit of members of the tribe who were not actually present at it. The hunt *did* take place, and however arduous, it was successful in that animals were taken, food provided, and men's prowess proved.

With the passage of time and seasons in which hunting is not possible, hunger might contribute to the emotion associated with the original successful hunt. The hunt is then re-enacted in general outline; its precise details might have been forgotten. That is, a process of abstraction takes place. The tribe then enacts an idealized hunt through dance, and that dance is not merely a *re*-presentation of an actual hunt, but a *pre*-presentation of what is hoped for: another successful hunt, demonstration of prowess, and a full belly. In this we see what the Greeks intended by mimesis, and what Plato believed to be "the very source and essence of all

---

[15] (London, 1951), p. 41.

art."[16] The hunt-dance does not represent nor is it mimetic of what another has done, but of what the dancer himself desires to do. "The habit of this *mimesis,* of the thing desired, is set up, and ritual begins. Ritual, then, does imitate, but for an emotional, not an altogether practical end."[17] "The origin of an art is not mimesis, but mimesis springs up out of art, out of emotional expression, and constantly and closely neighbours it. Art and ritual are at the outset alike in this, that they do not seek to copy a fact, but to reproduce, to re-enact an emotion."[18]

Ritual, then, is a stylized acting out of something fully and emotionally desired by a community; an imitation above all of that object. It is communal, not personal, and with the lapse of time, it tends to become abstracted from its origin; it becomes, in the case of drama, an imaginative projection of the original communal desire, losing none of its emotion, but losing its original outlines. Ritual becomes art when the artist takes advantage of the emotional associations of the rite in a context uniquely his own, in his own imaginative framework.

Such an account not only helps to establish the relevance of legend to toreo, it also helps to explain the attraction of the totemic theory of origin. It is safe to say that when ritual becomes stuck, so to speak, on its way to becoming either art or religion, it is the totem upon which it becomes stuck. Numerous rites have been recorded in Spain, archaic in flavor and not subject to precise dating, which may help to clarify our meaning. In the mountains of León, for instance, there was as late as the nineteenth century the rite of the bull dance. On the first day of May, young men wearing bulls' horns would simulate battle with young girls, after which men and girls would pair off, to sleep together in the barns until the following November, when they might (or might not) be legally married. The activity was seasonal and communal; the thing imitated and desired, obviously, was male potency as symbolized by the totemic bulls' horns, together with the continuity of the community which fertility would ensure.

Yet the bull as totemic object, as symbol of fertility, does not go far in explaining the origins of the modern corrida. Of far greater importance to our understanding of the origins of toreo is the ritual that did not become stuck at the totemic stage: the ritual of

---

[16] Harrison, *Ancient Art and Ritual,* p. 44.
[17] *Loc. cit.*
[18] *Ibid.,* pp. 46–47.

the marriage corrida. In the marriage corrida we may locate at least one missing link between the bull as merely totemic object and the elaborate, apparently mysterious elements of the modern corrida. Although the marriage corrida was recorded only at the beginning of the twentieth century, its origin may be traced at least as far back as the beginning of the thirteenth century.[19] In the regions of Hervás, Casas de Monte, La Zarza, and other parts of Estremadura, the nuptial ceremonies began two days before the actual marriage. The bridegroom and his friends would get from the slaughterhouse a bull, which they would tie by the horns with a stout rope. They would then "run" the bull through the entire village, luring it and "passing" it with their jackets as impromptu cape or muleta, all the while wounding the animal to insure a flow of blood. Once arrived at the bride's residence, the bridegroom would place in the bull's withers two *banderillas,* previously decorated by the bride. The bull was then killed, not by the bridegroom but by the local butcher. In the Camargue region of southern France, a similar rite called the *bourgine* has been practiced for centuries and is still practiced. Once a year, the newborn children and recently married women are brought face to face with a trussed bull to insure their fertility. (See Chapter 6.)

Such was the peasant ritual, but the ritual was not confined to the peasantry. Documents from the thirteenth century, both poems (*cántigas*) and an illustrative miniature recount similar marriage rites involving the nobility of Plasencia (Estremadura). Again the animal is tied by ropes, and in the miniature it has been pierced by darts and is about to be played with a cloak, or cape.

Corridas were associated with marriage for a very long time: the most ancient public announcement we have of a corrida dates from 1080, on the occasion of the marriage at Ávila of the Infante Sancho de Estrada to doña Urraca Flores. Alvarez cites further instances of corridas organized to celebrate marriages, all antedating the late mediaeval and renaissance practice of *rejoneo,** or knightly jousting against toros bravos.[20]

---

[19] See Alvarez, *Ritos y juegos,* pp. 93–110.

* *Rejoneo:* Toreo from horseback, in which the rider plays the bull with the horse itself, placing long banderillas, darts known as *rejones,* and killing with a long lance, also called a rejón. Rejoneo has little to do with the true art of toreo on foot; it is too showy, and the danger is risked by the horse, not the man (*rejoneador*).

[20] *Ritos y juegos,* p. 99.

In both the peasant and the aristocratic rite, identical elements are significantly present: the conjunction of marriage and a fiesta involving a bull; the bridegroom as protagonist and his friends as helpers and collaborators; the fact that the bull is secured by a rope rather than left free to attack; the emphasis upon the shedding of the bull's blood upon the garments of the participants rather than emphasis upon the death of the bull. If such emphasis is not misplaced, then the object or wish imitated in the marriage corrida is obviously the sexual act itself, with the bull playing the familiar role of insurer of potency in the male and of fertility in the female.[21] The marriage corrida may be said to account for many elements of the later art. The bridegroom is obviously the matador—but a matador who does not *matar* (kill); his friends are the cuadrilla; the luring of the bull, the placing of banderillas previously prepared by the bride, and the ritual staining of the garments of the bridegroom with the bull's blood, while totemic and magical in import, aid us in comprehending both the origin of the *tercio** of the banderillas, and our response to that tercio, often not a merely rational one. The marriage corrida further accounts for the quality of fiesta, the special gaiety of Spanish crowds at the plaza. One is assured that the fiesta is a fiesta because it is so often associated with a saint's day; yet we know that often corridas were in existence before the specific town's adoption of a saint. And in Mexico, where church and state have been separated, where traditional Roman Catholic practices are officially frowned upon, an identical or even greater gaiety than the Spanish sort may be seen.

Although the marriage corrida may account satisfactorily for a certain outline of the modern corrida, it does not account for the very elements that make the modern corrida an art form: the element of inevitability, the element of tragedy. The marriage corrida deliberately avoided any element of tragedy in the fact

---

[21] This interpretation is further borne out by the modern matador's frequent comparison of the *faena* (see footnote explaining the tercios) to the act of making love to a woman.

* *Tercio:* Literally, a third. It is used both of the entire *lidia* ("bull-fight"—see note on page 25), which is said to be divided into the tercio of the *vara* (from the picador's long pole tipped by the pic), of the banderillas; and the faena, which includes the *estocada,* or kill. Tercio also defines the division of the plaza into thirds: *tablas, tercio,* and *medios.*

that the bridegroom did not himself kill the bull; the death of the bull at the butcher's *puntilla*\* was incidental to the central ritual, which was, one must repeat, an occasion of gaiety and joy. No written record will give us the answer to why, when, and exactly how the corrida was transformed from spectacle to art. We may note that the change from rejoneo to toreo on foot was one stage in the process; that the invention of the muleta was another; but we cannot say that in the year X, torero Y became the first artist, as opposed to athlete. The emergence of the art was obviously a slow process, involving the character of the Spanish, the slow unfolding of techniques for dealing with toros bravos, and above all, the recognition, however obscure and however opaque, on the part of audience and toreros alike, that the corrida at its best could be an acting out of certain universal human expressions, a purging of emotions and passions akin to that which Aristotle described of Greek tragedy.

Comparative mythology again offers evidence to support the claims for toreo as art rather than as accidental, picturesque survival of savage custom. The origins in ritual of Greek drama are not only parallel to the rituals associated with early forms of toreo; they also involve the sacrifice of bulls, thus offering not only a symbolic parallel but an actual analogue to the art of toreo. To summarize briefly a complex body of work, scholars of the late nineteenth and early twentieth centuries,[22] following Aristotle's cryptic lead in the *Poetics* to the effect that drama originated in the leaders of the dithyramb, established satisfactorily the rite implied and the connection to later developments in drama. The word "dithyramb" itself meant a "leaping, inspired dance"[23] performed at Athens and elsewhere in Greece in the course of a

---

\* *Puntilla:* The dagger used by the *puntillero* to finish off a toro down but not out. Inserted properly into the vertebra at the base of the animal's skull, the puntilla produces instant death. Although the puntillero dresses in the suit of lights, he is not, correctly speaking, a torero. He may be a ring attendant during the week, or the local butcher, or an ex-banderillero.

[22] The first edition of Sir J. G. Frazer's enormously important *The Golden Bough* appeared in 1890; Jane Harrison's *Themis* was published in 1912, and her *Ancient Art and Ritual* in 1913. In these same years basic work was being done not only at Cambridge University but also by French and German scholars.

[23] Harrison, *Ancient Art and Ritual*, p. 76.

spring ritual. The ritual was a logical activity of a primitive, agricultural people; by it they hoped magically to renew the food supply after the winter "death." At the same time, an associated rite enacted the driving out or killing of winter, and the calling up of an earth spirit, or daimon, associated with the god Dionysos and with his mother, Semele. The ceremonies of driving out or symbolically killing had simply to do with times of famine, and what was being killed was hunger itself. Poetic references to a bull associated with these rites were clarified by archaeological evidence both from Greece and from Asia Minor, where that animal, garlanded and adorned, was summoned by young women for the purpose of sanctifying the proceedings. Harrison places great emphasis upon the role of the bull as sanctifier: ". . . the sanctifier is a Bull. A Bull who not only is holy himself, but is so holy that he has power to make others holy, he is the Sanctifier; . . . So holy was the Bull that nothing unlucky might come near him; the youths and maidens [of the procession] must have both their parents alive, they must not have been under the *taboo*, the infection, of death."[24] A prayer was said for the safety of the city and the land, and for the fertility of both soil and humanity. "All this longing for fertility, for food and children, focuses round the holy Bull, whose holiness is his strength and fruitfulness." The bull, which had been fed through the year at the expense of the state, in order to bring luck upon those whose bounty he partook of, was killed in the spring festival, his death providing the climax of the festival. To the question why an object so holy, so life-provoking should die, Harrison answers, "He dies because he *is* so holy, that he may give his holiness, his strength, his life, just at the moment it is holiest, to his people."[25]

---

[24] *Ancient Art and Ritual,* pp. 87–88.

[25] *Ancient Art and Ritual,* p. 89. The connection in the primitive mind between death and fertility is appallingly underlined in a Reuters dispatch from Lima, Peru, in *The New York Times,* August 10, 1965: "Recent reports said a large crowd cheered the death of the bullfighter, Pepe Huanca, from a stomach wound after he was tossed by a bull. The Indians [of Canas province] believe that the death of a torero means good harvests and increased wool crop[s]. Seven spectators who jumped into the ring to aid the torero were gored by the bull.

"Local authorities were unable to stop the bullfight because of the Indians' hostility, the reports said."

The bull was not sacrificed to a god, however, as one might expect from similar rituals throughout the primitive world. The flesh was divided among the citizens and eaten, in order to assure that the bull's strength be shared out, and that the good luck of the state be thus broadly based. At Athens when the flesh had been eaten, the bull's hide was stuffed with straw and the carcass placed upon the earth in a position to simulate plowing; thus a resurrection was suggested. With the passage of time, and possibly with the increasing sophistication of some communities, the place of the actual bull in the ritual was taken by the image of a bull-spirit, or daimon, ultimately by a bull-god. In this connection we are reminded that the woman followers of Dionysos wore bulls' horns, thus imitating the god, who was often depicted as having a bull's head.

That abstraction of the image of the bull from an actual animal to the god Dionysos is similar to the process by which the dithyramb became early Greek drama. The ritual dance was a periodic, communal festival, having a practical end in view: the assurance of the communal food supply in the new year. But when primitive, communal belief became strained, when doubt was cast upon the efficacy of the ritual, when magic gave way to skepticism, only the form of the ritual remained, a form which in Greece made possible the art of drama. Once skepticism about the magical procedure arose, the community ceased to participate and its place was taken by specialists—actors, in fact, whom the citizenry observed. The practical ritual became the impractical art of drama. The final transition was the substitution of the bull-dance, the primitive content of the ritual, by the material of Greek saga. And the drama was "impractical" and an end in itself; therefore it was an art.

Even in abbreviated form, this account of the origins of art in Greece will seem hauntingly familiar to the Spaniard or the Mexican who has spent his life in the climate of the modern fiesta. The garlanded and filleted bull of prehistoric Greece will remind the Mexican of villages in Yucatan, where to this day, on certain "ritual" occasions, bulls decorated with flowers and garlands are led through the streets before being fought in the plaza, often without picadors. The communal ritual involving the bull will remind the Spaniard of the fiesta of San Fermin at Pamplona and the public running and playing of the bulls there (a fiesta made impossible in the crescendo of publicity begun by Ernest Hemingway). The fact that the early Greeks actually consumed the victim to partake of his strength and fertility immediately recalls the macabre scene that takes place in Mexican plazas after the last bull of the afternoon is dragged to the butcher's space under the stands: there, crowds of boys and young men throw themselves upon the animal with paper cups and soft drink bottles to catch and drink some of the blood.[26] The custom of awarding an ear for superior work by the matador originated in the fact that the ear signified the award of the carcass as a whole at a time when matadors were less well paid than now; it remains a custom that reminds us of the communal eating of the sacrificed bull. In similar manner, to the aficionado the scholars' emphasis upon luck in their accounts of the spring rituals is very like the *suerte** he wishes the torero, the suerte for which the torero hopes and prays at every juncture in his career.

We are not suggesting that because the ritual of the dithyramb grew out of a primitive association between bulls and fertility, and that because the dithyramb developed into tragedy, the modern art of toreo is therefore to be directly equated with Greek tragedy. Rather, what we are attempting to establish is a certain coincidence of effect between tragedy and toreo, a coincidence which can be accounted for in the ritual origins of the two disparate arts. Whoever has seen a superb performance of *Hamlet* or of *King Lear* knows the haunting, unsettling effect of those tragedies; an effect that may persist for days, months, or years. What causes it to persist is that the effect upon the self is greater than the sum of the parts. It is not simply that one has witnessed a good performance of a classical text by competent actors, nor that the text is poetic rather than prosaic, even though the poetic idiom is essential to the effect in question. The effect is paradoxical in that it combines strangeness and surprise with recognition, the sensation of having been there before, *déjà vu*. As is the case of certain operas and

---

[26] In contrast, one remembers the elegantly turned-out women at private fiestas eating with gusto the testicles of *novillos* (three-year-old bulls) killed in the plaza by their admirers.

* *Suerte:* 1. Good luck. 2. Used of any *lance* or *pase* or other action to the bull in the ring. "The suerte of the varas" means the picador's work. (A *lance* is used to describe the torero's cape work only; a *pase,* or pass, is used only of the muleta.) A *verónica* is a lance; it may also be referred to as a suerte. A *natural* is a pass; it too may be called a suerte.

most music, the more familiar we are with the plays, the more profoundly we respond to them; and thus the sensation of strangeness or surprise has nothing to do with narrative unfolding of the unfamiliar; it is far closer to the repetition of the familiar, closer to ritual. Yet neither are these mysterious sensations learned; in no sense do they depend upon one's awareness of the ritual origins of tragedy, nor upon one's literary awareness of Shakespeare.[27]

Similarly, every aficionado remembers one afternoon at least when one of the great master toreros—a Belmonte, a Manolete, an Armillita, or an Ordóñez—confronted the ideal bull, frank, noble, and brave, to send the spectators away from the plaza transfigured by the resulting unsettling experience of strangeness, awe, and pathos—the very emotions of the spectator after a fine performance of great tragedy. Again, those emotions are evoked not only because of the nobility of the bull, the torero's *lidia*,* his finesse with the cape, his mastery with the muleta, or his single well-placed sword. The aficionado's response is disturbingly like memory, and the unfolding of the lidia seems a process of recognition. As with tragedy, the lidia to the noble bull has about it an aura of inevitability; it cannot be any different from what it is.

The rationalist who would explain the attraction of tragedy or of great toreo is forced to go to psychology, to Jung's theory of archetypes or to Freud in order to account for the irrational elements in those arts. We prefer to allow validity to the irrational and to agree with A. C. Bradley, who wrote of tragedies "at whose close we feel pain mingled with something like exultation. There is present . . . 'a glory in the greatness of the soul,' and an awareness of an 'ultimate power' which is 'no mere fate,' but spiritual, and to which the hero 'was never so near . . . as in the moment when it required his life.' "[28] The most hardened atheist cannot fail to sense about the matador and his lonely confrontation with the bull his resemblance to the priestly, a spirit of atonement, perhaps; an awareness of an heroic figure ever close, in

---

[27] Such learned awareness does exist, but it is a social response rather than a spontaneous one.

* *Lidia:* Literally, combat or contest. In toreo, it means the entire technique of dominating the bull and rendering him suitable for toreo, the artistic object of the fiesta, and a most important concept for which there is not even an approximate English equivalent.

[28] Quoted in Maud Bodkin, *Archetypal Patterns in Poetry* (London, 1934), p. 20.

the plaza, to a spiritual quality, for each moment there may be the moment that requires his life.

So it is that while toreo has its origins in profoundly Spanish rites and customs, those rites and customs reflect not only Spanish wishes and desires, but universal human ones. It is only superficially accurate to consider the fiesta as Spanish; in part, the universality of the art of toreo is the fascination that natural force as embodied in the toro bravo has for all humankind, together with the possibility of controlling, commanding, and benefiting from that force as personified by the torero.

On the one hand, the Spanish insist nationalistically upon sangre, yet at the same time they are the first to declare that toreo is art, not sport, and not primarily spectacle. Art, by definition, is universal, therefore cosmopolitan and international. To limit toreo to Spain or even to the Spanish cultural complex abroad would be the equivalent of limiting drama to ancient Greece, the art of the novel to Britain, or ballet to Russia. Good art is particular and universal simultaneously. When a work is only particular, as is the case of certain naturalistic novels, or pretends to be only universal, as in the case of certain neoclassical plays and paintings, the final product is provincial, limited, the reverse of the real thing.

The limitation of toreo is an accident of geography, zoology, and misplaced humanitarianism, not a limitation in the emotion created and expressed by the fiesta. The fact is that the toro bravo is native only to Spain, and that the most culpable ignorance married to sentimentality has prevented the spread of the breed beyond certain former Spanish colonies. Without the toro bravo there can be no toreo; we need thus to consider that magnificent animal before moving on to other components of the art.

# CHAPTER 2

# THE TORO

Having seen the domestic bull of the Greeks and the primitive aurochs of the early Iberians as fertility symbol, totemic object, as hero or villain of folk tales, as model for prehistoric cave drawings and bronzes, as inspirer of ritual, and as a force which seems to have triggered the imagination of the earliest artists that history records, we might now regard the toro bravo in his contemporary actuality. It is one thing to assay the evidence and to conclude that modern toreo originates in Spanish ritual and folk custom. It is quite another matter to see a brave and noble bull in the plaza just as he leaves the *toril*,* first at a trot, then at a canter, head and horns high, his senses completely alert, his hide shining with health and vitality. Such an animal is an event in nature, one which we know in the pit of the stomach, suddenly and viscerally, just as we know, whether our knowledge of toreo be slight or profound, that the events to follow in the lidia should not be trivial, ordinary, false, or dull. The death of the bull is an occasion, one demanding a nobility in the torero at least equal to the nobility of the bull.

The visceral knowledge that the true aficionado discovers in himself at his first corrida and never loses accounts for two contradictory attitudes: for the addiction of the aficionado that may equal or exceed the customary addictions, whether to God, women, drugs, drink, tobacco, power, or wealth; and for the hatred of the abolitionist which is expressed with the venom

---

* *Toril:* The wooden gate separating the *chiqueros,* or stalls, where the bulls to be *toreados* ("fought") are confined, from the plaza.

reserved for Satan, hydrogen bombs, usurers, pederasts, morticians, bankers, book publishers, and abortionists. That visceral knowledge is feared because it is not a product of education, nor can it be bought or otherwise acquired. To the man who lacks it, it smacks of the occult, the fake, or the recherché. It is similar to that faith without which religion is impossible. Or if Nietzsche's terms (from *The Birth of Tragedy*) be preferred, it is Dionysian rather than Apollonian: irrational in essence rather than ordered, rational. Without such knowledge, *afición*\* is impossible. But because it is Dionysian and irrational, it cannot be written about convincingly; it can only be alluded to, in the knowledge that the possessors of it, happily very numerous, will recognize it for what it is.

We are concerned here, however, with another order of knowledge which *is* logical and which may be ordered rationally: that entire range of knowledge about toreo which is expressed in craft, which is the product of observation and experience and which has been handed down from torero to torero through words and example for some two centuries or more. In brief, without an awareness of the bull well beyond the visceral, one cannot study properly the work of the torero nor assess all that occurs in the plaza. Visceral knowledge alone produces an unfortunate romanticism which is the curse of the fiesta, while toreo is among the most classic of the arts.

In the literature on toreo in Spanish, French, and English, the importance of the bull, his true place in the scheme of things, and above all the abuses to which he may be subjected have been slighted in a degree that amounts to evasion. The literature in Spanish, with a few noble exceptions, uses an evasion different from the literature in English. Most Spanish writers know a great deal about the bull, his pedigree, and all the circumstances that precede his presentation in the plaza; they also know how to observe the bull in the plaza. The difficulty is that they assume a high degree of visceral knowledge in their public, knowledge which very often is lacking. In other cases they may simply have been bought off. Writers in English suffer from other disorders. Often they may be ignorant, simply failing to realize the place of

---

\* *Afición:* What the aficionado has—passion, knowledge, dedication to the entire fiesta. Also used of sport or any activity in life, but essentially a term reserved for toreo.

the bull in relation to the torero; in other cases they approach the fiesta with a culpable romanticism, wishing to play down any factor which may detract from the fiesta before the scrutiny of the skeptics or the abolitionists. In still other cases, they suffer from egomania, from the inability to see anything about the art but their own usually marginal participation.

The writer in English has a special problem: our language itself is against us when we use the word "bull." Our semantic associations are all wrong where the fighting bull, the toro bravo, is concerned. We speak of the bull in a china shop, a bull of a man, of a bullish stock market, of bull sessions, which in turn implies the coarse, scatological variant. Usually the implication is that of brute, stupid strength, of gracelessness, or in the impolite usage, of a baroque lie. At the same time, as a country we North Americans are usually too industrialized, too irreligious, too remote in time and distance from the primitive association of the bull with the gods to respect in the ancient sense the power of the bull, and too citified or suburban to be able to see his beauty. In countries where the toro bravo is bred, however, the nasty associations of English not only do not exist, but a vast number of terms have currency by which to describe the physical points of the bull, his age, his horns, his color, to say nothing of a large and subtle vocabulary for his character. In Spain and in Mexico, the bull is recognized as one of the most splendid animals in nature; credit is given him for his beauty, his agility, grace, and his marvelous, controlled strength. Vocabulary, that is to say, is preceded by fact, by long association, observation, and judgment.

In Madrid, in Mexico City, or for that matter in any city or village where a corrida is to be held, nothing is more interesting than to go before noon to the plaza to see the people lined up for tickets to the *apartado** or *sorteo.** If the city is Madrid on a Sunday morning, entire families—fathers, mothers, aunts, uncles, and children—will have been to ten o'clock Mass, then will have

---

* *Apartado, sorteo:* The drawing by lots to determine which matadors shall torear which toros. Six toros make up the usual corrida. The animals are grouped in pairs by common agreement among the matadors' representatives and the *ganadero* (the breeder) as to physical characteristics such as weight, length of horn, and other genetic factors that produce excellence or defect. The apartado also refers to the next step, the separation of the animals into their respective stalls.

gone on foot or by subway, bus, or car to the plaza, where for payment of five pesetas they may observe the toros in the corrals; observe, if they are lucky, the actual drawing of the lots by the banderilleros or apoderados, and best of all, see the maneuvering of the bulls from the corrals to the chiqueros, where the animals will wait in the dark and quiet for the late afternoon finale to their lives.

Although the business types who run the plazas seem to ignore the fact, these are the people upon whom the future of the fiesta in large parts depends. More often than not, such people have remarkable taste, judgment, and historical and contemporary knowledge of toros and toreros; they are unimpressed by sudden reputations and by startling fakery. They have the mad dedication increasingly necessary for a poor man in Spain or Mexico to husband his resources for the price of a ticket. Often they can afford none at all, but are content with the sorteo. There was an old man in Madrid, his face like a relief map of geologically difficult country, who came to Las Ventas every Sunday, always to the same place above the corrals, sunny but sheltered from the wind, where he could easily see the passage of the toros to the chiqueros. In the hour or so of the sorteo he would smoke two cigarettes. One he would take from a package of Celtas and smoke halfway, then empty the unsmoked tobacco into a flat tin. The second he would roll from the salvage in the tin. That was his tobacco ration for the week. He had not been able to pay for a ticket to an actual corrida for many years, he said, but he never missed the sorteo and the opportunity to look at the toros. He studied their conformation, their horns, the condition of their hide; he noticed every flick of their ears, and how they followed objects with their eyes. He knew their exact age, and whether the weights listed in the newspapers were accurate, or, as is more usual, exaggerated. He could pick out the *mansos** with eighty per-cent accuracy, which is better than most toreros can do. He worked hard in that hour, studying the toros with the same intensity as the toreros who were actually to face them. Yet when I asked him to come to the corrida as my guest, he refused. He said he was a

---

* *Manso:* Tame, cowardly. That toro which, for defective heredity or some other cause, will not charge. Under the regulations, if the toro refuses to take the pic, he is supposed to be returned to the corrals and one of the reserves sent in. A *mansurrón,* a cowardly toro, is dangerous for the toreros and its lidia often boring to the spectators.

*torista,* not a *torerista,* and that he was of an age where the corrida would exhaust him. "I take my pleasure in seeing the toros here," he said. "Then in the afternoon, back in my room I lie on my bed and imagine the perfect lidia to each of them. That is excitement enough for an old man."

The old man was an extreme example of a type often met in Spain and in Latin America, but rarely met in North America or in Northern Europe, the torista. The torista exalts the toro over the torero to the point where he will ignore and despise the man's best achievements. He observes everything that takes place in the plaza from the bull's point of view, looking on the toreros' work only as a necessary distraction to what really matters: the toro's performance. He will be more disturbed at seeing a banderillero cape a toro into the *barrera** than at seeing a matador receive a grave *cornada.* The torista is not inhuman or hard of heart; he merely tries, consciously or unconsciously, to correct what he sees as an imbalance caused by ignorance between the integrity of the animal and the exaggerated reputation of the torero.

Again, the literature in English tends to be the work of torer- istas, not of toristas, if only because the work of the torero is human and more immediately accessible to the neophyte. Even *Death in the Afternoon,* which remains the best work on the subject in the language, is limited by Hemingway's comparative indifference to the toro; he pays lip service to the place of the toro but gives his fullest attention to the torero. That limitation becomes crippling in the journalism of "The Dangerous Sum- mer."[1] Whether in English or Spanish, the vast majority of ex- toreros' memoirs or autobiographies are the work of toreristas, intent upon glorifying themselves and their careers rather than upon discussing the full art.

The complete aficionado is neither torista nor torerista. While agreeing with the torista upon the importance of the animal, he will neither ignore, exaggerate, nor deprecate the work of the torero. Like the torero himself, the aficionado cannot emphasize

---

* *Barrera:* The fence around the ring. Barreras refer to the first range of seats nearest the *callejón,* or the alleyway between the barrera and the wall of the stands proper.

[1] The situation has improved in English since the publication of Angus McNab's *The Bulls of Iberia* (1957), and of Luis de Asca- subi's *Of Bulls and Men* (1962). Both men are *toristas* with a vengeance.

men at the expense of knowledge of toros, nor toros at the expense of knowledge of lidia. The acquisition of such knowledge is a lifelong task, for the variants that go into the production of the toro in the plaza are great. The observer who makes only crude distinctions along the lines of large versus small, three-year-old novillo versus five-year-old toro, while at the same time claiming a nice discrimination in judging a torero's cape and muleta work is in fact deluding himself. He is like the *novillero\** who confronts every novillo with the same suertes in the same sequence. He cannot master his art, for he is unaware of the true nature of its components. For the novillero, only observation and experience can supply his deficiency, always assuming the disposition to learn, together with the indispensable talent and intelligence. For the aficionado, reading and observation may in part substitute for the immediate experience of the torero, but the aficionado too must be able and eternally willing to observe and to learn through observation.

It is a common assumption that contemporary bull breeding is decadent, that the modern toro is a shadow of his ancient proto-type, that the contemporary torero is a shameless, money-loving coward, enforcing upon breeders his degenerate standards. To the historian of any of the arts, that assumption of decadence has a familiar ring. We have been assured that Joyce and Proust "killed" the modern novel with their experiments, and that in any event the public wants fact, not fiction. We are constantly assured that the theater is dead and does not know it; that modern painting and music are in a cul-de-sac of their own construction. A modicum of truth may be contained in these accusations of deca-dence, but the full truth is far more complex than the popular reduction. The fact is that great art has always been rare, the arts have always been full of fakes, leeches, and crooks, while it seems to give comfort to some persons to beat the living over the head with the achievements of the great dead. Because our artists in the fullest sense represent us, we long for them to be unassailably

---

*Novillero:* The neophyte who, while gaining experience, faces not toros (four-year-olds and up) but novillos (three-year-olds). He is a matador de novillos, or adolescent bulls. In fact, the novillero may often have to face five- or six-year-olds that the full matador does not care to risk.

great; we want a masterpiece with our Sunday morning coffee and oranges. But when our contemporaries do not oblige, we turn on them. We resent having to identify the artists' failures with ourselves; thus the aficionado's exhaustion and depression after a poor corrida, in contrast to his exultation after a good one.

The charge of decadence in modern toreo involves more than an emotional rejection of the present on the part of the middle-aged purist. The same, of course, must be said for fiction, painting, or any of the other arts. The charge rather reflects a conscious awareness of fundamental change, together with anger or despair, half-realized or realized virtually not at all, at the failure of the individual to be able to account for the reality before his eyes. This in turn leads to hostility and rejection of the event, whether it be a canvas, a novel, or a style of comporting oneself before a toro. The changes in question occurred over a fairly long period: in poetry, they date from Baudelaire's work; in the other arts, from the turn of the century, with great acceleration in the decade of World War I, or between 1910 and 1920. What is involved, of course, is a fundamental change in European sensibility; in order even to discuss that change, one must try to enter the difficult country between public event and private sensibility, between the demands of art and the demands upon the self by the artist working within his art.

In moving from the contemporary reality in toreo (or any other art) to the criticism of decadence, one encounters what one may call the conservative illusion. The conservative illusion is that side of our social nature which prefers the familiar to the strange, the past to the present, the established to the revolutionary. According to the illusion, these things are not only to be preferred, but they are invested with irrational value to a point where the past reality, always pitted with imperfection, is remembered as golden and perfect, in proportion as the present appears a sorry thing, unappetizing and unworthy. The sociological term "cultural lag" may help to define the conservative illusion, although it is inadequate in that it focuses too narrowly upon the temporal factor. The conservative illusionary does not actually lie to himself; he merely ceases to make the effort to adjust his mind to a constantly shifting panorama of reality, admittedly an exhausting effort and therefore a vice of age. Few human beings over twenty-one do not experience the impulses of the conservative illusion in some degree. The danger arises at the point where illusion supplants truth, induces blindness to actuality, and where illusion is transformed into delusion.

Contemporary art may be seen with profit as the effort to dispel the conservative illusion of Western Europe in the last century and a half. In part, nineteenth-century history is the record of political and social attempts to deny certain realities: after 1789 and Bonaparte, the pretense was that the French Revolution and ensuing uproars had never occurred; 1848 was regarded as an aberration, and 1870 as an abomination. Grandiose illusion was substituted for recalcitrant fact. Material progress was called spiritual triumph; cash dividends were confused with God's grace; conquest was called pacification. The hog was encouraged to behave like the poodle. The official version of social reality, in short, was very far from social fact. The 1914–1918 war put an end to all that; its actuality was so oppressive that neither illusion nor delusion could survive it. The lines of relationship between art and social event—what we loosely call politics—are mysterious; some would deny their very existence. That we are dealing with sensibility is apparent; in such an area, nothing can be proved, all must be suggested.

Since Spanish history is not identical with that of Northern Europe over the years in question, it might seem that the above is irrelevant to Spain, and to toreo. All that differs, however, in the case of Spain, is the chronology. A change in modern Spanish sensibility has undoubtedly taken place, one which has worked a tremendous change in what the public wants, will accept, and will demand in the plaza. But those changes, in turn, derive from changes in the toro, the basic animal. At the same time, the recent history of toreo may be shown to prove a direct relationship between social event and art with a particularly pure savagery.

That the contemporary toro differs from the toro of the nineteenth century is a fact. Selective breeding, in part the result of an increased knowledge of genetics, in greater part the result of advice and pressure upon breeders by toreros, accounts for the changes. Yet the assumption that toreros exerted pressure for changes upon breeders out of fear of the nineteenth-century monster is simply not true. Rafael Guerra, "Guerrita," for example, one of the legendary matadors of the period whose name is always invoked with awe, is known to have been among the first to urge the breeders of his day to refine their system of selection to a point where their toros would be more amenable to fine lidia—so that, in fact, the modern faena might become possible.[2] It can be argued that before the change in the toro, the work of the torero was little more than athletic and brave, defensive in character to the point of the *estocada*.* Criticism has not yet come to terms with the change. It is illogical and unfair to approve the modern faena to the comparatively small, four-year-old toro, and to regret the passing of the five- to eight-year-old, very large toro of the past. The modern aficionado who regrets the past should be very clear about what he is regretting.

One has only to look back into the files of *La Lidia*, to read certain of the early manuals of tauromachia such as that of Montes, to read travel literature like Théophile Gautier's *Voyage en Espagne,* or to consult governmental regulations of toreo of the past, to realize that, while certain elements have been lost, a good deal has been gained through modern changes. The nineteenth- and early twentieth-century toro was by modern standards a monster. He was at least five years old, he might weigh 700 kilos, and he was armed with a formidable sweep of horn. Because he was older, not necessarily because he was larger, he was more dangerous and more possessed of *sentido*.† (Size is a psychological factor, both for torero and audience; but a small, fast toro with sentido is much more dangerous than a large, frank, noble one.) Before 1928, when the *peto*‡ was introduced, the work of the picador was more prominent than it is in the modern corrida. Unprotected horses, powerful, wise toros, and incompetence on the part of the picador frequently meant the grievous wounding or death of many horses. Hemingway claimed to find the sight of a horse treading its entrails comic; the reader may form his own judgment of that. When we read of toros of the golden age taking twenty or thirty pics, we need to remember that the pic itself was smaller, and

---

[2] José Alameda, *Los arquitectos del toreo moderno* (Mexico: B. Costa-Amic, 1961), p. 12.

* *Estocada:* The *suerte de matar.* (Matar: to kill; hence matador.) The kill is performed with the *estoque* (also *espada*), or sword. Techniques of the estocada are discussed in Chapter 4. Espada means any sword, but only the matador uses the estoque, which is curved at the end for better penetration to the toro's aorta. Espada is also a rather archaic term for matador.

† *Sentido:* A quality in the bull which defines rapidity of learning to distinguish man from lure, and his accuracy in attack.

‡ *Peto:* Mattresslike protector for the picador's horse.

because of its shape, less capable of damage than the modern pic. The modern toro that takes three pics may be no less brave than his ancestor.

We are told that the glory of the early corrida was the emphasis upon cape work in the *quites** necessitated by the large number of pics to the toro; the variety of lances practiced by the matadors, and the satisfaction to the toro of getting his horn into the living flesh of the horse, as opposed to his frustration at encountering the peto. No question that the contemporary torero neglects the cape to exalt the muleta. But, if one reads between the lines, one learns that the toro which drew blood by wounding or killing a horse was very likely to take up a dangerous *querencia†* at that point; second, that much of the vaunted cape work was done not by the maestros, the matadors, but the *chulos,* the young apprentices who performed some of the tasks of the modern banderillero. Francisco Montes' proposals (in 1836) for reform of the fiesta are eloquent: among other things, he deplores the substitution of inferior toros for those announced; the employment of grossly untrained, incompetent picadors and chulos; the habit of matadors of allowing chulos or fellow matadors to kill toros that seemed unlucky. And in the case of mansos, Montes proposed that they be played with the cape, leaped over, and otherwise tormented, in order to divert the public and give them their money's worth. Finally, and most important, that they be killed not by the matador's sword, but that dogs be turned on them to worry them to death.[3]

Most eloquent of all was the nineteenth-century regulation requiring at least two passes with the muleta before the estocada. Federico M. Alcazar writes that before Belmonte, nine out of ten

---

* *Quite* (keé-tay): The action of removing the toro from the horse or from a man. Quites are of two kinds: the formal cape work after a pic, and the quite as a *recurso* (recourse)—as when the bull is about to gore a man on the sand. See also footnote on page 145.

† *Querencia:* Literally, a preferred place. A place in the ring in which the bull feels comparatively safe and where he is dangerous, for in effect he says, "Come and get me." The toril is a natural querencia, and most moribund toros move there to die. A warm place in the sun on a cold day, or a damp patch of sand on a hot day may account for other querencias. Some cannot be accounted for at all. It is a trick of flashy toreros to give a dangerous-looking pass or lance to a toro on his way to a querencia; the animal is not then thinking of man or lure, but of his favored spot.

3 *Tauromaquia completa* (Madrid, 1836), pp. 266–277.

toros were fought *por la cara*\* [4] That is, the entire sense of the earlier corrida worked against the long, varied faena. The toro with his years, sentido, and armament was dangerous, and the emphasis accordingly was upon reducing his power in the prolonged suerte de varas, in spending more time and appreciation than is customary today upon the placing of the banderillas, and of course full emphasis upon the kill. If the very large, earlier toro were to be killed at all, great domination was required on the part of the matador, great care was necessary to insure that the toro was fixed in the cape. Yet much of the work with cape and muleta was of necessity defensive, and because the toro was cited from in front (*de frente*), at considerable distance, his charge was likely to be so rapid as to forbid the linked passes so dear to the modern afición. At the same time, again reading between the lines, the chulos were liberally employed to take the toro's attention as he came out of the pass, and to line him up for the next pass which the matador might want to make.

This is not to deprecate the style of the past; far from it. The necessity for authority, for *dominio*† in the plaza, produced a line of great matadors; those men spent years as chulos in learning their work. They placed their own banderillas, they had to have a knowledge of lidia, they were frequently very fine with the estoque. But when the aficionados now in old age lament the past, we (and they) should be very clear about what they are lamenting: magnificent, savage animals, although not all so, as their memories would select. A large number of mansos was sent to the plazas in the days of Montes, Lagartijo, Frascuelo, El Espartero, and the other gods. The white-haired aficionado laments a spectacle more often than not dominated by the picador, an equine auto-da-fé in which many horses in the course of an afternoon were gutted in the plaza, to be finished off by the puntilla, or to be hastily sewn up and to reappear until such time as they received a mortal cornada. They lament a faena often made up of a few flaps of the muleta in the toro's muzzle to square him up for the kill. And they lament a public that was diverted by the prospect of a toro torn to

---

\* *Por la cara:* "In front of the muzzle"; any suerte in which the toro does not pass the man is por la cara.

[4] *Tauromaquia moderna* (Madrid, 1936), p. 99.

† *Dominio:* Domination. *Mando* means the same and is more commonly used by toreros.

death by dogs, while they seem to prefer athletic agility on the part of the matador to grace and fluency of movement. Whatever their disagreements, old and young have no quarrel about the necessity for certain basic standards in the toro de lidia; the argument about mere size should not obscure a community of agreement.

Our intention is not to write one more treatise on the breeding, testing, and marketing of toros bravos. That has been done, and handsomely, by others: by Cossío in Spanish, and by McNab and Ascasubi in English. We want, rather, to indicate how the breeder's work affects both the torero and the aficionado in the contemporary plaza. The ideal breeder would need to combine many antithetical qualities: he must be both scientist and artist, businessman and philanthropist, torista and torerista. He must be endowed with instinct, afición, insight, honesty, patience, land, and capital. That he is rarely or never met in life is not surprising. When we see a shameless mansurrón in the plaza, or a toro willing but weak on his feet, we may trace the defect back to the deficiency in the *ganadero*\* of one or more of those saintly or worldly qualities. Given the royalist, retrospective, and agricultural stamp of Spanish society, the breeding of bulls has always been undertaken either by members of the hereditary nobility who possessed the necessary land, capital, and spirit, or by that other aristocrat, the retired torero. Latin-American breeders, in the main, have followed the Spanish pattern, in spite of revolutions and social upheavals.

One of the nagging problems of the modern art of toreo is that breeding is not only a delicate and demanding process but also a huge business, involving major profit or loss, and the livelihood of thousands upon thousands of human beings. Indirectly, the presentation of corridas in Spain and Mexico accounts for a large although incalculable percentage of the tourist traffic, and therefore a significant percentage of the national income. As a result, considerable pressures are exerted upon the breeder to diminish his standards, to pass as brave a dubious animal after the testing, and to send inferior strings of toros to the plazas. Over the short run, such practices will produce handsome profits and encourage the unscrupulous everywhere, but only at the expense of debasing

---

\* *Ganadero*: Cattle-breeder, owner, or in charge of the ganadería, or ranch. *Finca*, a country holding, is also used instead of ganadería.

the integrity of the fiesta, and, as is conceivable, of eliminating it as an art form. Another special threat to the fiesta has to do with the relationship between genetics, history, and politics. Although there are two hundred and fifty-nine ganaderías of toros bravos in Spain alone, the breeder everywhere depends upon perilously few blood strains that have come down to us from the organization of the first Spanish ganaderías in the seventeenth and eighteenth centuries.[5]

The oldest strain is the Jijona, dating from about 1606 but today extinct. The bloodline has been absorbed in the Vistahermosa strain. In about 1690, the Marquis of Santa Clara organized a stud of the small, red Pyrenean toro, later known as Carriquirris. The Carriquirris were brave but difficult, and too small for the heroic age of toreo. Thus today the line is virtually extinct in Spain, although it survives in the Atenco stud in Mexico. In a period of thirty-five years in the eighteenth century, the four great bloodlines that made modern toreo possible came into being: the Cabrera, in 1745; the Gallardo, about 1750; the Vistahermosa, in 1775; and the Vázquez, in 1780. For a century, the Cabreras, an Andalusian strain developed from many localities in the Seville region, were noted for their size and bravery. They also became noted for sentido, their ability to distinguish the torero from the lure, thus diminishing their popularity. In 1852, Don Juan Miura bought the Cabrera stud and combined it with other Andalusian strains to produce the magnificent and murderous Miuras that we still see occasionally today.[6] The Gallardos were a cross between the small bulls of Navarre and large Andalusian cows. They survive in the modern Pablo Romeros, which also combine Jijona, Cabrera, Vistahermosa, and Vázquez blood.

No breeder, from the seventeenth century to the present, has consistently equaled, much less surpassed, the qualities of the

---

[5] The reader hardly need be reminded that the fighting bull is native only to Spain; one mentions it here because of Agustín Linares' claim in *El toro de lidia en México* (Mexico, 1953), p. 15, that toros bravos were native to Mexico, too. They were not.

[6] The stress must be placed upon "occasionally." In recent seasons, the Miuras have displayed their traditional conformation but little else. The strain has undergone an alarming decline, having run to weakness and comparative timidity. Even their notorious sentido has diminished. Yet the Miura is still the only strain that can fill a plaza, irrespective of the toreros on the *cartel,* the program.

Vistahermosa breed. Uniform in origin, unlike the Cabreras or the Vazqueños, the Vistahermosa is noted not only for his nobility and frankness but for his beauty. Of good size but not monstrous, he has small hoofs, fine horns, a small dewlap, and a long, silky tail. While Vistahermosa blood is present in a large number of herds in Spain and in Latin America, the strain still exists in its purity in the Murube herd, owned by the Urquijo family.

Like the Cabrera, the Vázquez strain was of mixed Andalusian origin, and the Vázquez was similar in characteristics to the Cabrera. Their repute in the early nineteenth century was such that in 1830, at the death of Vicente José Vázquez, King Fernando VII purchased the greater part of the stud; upon his death, it was again purchased by the Duke of Veragua. The Vazqueños survive undiluted in the Concha y Sierra ganadería, while again they have contributed their qualities to numerous modern strains.[7] These genetic facts are of course well known. They are cited here simply to emphasize that bull breeding is a selective process and that the nature of the selection ultimately is determined by public sensibility. The Vistahermosa strain came to dominate the Jijona or the Cabrera because of the growing importance of the muleta. The muleta in turn reflected a stage of refinement on the part of torero and public, an awareness that the fiesta could be more than public savagery; that it could, in truth, be an art.

Contemporary toreo is dominated by two extremely important events: the emergence of the toro specifically bred to produce a certain type of lidia in the period coinciding with the careers of Juan Belmonte and Joaquín Rodríguez (Cagancho), the former having taken the *alternativa** in 1913, the latter in 1927. The

---

[7] The most lucid discussions in English of relationships between bloodlines and the modern bull are those of Ascasubi and McNab.

* *Alternativa:* The aspiring matador is called a novillero because he faces (in theory, not often in practice) novillos. He is a matador de novillos. When he is judged to be sufficiently experienced, when he has established *cartel*—which cynically may be understood as his being a good financial risk to empresarios—and appears to be solidly on the rise, he will undergo the ceremony of the alternativa and thereafter be a matador de toros. He receives his new status during a corrida from the senior matador of the day, who is his *padrino*, or sponsor, in the presence of the number two matador, the *testigo*, or witness. The padrino cedes the first toro of the day to the ex-novillero, thus alternating the normal order of things; hence alternativa. The ceremony will take place either in the young man's

second event was of course the Spanish Civil War, which broke out in July 1936. That anything of cultural value survived the Spanish Civil War is a tribute to Spanish character; the same may be said of the Mexican Revolution of 1910–1917, although in a very different context. That toreo survived is further witness, if witness be needed, to the fact that toreo fulfills a profound human need. In Spain, the immediate effect of the outbreak of the Civil War was the virtual suspension of corridas and the destruction of many of the herds. In hungry times the animals were slaughtered for food, or wantonly in political protest against the landowners. At considerable personal risk, many ganaderos managed to preserve the blood strains by hiding away a few seed bulls and cows in caves or other remote areas. The imposition of Franco's peace by no means meant a return to pre-Civil War conditions, for the years of World War II were almost as wretched for the Spanish as if they had been combatants. Scarcities of all sorts, including meager fodder, were exacerbated by a series of dry years, lasting to 1950.[8]

It is necessary to remember that the classical age for the toro bravo in a first-class plaza was five completed years, and the classical minimum weight 500 kilograms (2.2 pounds to the kilo). By royal order of 1919, four-year-old bulls were allowed provided they came up to the classical weight. In 1930, a new regulation permitted the recognition of four-year-olds weighing only 470 kilos as toros; this was *de jure* recognition of the new aesthetic introduced by Belmonte and others, and was in the main welcomed by the public. But the changes in standards were of another order altogether. Whereas the changes of 1919 to 1930 represented choice and alteration in public sensibility, the changes between 1939 and the present represented the force of necessity together

---

home town, or in the city in which he is best known; it will then be confirmed through repetition in the capital city: Madrid, in Spain; Mexico City, in Mexico. Until recently, all toreros, banderilleros, and picadors too went through a form of alternativa ceremony. Now, unfortunately, the rite applies only to matadors. Matadors' seniority, and therefore the order in which they torear, is determined rigidly by their dates of alternativa.

[8] The authors are aware of the possibilities of ludicrousness implicit in the juxtaposition of horrors such as the Civil War and World War II with a (perhaps minor) art such as toreo. We write, however, in full consciousness of the war rather than as flaming-eyed fanatics incapable of proportion.

with cynical profiteering at the expense of the dignity and integrity of the fiesta itself.

Throughout the bad years, the authorities were forced to tolerate underage and underweight animals in the plazas; novillos weighing as little as 250 kilos were regularly fought as toros. In 1943, the regulation demanded a minimum of 423 kilos in first-class plazas, but this regulation too was frequently violated. The practice of levying fines upon the breeder in proportion to the amount a given animal was underweight had the effect only of increasing the price of the animal to the empresario, who in turn made up his loss by raising ticket prices. If the regulations were flouted in major plazas during these years, procedures in minor plazas may be imagined. Calves the size of foxes were fought as novillos, and *utreros** the size of dogs were fought as toros. Widespread toleration of underage and underweight fighting stock was unfortunate, but it was at least understandable, nor was it necessarily immoral, given the bleak realities of the period. Widespread toleration of horn shaving, however, in the years between 1939 and 1953 was not only immoral, it was an attempt by all involved to murder Spanish toreo. What was done to bulls and to toreo might be compared to selling off the original paintings in the Prado and substituting badly executed copies, or to supplying dud ammunition to one's own troops in time of war.

The narrative of the revelations in 1952 by the Conde de la Corte, Domingo Ortega, by the radio critic Curro Meloja, and above all by the matador Antonio Bienvenida has been well told.[9] The mere narrative, however, does not adequately register the complexity of cause and result in the abuses committed, nor does it take into account the Spanish public's part in the episode. At the risk of emphasizing the obvious, one must remind the reader that horn shaving (and other abuses to the toro) creates a parody of the fiesta because it upsets the toro's timing, and therefore allows the torero to take "risks" that look suicidal but are not so. The toro's horns are not actually shaved; we translate the Spanish idiom (*afeitar*) literally but fail to translate the cynical understatement of the word. Rather, the toro is lured into a narrow corral, trussed with ropes to the point where he is immobile, and

---

* *Utrero*: A bull between two and three years old. Before that he is an *eral*—one to two years old.

[9] By Angus McNab, *The Bulls of Iberia,* ch. 16.

two or three inches (called "the diamond") are sawed off each
horn with a hack-saw. The entire horn is then reshaped by filing,
including a sharp point, but the toro has been raped of his lifelong training in the precise use of his horns. The effect upon his
attack might be comparable to that of a tennis player who radi-
cally alters the weight of his racquet before a match, or of the
amputee who feels sensation in an extremity that is no longer
there. After filing, the horn may be rubbed with mud and dung to
dirty up the dirty work (not, as Hemingway reported in "The
Dangerous Summer," with crankcase oil; the smell would give
away the job to the unbribed, and unless the filing were quite
artistic, it would be made obvious by oil). Whoever has tried to
force pills down a cat's throat is prepared to appreciate the effect
upon the toro of being trussed by ropes and violated by the saw
and the file; in addition, if the saw cuts too far down, tissue will be
torn, and pain and perhaps fever follow, just as though one were
to cut deeply into the flesh of one's nails.

Horn shaving is only the most notorious of the range of abuses
to the toro of which the aficionado should be constantly aware.
Perhaps the most common abuse takes place before the toro gets
anywhere near the plaza; that is the practice of gorging the animal
on grain in order to pass off a novillo as a toro, or to insure that an
inferior toro will make the required weight. A related practice is
to feed the animals on straw in winter to economize. They will look
reasonably fit, but they will be weak on their feet. The effects of
overfeeeding are the same to the animal as to a man. It will be
short of breath, weak, and uninterested in responding to the
torero's lures. When, as so often happens, we see a splendid-
looking toro that seems to want to take the pic but simply stands
panting, and after one or two pics falls down, we are witnessing
the overfed toro rather than the manso. Similar symptoms may be
caused by still other and more wicked abuses: after an *encierro** is
sold to an empresario, it becomes his to transport as he sees fit to
the plaza. In the days before railroads and trucks, the animals were
driven by night to the plaza; now they are herded into wooden
compartments and usually driven by specially constructed trucks
to their destination. The length of the journey alone, during
which the animals take neither food nor water, weakens them and

---

* *Encierro:* A string of six or more toros (often two reserves are
  included) to be toreados in the plaza. Ideally they are matched for
  appearance and brave qualities. Corrida is also used in this sense.

creates the familiar apathy which we see all too often. Still other abuses often indulged in during the golden years of horn shaving, always with the intention of weakening the animals to make them easier for the torero, were the practice of injecting novocaine into the kidneys or beating the animal in the loins with a sandbag. All of these abuses have the effect not only of weakening the toro but also of diminishing his bravery and of upsetting his natural re-actions. Since the toro's source of strength for the charge is the muscles of the lower loin, the result of any of the above abuses is rather like that of a six-cylinder motor in which two cylinders are dead.

The file, the saw, the needle, and the sandbag are all used in comparative secrecy; thus their use is difficult for the layman to detect and to protest. Another order of abuse is practiced in public and needs to be protested loudly whenever it occurs. In spite of the toro's great strength, the animal's musculature is as delicate and as subject to strain as that of a thoroughbred. Hence, when a matador permits or instructs his banderillero to double the toro in the course of running it (*bregando*) preparatory to the matador's own preliminary cape work, he is encouraging a serious abuse. The toro is subjected to strain by being forced to turn rapidly; his testicles may be injured; his entire attitude may be, as the Spanish so precisely put it, *descompuesto* (discomposed). It is even more serious when the banderillero forces the toro to smash into a *burladero*.* An uninstructed public will often laugh when this occurs, although it ought to call for a stiff fine to the torero responsible. The effect upon the toro is exactly the effect such a trauma would have upon a man. The beast is dazed, discomposed, weakened, again deprived unfairly of a portion of his bravery. A more subtle variation upon that abuse is the picador's frequent practice of allowing the toro to smack into the peto. Here it should be explained that according to article 85 of the current *Reglamento Taurino*, the peto is supposed to weigh no more than 30 kilos; the use of a heavier peto than this is to be punished by a fine of 2,000 pesetas. The point, of course, is that the use of a very heavy peto in itself is an abuse; it is common knowledge that the petos in standard use in Spain and in Mexico weigh up to 100

---

* *Burladero:* A narrow wooden shield about one foot inside the plaza from the *barrera*, permitting the toreros to slip to safety when necessary but not wide enough for the toro to pursue them. The burladero permits the torero to *burlar* (deceive) the animal.

kilos. While the toro strains to overturn the combined weight of picador, horse, and peto, the picador all too often uses the pic virtually to immolate the toro, rather than as an instrument to impede the charge and allow the horse to pivot to safety. It is also a common abuse for the matador to be reluctant or dilatory in making the quite, thus allowing further punishment from the pic and further muscular strain to the toro.

In 1952 when the Conde de la Corte said that he would not send his stock to plazas where their horns might be shaved, when Domingo Ortega said that he had regularly shaved horns to order but would do so no more, and when Antonio Bienvenida refused to fight animals whose horns had been shaved, there were shouts, yells, howls, and roars from the press and the public. Such outcry was followed by long-overdue changes in the regulations which, if enforced, offered the possibility of eliminating the abuses. That outcry was fascinating in its vehemence, for it had the false accents of him who protests too much; one is tempted to think that it could occur only in a land where *pundonor** is on every tongue. Everyone in Spain who knew anything about the fiesta knew that horns were regularly shaved, and knew furthermore that a generation of figuras had made their reputations through their maneuvers to toros which had been deprived of their energy and bravery through one or more of the common abuses. As many commentators have pointed out with a good deal of *Schadenfreude,* it did not seem accidental that a wave of retirements occurred with the new regulations, including that of Litri, Dominguín, and Arruza. What appears to be involved in the whole question of the abuse to the toro, the public toleration of that abuse, and the cynical outcry when, finally, abuses were denounced by some of the very men who had indulged in them, is a national inherited attitude towards the fiesta, and the effect upon the Spanish public of the Civil War.

Both Spain and Mexico have preserved with a disturbing and often wonderful purity certain communal gestures that speak for deeply rooted psychological motives in us all, but that are virtually lost in highly industrialized countries. Among these gestures is an ambivalence toward a loved or respected object that creates moving spectacles of devotion on the one hand and may on the

---

* *Pundonor:* An almost excessive sense of honor; *noblesse oblige;* sense of duty to one's calling, one's fellows, and oneself.

other hand be responsible for orgies of blood. Thus while the toro is accorded a respect approaching veneration, he may also on occasion become an object of savage ridicule, and ultimately of hatred. Anyone who has attended a provincial fiesta at which a calf is let loose among the crowd understands the import of these words. The calf is prodded, kicked, played with items of clothing used as capes or muletas, perhaps jabbed by knives, and otherwise tormented in a manner to chill the blood. All the while, waves of laughter follow every antic of each country lout. Such treatment to the animal is a vivid reminder that until at least a century ago, difficult toros in the plaza might be hamstrung with the *media luna;** that frequently the plaza would be invaded by the public, perhaps bored with the toreros' work and ready to inflict its own lidia upon the wretched toro; that dogs were frequently used to dispatch a dangerous toro, and nitric acid used to incite a manso.[10] One is reminded of the genuine fervor of Spanish and Mexican Catholicism, and of the savagery to churchmen in time of civil war and revolution. An ordered society may have its rule of disorder, its *festum fatuorum;* the country of the marriage rite is also the country of the wretched *charlotadas†* in which culls from the encierros are burlesqued by clownish toreros. An urban psychological parallel is the husband who beats his wife because, among other reasons, he loves her; or the wife who shoots her husband while caught up in the terrible love-hatred polarity.

This is to say that abuses such as those of 1939–1952 in Spain need to be understood, in part at least, in terms of a given society's definition of cruelty, in terms of that society's toleration of given modes of conduct. Cruelty may be defined according to both a relative and an absolute scale. What is socially acceptable in one country is regarded as barbarous in another. In contemporary Germany, for example, educated middle-class parents who wish to go out for an evening and lack servants will tie their infant to its bed and leave it alone in their quarters for hours on end. This would be regarded with horror in Spain or Mexico, where infants

---

* *Media luna:* The mediaeval pike having a blade in the shape of a half moon.

[10] Théophile Gautier, *Voyage en Espagne* (Paris, 1914; 1st ed., 1843), p. 345.

† *Charlotada:* Comic toreo; from "Charlot," the French affectionate diminutive for Charlie Chaplin.

are treated as young royalty, irrespective of family income. What foreigners regard as cruel is always a product of indifference, perhaps of a lacuna in the sensibility of the given society. Where cruelty must be assessed on the absolute scale, where it indicates moral failure, is the point at which the individual takes positive pleasure in the suffering of a sentient being. The Mexican *campesino* (peasant) whose burro plods along the road laden with charcoal and suffering from an enormous saddle sore covered with flies is not being cruel, merely indifferent. The campesino's sufferings, in any event, are greater than the burro's. His standards of cruelty begin at the point where the wrong is greater than his own.

Insofar as the abuses in question were tolerated by some of the public as a product of the traditional love-hatred expressed for the bull, they are not to be charged simply to cruelty. The difficulty is that, as has been said earlier, a large percentage of the public not only knew of the abuses but also applauded the results in the plaza. This was not only cruel to the toro; it was a conscious reduction of the dignity and meaning of toreo, very like the phenomenon of anti-intellectualism and McCarthyism in the United States a few years ago. Just as McCarthyism has been explained as a manifestation of the effect upon a large public of the Cold War, so in Spain the combined toleration and applause of such things as horn shaving can only be explained by the Civil War. War in any guise, to indulge in truism, is a moral outrage which takes its toll.

The career of Manolete (Manuel Rodríguez y Sánchez) is interesting within the perspective of public reaction to abuses to the bull. It is considered bad manners to recall that Manolete's heyday coincided exactly with the period of most widespread abuse. His apologists do him disservice by covering up the fact that many of the animals he faced—no one will ever know exactly how many—were shaved or otherwise incapacitated; Islero, the Miura which killed him, had been shaved. The truth is that Manolete was among the greatest of matadors in spite of the fact that many of the animals he fought had been *arreglados*.* Manolete himself was not personally responsible for those animals; the truth is that he was so valuable a commercial property that the businessmen who surrounded him did not want to lose one day of his money-making

---

* *Arreglado:* Arranged. A polite and therefore nastily ironic term.

47

capacity, therefore they attempted to insure that his career would be long and always more profitable. The public understood this, if only in its bones; the public therefore was terribly exigent, more so than in the case of any other torero we know. The public was exigent out of its own guilt; Manolete was obedient to that exigence to the point of his own death; also, no doubt out of guilt, at least in part. In one sense, his death was a suicide: "You tell me I am in no danger. I shall show you the danger of this Miura, whose horns are shaved. Is this what you want, this cornada? It is yours." Only in such context does the mourning for Manolete make full sense, a requiem that continues these many years after that mortal afternoon in Linares.

Since 1952, abuses to toros in Spain have been the rare exception rather than the rule; in Mexico they were never common, although they may crop up at any time in any plaza in the world. What, then, of the normal toro whose horns have not been shaved, whose physical condition has not been altered by surreptitious meddling? While avoiding anthropomorphism, let us imagine a corrida de toros in Las Ventas, Madrid, or in Plaza México from the standpoint of the animal rather than from the more customary standpoint of the matador. The encierro of eight bulls (two reserves) are between four and five in age, as proved by the four growth rings (*rodetes*) visible at the base of their horns. Their weight varies from 480 to 575 kilos; their tails are short and silky, their feet small, their hide gleaming black, their horns neither turn in excessively (*brocho*), nor are they excessively open (*corniabierto*) and therefore ugly to the eye and difficult for the toreros. One of the reserve toros, however, has splintered (*astillado*) a horn during the unloading from truck to corral, and toro number three is a *bizco*, which is to say that one horn has developed lower than the other, in this case, the left one. They have been in the corrals for five days before the corrida; long enough to settle down after their trip by truck from the ganadería to the plaza, but not so long that they have had time to become sluggish from lack of exercise. At the sorteo at noon on the day of the corrida, one of the matadors, all three apoderados, and various members of the cuadrilla spend long periods of time looking at the toros in the corrals, with the withdrawn, meditative appearance of men at prayer. They observe that toros one, three, and four have more pronounced muscular development in the shoulder, upper loin, and haunch areas than the others, indicating better possibilities for performance. Number six has a noticeably short neck; this is bad, for toros with short necks fatigue easily and tend to hook (*atropellar*) more readily than others. The difference in physique is rather like that of the boxer with long arms who will reach out for his opponent, as against the boxer with short arms who will move in and under his opponent's guard. The torero studies the faces of the toros; none is *cariavacado* (cow-faced). This torero learned as a novillero that the toro with a long, flat cow's face is dangerous because of its angle of vision, its eyes being so set that it can more readily distinguish the man from the lure. In any event, a cow face is a kind of throwback, for it is not a quality bred into the animal. None of the beasts has the stuffed, overfed look of animals that have been raised lean, then overfed for a few weeks for sale. Five and six are slightly swaybacked, a possible source of weakness. One and seven, unlike the others, display nervousness; they paw the earth and occasionally hook at their neighbors. The *mayoral*\* explains the accident to the astillado when questioned by the picador; he has no explanation for number one's jumpiness, however. The other toros are bored by their companions' nervousness. They are alert but at ease, rather withdrawn, like the toreros who study them. Their ears move, they seem to smell the air from time to time. They look like the aristocrats they are. On the whole the toreros are pleased, although they do not admit it. They do not like the age and weight of the animals, although they respect them; they would prefer horns a little more brocho. A *palotazo*† from a brocho could mean a cornada from these bulls. All agree to protest the possible use of the astillado; they will petition that the gray (*cárdeno*) left over from the previous corrida be used instead if necessary. The cuadrillas agree on grouping one and four, two and three, five and six. During the actual sorting into the chiqueros, nothing untoward occurs. Number one in his nervousness gives the *cabestros*‡ some difficulty, but the others go like gentlemen swiftly to their stalls, to wait in darkness and quiet for the late afternoon. The astillado remains in the corral, awaiting the outcome of the protest.

---

\* *Mayoral:* Foreman of a ganadería.

† *Palotazo:* A blow from the side of the horn.

‡ *Cabestro:* Steer. The cabestros are trained to herd the toros bravos, which, having the herd instinct, are usually gentle in a mass, dangerous only when isolated.

**49**

Concerning the manner in which the toro enters the ring from the toril, the aficionado is bound to have read something like this: "As he [the toro] hurtles into the arena, flaunting his murderous intent, there are enough living targets for his deadly weapons that the arena must seem like a fighting bull's paradise."[11] He will have read it, but he will not have seen it in life, for that is not what happens in life. Ernest Hemingway may have originated this particular notion when he wrote in *Death in the Afternoon* that the brave bull enters the ring "confident, fast, vicious and conquering." Barnaby Conrad and other romanticists of toreo have sharpened the ambiguity into full error, frequently repeated in English.[12] Spanish writers know better. Such remarks reveal a confusion in the writers' minds between *nervio** and bravery. It is possible that a toro which has been fought before and therefore has unnatural sentido might come out of the toril looking for something to kill. But toros supplied in any organized corrida must be certified as *limpios.*† In its habitat on the range, the toro bravo is no more aggressive than, say, the stallion. Bravery, *bravura,* defines the toro's reaction to challenge, its willingness to attack, not its disposition to seek out trouble. Bravery may be further understood as the toro's instinct for liberation.

In theory, but not always in practice, a very brave toro will come out of the toril at the gallop and will turn neither left nor right, but proceed at a gallop directly across the ring in a straight line. The toro is said to make its "natural" exit from the toril

---

[11] G. Erik, "Towards Understanding of the Incomparable Fiesta Brava," *Toros,* VII, No. 4 (April 1963), 10.

[12] See Tom Lea, *The Brave Bulls* (Boston, 1949), p. 250: "The package came hurtling from the door. In the center of the plaza it stopped, head up, searching. It stood trembling, lusting to kill." And Juan Belmonte's translator or ghost writer may have been responsible for the statement in *Juan Belmonte: Killer of Bulls* (London, 1937), p. 7, that the bull is "wild and savage" when it enters the plaza. The most grating example is in Barnaby Conrad's nonbook, *The Death of Manolete* (Boston, 1958), p. 84: "The 'gate of frights' clanged open and out of it slammed Islero the last bull of his [Manolete's] life, whirling around and looking for something to kill." (Printed just like that on the page. How do wooden gates "clang"?)

* *Nervio:* Nervousness, jumpiness; what the British mean by "nervy." Hemingway mistranslates nervio as "strength or vigor."

† *Limpio:* Clean, never before caped.

when it turns to the left and circles from left to right in the tablas. When the toro turns to the right upon entering the ring, he is said to make a *salida contraria* (opposite exit). Although these terms have lost their original significance, they are still used as a reminder of the times when the picadors took their place in the ring before the toro's release. At the same time, the toro's exit is frequently a gauge to his degree of bravery: very brave, straight ahead; average bravery, natural, or left; toro of sentido or sometimes outright manso, salida contraria. These neat classifications

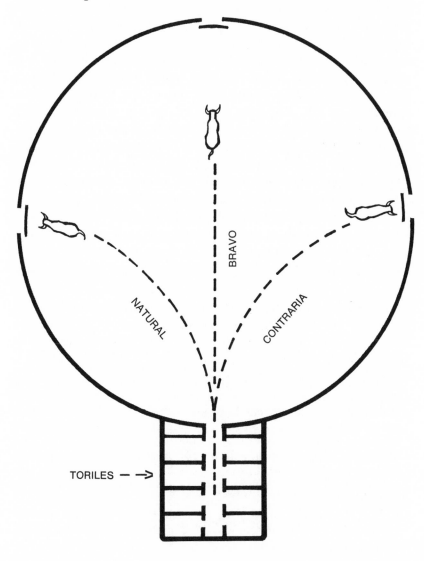

may be upset by the manner in which the toro is treated in the callejón, just before his exit, as well as by the side on which the toril door is hinged. But in general the exit to the left is normal, in toros as in men. It may be associated with our habit of looking from left to right for our seats in a theater.

The average toro de lidia as well as the manso is looking for his natural habitat when he enters the ring: namely, the open range. In the stall, all was dark. When the door swung open, the mayoral or an attendant placed a short barb with the *divisa* of the ganadería in the toro's *morillo,** thus inducing a possibly false *alegría.†* But the bright light of the plaza and the noise of the crowd are unnatural and may often be upsetting. The toro's impressions are therefore confused, and his normal impulse is to get away. The manso will of course sometimes leap the barrera repeatedly in his search for peace and quiet.

The senior matador has decided to take toro four first; he likes to start off well, and number four promises to be better than number one. At the sound of the trumpet, the plaza attendants open the heavy door of the chiquero by manipulating manila ropes. A second attendant smacks the wall near the toro's flank, and the toro lopes through the opening in the direction of the light from the toril, which has also been opened in the meantime. Just before toro four reaches the opening of the toril he pauses, suddenly aware of the rumble of noise from the crowd. As he does so, the mayoral, who has fixed the divisa of the ganadería in the banderilla stick, plunges the barb with the bright ribbons in the toro's neck, and the toro moves forward at a canter into the plaza. He carries on well toward the *medios* like a *toro muy bravo,* but then he veers to the right toward the tablas and pauses, startled by the roar of the crowd as he exploded into the open. The crowd has been pleased at the toro's condition and first indication of bravery, but when he stops, shouts of "manso" are heard from the sunny side. As yet there has been no cape flapping. The senior matador, who knows and likes this breed, has told his *peones‡* not to show a

---

\* *Morillo:* The hump of muscle in the nape of the neck that swells markedly when the animal is enraged.

† *Alegría:* Gaiety, merriment. Used of a toro that seems to charge gaily in his willingness.

‡ *Peón:* Another term for banderillero, deriving from aristocratic rejón, when the person who caped the bull to the horse was in fact a peasant (peón).

cape until he gives the signal. Now, as though to answer the insult of manso, number four takes off around the ring at a good clip, and the matador allows him to make a full circle before nodding to the banderillero in the burladero to the matador's left, across the plaza from the toro. The toro catches sight of the banderillero's cape held high, and hears the man's call. He wheels and charges frankly and swiftly, having to turn in a fairly sharp arc as the cape changes position mysteriously. The toro then pauses,

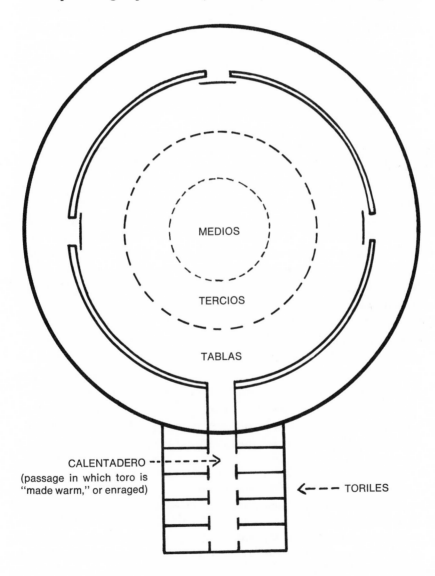

MEDIOS

TERCIOS

TABLAS

CALENTADERO --|-- ----- >
(passage in which toro is
"made warm," or enraged)

<---- TORILES

while the man throws the cape upon the ground and runs at an angle to him. The toro pursues, and while it charges the cape it gives short, rapid stabs, not quite hooks, with the tips of its horns, first with the right, then alternating with the left horn (*puntear*). The matador has seen enough; he calls off the banderillero, who performs a rough *recorte** to fix the toro gently before he disappears behind a burladero. Number four has shown speed, frankness, good vision on both sides, and a disposition to puntear. He may favor the right horn, but probably not. He is strong; he has good feet.

Number four has watched the banderillero disappear, and now the target again appears over his shoulder. The toro wheels and stops to study the cape, which now advances toward him as the matador cites, moving up on the toro's territory, challenging the animal by voice. At twenty feet the toro lays back his ears and charges fast, lowering his head after the high *cite†* and almost forgetting to puntear; twice again the process is repeated. First the cape is high, then lowered and far out from the torero, in the "teaching" lance preceding the true verónica. The toro has learned to follow the cape in these first fast lances, which complete the brega of the banderillero. After having moved at speed for almost five minutes, number four begins to breathe hard. He is tempted to open his mouth but he does not do so. He would like to move to the center of the ring, but the enemy remains near the barrera. Again he charges, more slowly now; he wheels, charges, wheels and charges again and yet again, in rhythm to the cite and flow of the cape. He is definitely winded, but again the cape is directly in front of him, as the matador cites for a media verónica. Again he charges this easy target, circles tightly to pierce with his left horn, but again the target vanishes, and now he must stop to draw breath and gather strength. The matador is walking insolently away, but the toro cannot or will not follow; a movement on the opposite side of the ring shows him yet another target, as a banderillero distracts him from the slowly moving matador. Now his head begins to feel heavy; the constant reaching for the moving target has begun to tire him.

---

* *Recorte:* From *recortar,* to shorten. Any one of numerous lances and passes, such as the *media verónica,* in which the torero "shortens" the bull's charge and fixes the animal at its conclusion.

† *Cite:* From *citar,* to provoke the bull by motion of the lure, by voice, or with the body.

The sight of the picador's horse infuriates the toro. This is more familiar; memory of the *tienta** stirs and fires him to a prompt charge, his weariness forgotten. To the cheering of the crowd he is upon the horse with a slash of horn and a mighty heave to overthrow the animal before the picador has been able to use the iron. The toro pushes at the unyielding peto to disembowel the horse, but again his first target is there in the corner of an eye; he must dispatch that. He is led off by the cape, only to see still another horse nervously approaching. He wheels from the cape and answers the picador's shouted challenge. This time the picador is ready, but the toro ignores the iron in the muscle of his shoulder and again he forces the horse back, off balance, up and over. The picador slides out of the saddle and lies still, playing dead, near the toro, who chooses to ignore him and to slash again at the peto protecting the horse. The matador does his first formal quite, and now the toro's charge is distinctly slower, allowing two neat *gaoneras.†* Twice more the bull goes to the horse, taking two more heavy pics. His power is somewhat diminished; he is not able to overthrow in these latter charges. He feels the pics and bleeds a good deal; the mouth is now open for half a minute at a time, then closed again. Seeming to heed the crowd's shouts, the president changes the tercio, although the toro is fully willing to go yet again to the horse. The matador thinks that the toro perhaps should have had another pic, but it is too late to do anything about it. And better one pic too few than one too many.

Resisting an urge to trot to the medios, the toro makes an uneasy ellipse, returning to the tablas, that area from which his enemies seem to emerge. He experiences satisfaction mixed with rage; he has dealt twice with the horse, but he has not been able, in spite of his exertions, to catch the vanishing capes. He is winded, and his sides heave. His shoulder muscles pain him, and his head is considerably lower than before the suerte de picar. Because one of the pics has penetrated on the right of the spine rather than on top, where it belonged, the matador tells the banderilleros to quarter on the left, not on the right as most

---

* *Tienta:* The process of testing for bravery at the ganadería both of breeding cows and of young bulls.

† *Gaonera:* A lance in which the torero holds the cape behind his back, citing the toro from in front on one side, then turning as the toro passes to cite it on the other side. Named for the great Mexican matador, Gaona.

banderilleros seem to prefer. The matador does not want to encourage the toro to favor one side, thus the banderillas to the left might counteract the pain and physical damage on the toro's right side. Again number four charges frankly at his new enemy, the running man who three times quarters to place the barbs inside the tightest ellipse the toro can manage. The pain of the banderillas is different from the heavy pain of the pic; the toro can fight this sort of pain by tossing his head and bucking. The clattering shafts annoy him with their noise and weight. But he learns to accept them, however angrily.

The appearance of the matador alone in the ring with muleta and sword at the change of tercio conveys to the toro a sense that now he confronts his ultimate enemy. He is both soothed and determined by the elimination of many targets from his view. He comes to the muleta willingly, only to be doubled severely upon himself. The matador perhaps punishes too much, in the theory

*Gaonera*

that the toro needed one more pic. The toro is slowed, and proceeds more cautiously, with less alegría than he displayed for the cape. Now his intelligence indicates that the man is his enemy rather than the muleta, but his instinct forces him to charge the moving cloth, aided by the man's cajolery and encouragement. In spite of his annoying pain and unaccustomed slowness, the toro seems almost to be in conspiracy with the man to carry out the man's intentions. Yet the toro's dominant and persistent aim is to triumph over the moving target, to throw it high, to kill it by repeated attacks with his horns. Near the end of the faena, as the toro passes the man's chest in a *pase de pecho*, he realizes that he has been vanquished, that he has been deprived of any possible victory over the cloth or the man. Yet his deprivation is a triumph, too, for he has extended himself to his utmost. He seems to say to the man, *"Mátame"* (kill me). His mouth is shut, although he needs air urgently; his instinct is not to give in to that need. His

pain is generalized, not particular to any single wound. He knows that it is time to die, and he stands, feet together, allowing the man to aim the estoque carefully. But if it is time to die, it is also time to kill, and he lunges again at the man, causing the man to hit bone; the sword leaps in the air and falls to the sand. The matador to this point has been assured of two ears; now he will be fortunate to get one. He lines up the toro, first doubling him sharply to tire away another such premature charge. This time a three-quarter sword follows a good *volapié*.* The toro knows that he has been killed, although he does not die at once. He moves at a walk toward the toril, to die, in a sense, closer to home. He cannot reach the toril, and with the most beautiful of all taurine movements, he neatly folds his feet beneath him, lowering his weight to the sand, and dies, mouth shut, eyes open, his body extending on its side with the ebbing strength of severed arteries.

Toro number two lacks the *codicia*† of toro four, and while he leaves fast from the toril, he moves to his left along the tablas, in the manner of a manso. Requiring careful lidia to instruct him and fix him in the cloth, the toro is instead allowed to crash into a burladero, a trauma which both frightens and stuns him, then is doubled excessively by the banderilleros. As a result, instead of taking the matador's cape, he runs off, requiring the matador to pursue him. When the toro does turn at bay, he charges feet first, hooking to the left in a manner to discompose the matador, who does not in truth know what to do about it. He hopes that the pic will teach the lesson that he himself has not given, so he instructs the junior picador to punish the toro. The toro at first wants no part of the horse, and requires a good deal of bregar to get him to charge, to the boredom of the spectators. At length he does charge, and fairly well. The pic goes in too far back, while the picador pivots his horse on the pic in a *carioca*.‡ The entire process is repeated, without a quite, injuring the nerves in the upper loin

---

* *Volapié:* The estocada most commonly seen today, in which the matador moves on a toro *parado* (stopped), *vol a pié* (feet flying), to give him the force necessary to penetrate and the speed needed to make his exit from the horn.

† *Codicia:* The toro's avidity to charge again and again, rapidly, in order to get his target. *Codicioso* means greedy.

‡ *Carioca:* An abuse in which the picador, having inserted the pic, moves in a semicircle, blocking the toro's exit to the torero and inflicting heavy punishment.

and weakening the toro unduly. The toro lopes off from the horse to the sunny side, where it seems to have spotted a man in a blue shirt in the lower *tendido*.* It takes up a querencia very near the barrera, the toril, and the blue shirt, although the matador does not at first realize that fact. Although he has seen that the toro favors the left horn, he starts his faena on the right and is promptly caught, dangerously near the barrera. He is unhurt, and he foolishly repeats the maneuver, confusing mando with *amour propre*. The toro leaps at the muleta, half passing the man and nearly catching him again. The matador knows that he has failed with this particular toro; he cites for a natural, settles for work por la cara, and kills badly. He damns the ganadería, unwilling or unable to admit that his own banderilleros had spoiled the toro in the first minute of the lidia.

Toro three, the slightly bizco, was intended for use as a novillo; he was not sold in his third year and now is part of the encierro only because of a sizable reduction in price. This is cold comfort to the junior matador, who has not had the alternativa so long that he can not remember many bizcos and the problems they may cause. The bizco is neither so brave as number one nor a manso like two; he is *regular*.† He has always favored his normal, or right horn. He charges well on the right side but virtually refuses to charge on the left; further, when he comes in on the right, he cuts in toward the torero alarmingly (*se cuela*).‡ This can make the kill difficult. The bizco takes the pic fairly well, once, twice. No quites are attempted; the sticks are again to the right, to try to correct the tendency to swerve. In the faena, although the muleta appears again and again on his left, the bizco refuses, pawing the earth and roaring in anger. The toro knows from engagements with his brothers on the range that he is inaccurate with his lower horn. He can parry but not lunge, and he shifts his hindquarters about, trying to put the cloth in range of his good right horn. The

---

* *Tendido:* The range of seats above the barreras. "The tendidos," used loosely, means all the seats in the plaza.

† *Regular:* Adequate, O.K. Or it may be a critic's understatement for a complete disgrace, a *fracaso*.

‡ *Se cuela* (infinitive, *colarse*): An alarming tendency on the part of the toro to run in on the torero in the course of the charge. The tendency may be caused by excessive sentido, by poor lidia—too much time spent in placing banderillas, for example—or by the torero's misjudgment of the toro's distances.

matador, angry, begins to cross the horns and to advance to force a charge. Suddenly the toro does charge, butting the matador to the sand, then wheeling fast to gore. He is too eager, and his first thrust misses the stunned man, lying face down. In a trice the senior banderillero has sprinted to the scene, throwing his cape in the animal's muzzle, then working him away from his matador. The other toreros pick up the matador, who once on his feet tells them he is all right and will go on. He chops *trincherazos** at the toro, lines up for the estocada, and places a cowardly sword in the lower neck *al cuarteo.*† The toro walks towards the toril, staggers, and folds its feet beneath it, to be finished by the puntillero.

Toro one, the senior matador's second, had been nervous and

---

\* *Trincherazo:* A pass por la cara that doubles the toro and punishes it.

† *Al cuarteo:* On the quarter. Cowardly, because the matador attempts to get inside the toro's turning circle, as a banderillero does legitimately when placing banderillas.

The *verónica* is the most difficult of all *lances*

difficult at the apartado, we remember. He comes out slowly and cautiously, making a figure eight between the toril and the tablas to the right. The matador decides to bregar the toro himself; he is angry at himself for cutting only one ear from his first, and he will not risk discomposing this one. He works the toro with *largas** and a slow *remate,** then delivers five lovely verónicas and a *media.*†
The toro grows before our eyes, falling into the rhythm and mando of the matador. He takes the horse bravely, receiving four well-placed pics. After two sets of banderillas, he has not been excessively punished. He awaits the muleta quietly, then charges, without hooking, in short ellipses. The matador treats him gently,

---

* *Larga, remate:* In the larga, the cape is trailed in the sand with one hand as the torero runs (bregar) the toro. A remate is a lance or pass to conclude a series and to stop the animal.

† *Media:* Short for media verónica. The toro is cited from the front, then the cape is gathered in at the waist, causing the toro to circle tightly for a remate.

The *media verónica*

never doubling him, but beginning with *ayudados por alto,*\* educating him to the muleta, encouraging and cajoling him throughout. Now the toro's nervousness has vanished; he is that rare and fine combination of alegría and *nobleza.*† When at last the toro tires in the faena, the matador knows full well, as if the toro had literally spoken aloud the surrendering words, "Mátame." The first sword is virtually perfect, and the toro is dead before his body hits the sand heavily, feet in the air. We have not had to face the pathos and beauty of the foot folding. This is another sort of beauty, and the matador has his full award, of two ears and three *vueltas;* in the provinces he would be given the tail, a hoof, and the plaza if it were the crowd's to give.

---

\* *Ayudado por alto:* A pass in which the torero stands feet together, the muleta in both hands. As the toro charges, the torero raises his arms and rolls his wrists, causing the toro to rise into the empty air. A form of trincherazo, and properly done, a beautiful pass.

† *Nobleza* (or *noble*): Nobility. Used of a toro that follows the lure without evil thoughts of catching the man.

*Ayudado por alto*

Number five, slightly swaybacked, proves weak in the feet although willing. The second matador again allows his cuadrilla to punish the animal too much, in spite of the senior matador's advice, which he resents; as a result he cannot get a faena from the animal, whose blood is pumping over his withers from the needless picing. The toro actually fights the man, and the man the toro; we see not toreo but lucha, a true bullfight. Inevitably, the toro senses the man's ineptness, discomposure, and fear, and becomes all the more difficult. Inevitably, the result is whistles to the man, well-earned, and to the toro, quite undeserved. The animal has appeared manso but was not so. Again the superstition of the fifth toro never being poor is disproved, as so many superstitions of toreo are disproved constantly.

Number six, short-necked and more pronouncedly swaybacked than five, proves a *manso perdido*.* He refuses to leave the toril even after the barb with the divisa is placed; when finally he ambles into the ring, he turns to amble back again, only to find the gate closed. When the banderilleros approach, he refuses to charge, attempting only to hook at the capes without moving his body. When at length he does move, he lopes thirty feet and leaps the barrera, to the amusement and increasing disgust of the crowd. Back in the ring, he wants no part of combat; perhaps because of his short neck, he has never charged but has let the enemy come to him, to parry and defend himself but never to take the offensive. Men in the crowd are making witty and semi-obscene speeches to the president, who signals for the horses. When they appear, the manso again leaps the barrera. At length the steers are brought on, and number six is dispatched in the corral by the butcher's puntilla. The cárdeno which takes his place is fat from his ten days in the corrals. The junior matador, still shaken up from his butting by the bizco, seems to lack heart. The cárdeno deteriorates as the lidia progresses, becoming more *bronco*† and discomposed, more defensive at the muleta than at the cape. Two swords and four *descabello*‡ attempts are necessary to dispose of him, messily and unpleasantly.

---

* *Manso perdido:* Utterly and completely cowardly; the bull that defies Belmonte's statement that "every toro has his lidia."

† *Bronco:* Rough, hard to cope with.

‡ *Descabello:* The act of killing a toro that is motionless, dying, but still on its feet, by severing its spinal cord. (Infinitive: *descabellar*.)

If our hypothetical corrida demonstrates anything, it demonstrates that the accepted division of the lidia into three tercios or acts is a division from the point of view of the men, not from the point of view of the toros. The textbooks state that the tercios correspond to the toro *levantado\** for the cape and the horse; *parado\** after the *puya\**; and *aplomado\** for the muleta. In fact, the toro may undergo either fewer or more than these three states, depending upon his physical state first, and depending further and importantly upon the nature of the lidia to the toro which the matador may determine upon. The *toro huido†* (or *suelto†*) may remain levantado throughout all three tercios demanded by the rite; he may never receive the necessary pic-work, and never be slowed down by trincherazos sufficient for a proper faena. He may take the sword and so die, still levantado. Again, the overfed toro, or the toro in poor physical condition, may come out of the toril either aplomado or even parado, and remain in that state until his death. More commonly, we observe the basically brave and noble animal which comes out levantado, is rendered parado by the pic, and which in the faena may alternate between aplomado, levantado, and parado once more.

Above all, one must insist upon the fact that the matador's triumph or fracaso depends upon his observation and correct interpretation of the individual animal, upon its conditions before the corrida from birth, its blood lines, the behavior of its brothers in other plazas, any record the torero may find of its performance in the tienta, and any information he may glean from the *vaqueros‡* and the mayoral of the ganadería. The matador must further know instantly or by intuition before its occurrence of the change actual or immanent in the toro's physical and psychological disposition during the few minutes of the lidia. Failing this, he

---

\* *Levantado, parado, puya, aplomado:* The bull is said to be levantado—literally elevated, full of power—as he enters the ring; parado, or stopped, after the pic; and aplomado, leaden, at the end of the faena. The puya is the iron shaft at the end of the vara, or pole, of the picador, which in Spain is now required to be fitted with a *cruceta,* or crosspiece on a universal joint, to prevent the abuse of the carioca, and excessive penetration.

† *Toro huido:* From *huir,* to flee; used of the toro that runs away. *Suelto:* Literally, loose—used of a toro that will not remain in the lure but tends to run off.

‡ *Vaquero:* Ranch hand, herdsman.

can only give passes, in Domingo Ortega's famous words, but he cannot torear. Nor can he be an artist of torero, nor even a good journeyman. If he survives at all, he will survive in the profession through tricks and perhaps through abuses to the animal such as we have seen, abuses that will allow him to predict or to ignore the toro's true nature. Thus we see how easy it is to become a torista and to share that fanatic's contempt for the torerista.

CHAPTER 3

# THE EDUCATION OF A TORERO–I

CERTAINLY ONE REASON for the fascination of toreo is the fact that in the plaza a man places himself in a unique relationship to an animal. That animal is a wild beast, no matter how beautiful or brave, capable of wounding grievously or killing the man, in spite of which the man contracts with his own personality, his own inner being, to deny his natural fear, to control his body through the exercise of his intelligence and will, and thus to control the toro in such a manner as to evoke an intense emotional response in himself, and by his projection of that emotion, in the spectators. The man's engagement with the toro in the plaza is brief in time, as we understand the time of the clock face, but infinitely long to the torero because plaza time is not clock time. Plaza time is the time of happiness, despair, love, or catastrophe, of events mensurable only by their intensity, not by their duration. Toreo, however, differs from love or despair because in his confrontation with the toro the torero violates the chain of being, order in nature. Communication between torero and toro is of a special, ritual kind. It is love-death communication: because without a degree of love between the two, neither toro nor torero can fulfill his individual quality; death, because the toro in fulfillment of the ritual must die, and his death is admirable and handsome in proportion to the quality of love that has been demonstrated by the matador and his entire cuadrilla from the moment the toro enters the ring. Unlike relationships among human beings, the torero's relationship to the toro is virtually impossible to falsify. Human beings lie, deceive, flatter, engage in all manner of evasion, and no one is particularly surprised. Society even seems to demand such behavior, and fallible man is ever happy to oblige. The torero in the plaza, however, has left behind the practices of sophisticated social behavior; he has taken upon himself the simple but astounding duty of honesty before a creature incapable of dishonesty. No matter what his recourses, no matter his degree of fear, once he has begun, the torero must go through his ritual acts, if only from his knowledge that cowardice or dishonesty before the toro are dangerous. The torero's greatest physical security lies in his bravery, knowledge, and control.

A corrida, then, whether good, bad, or indifferent, contains certain naked, elemental, and profound elements which, when comprehended even partially, may be exhilarating and life-affirming or frightening and threatening; the spectator's response will depend upon his character, conditioning, and his openness to experience. Art always has something terrifying about it, if only because it takes us into reality, but not everyone can stomach reality. Much of life is given over to evasions of reality, wherever it might manifest itself. It is not necessarily romantic to say that industrialism is a way of substituting the synthetic for the real, of taking a product in nature and transforming it repeatedly into something else. The more advanced technologically a society becomes, the more difficult it is for men to cut back through fabrication and metamorphosis to the original reality. Therefore it is no accident that toreo has flourished in agricultural societies, and that objections to toreo flourish in industrialized societies. The people who rant about barbarism and cruelty in the plaza are not necessarily displaying fineness of sensibility, rather the opposite. They often affirm a system of values which prefers the polite lie to the unsettling truth, an enclosed, safe existence to openness and risk of emotional extension. The corrida is an invitation to just such an extension and exploration of the self; the prime agents of that exploration are the toro, as we have seen, and the torero, whom we must next regard.

T. S. Eliot wrote of tradition in relation to the poet: "It cannot be inherited, and if you want it you must obtain it by great labour." The same must be said of the torero. His craft and art is in the strictest sense traditional, bounded as it is by ritual and by the animal; to master that tradition requires great labor. (At this point we may note parenthetically one further denial of the notion of sangre. Afición is not inherited but acquired, just as the action of extending the elbows away from the body instead of pressing them to the body for protection when the toro charges is not inherited but acquired.) Mastery also requires dedication, training, humility, intelligence, and character. In no aspect of the fiesta has greater disservice been done to truth and dignity than in the assiduous cultivation of the notion of the torero as movie star, sex symbol, rakehell, and conquering hero. Shoddy prose fiction, films, journalism, and now television have fabricated an idea of the torero as an urchin of the streets one year, a dominator of toros the next who has earned millions by his feats in the plaza, bought his arthritic parents a Rolls-Royce to park outside his twelfth-century castle, seduced all the most beautiful women of the day, married into the Spanish royal family, and retired at age twenty to spend his days in the company of Pablo Picasso and God the Father. No mention is made of how this folk hero has acquired his mando over either bulls or banks. He simply is presented as possessing innately the art and craft necessary to his early apotheosis. Although it knows better, the public often goes along with the lie. In recent years, our distaste for middle-class mediocrity and our collective hunger for the admirable, the truly heroic, are such that we knowingly blind ourselves to certain realities, even when the reality may be more interesting than the public lie, as is the case in the making of a torero. In Spain and in Latin America the figure of the torero as a man apart—Byronic, bohemian, doomed, and damned—is a pure product of the romantic movement at its height. One recalls that romanticism and the emergence of toreo as an art coincided in time; the early nineteenth-century torero obliged the *Zeitgeist* by dressing in public *a lo Andaluz*, and by otherwise setting himself off from the run of men by his mien, his diction, his total public display. Obversely, this meant concealing the hard work, the discipline, and the dedication necessary to his mastery of an art classical, not romantic, in cast. The Spanish say that "the torero should smell of wine, tobacco, and women." For a century the torero has lived up to that saying insofar as public acceptance required him to, all the while leading a double life, a parallel existence the outlines of which did not and could not belong to the romantic cliché.

Reality, to repeat, is different from and far more interesting than the Valentino–Errol Flynn–El Cordobés construction. When Juan Belmonte said *"El toreo es, ante todo, un ejercicio de ordén spiritual"* (above all, toreo is an exercise of a spiritual order), he established a necessary antidote to the vulgar, romantic conception. In only one respect is the romantic conception of the torero's origin correct, and even there it is only partially so. It is true that, for the most part, toreros emerge from poverty; what is often glossed over is the fact that they emerge very often from families of toreros. This is not accidental, for the aspiring novillero must have authoritative instruction in every aspect of the fiesta. He cannot get it from the clouds; if he lacks a relative who has been matador, banderillero, or picador, he must have the luck to be taken up by someone who will see that he gets the necessary instruction. It is just at this point that the majority of the thousands of boys who turn up each year as aspirants are predestined to failure. They may be brave and willing, but without proper instruction before their bad habits become engrained, they cannot survive in the profession. Exceptions to the rule of poverty of course exist, as do exceptions to the rule of a torero in the family. Manolete's father, uncle, and grandfather were toreros; Paco Camino's father was a torero; Dominguín's father was a torero; Ordóñez' father was the famous Cayetano Ordóñez, Niño de la Palma; Joselito's brother was El Gallo. Mexico is rich in families of toreros. Among their names are the following: Espinosa (of whom the great Armillita was one), Balderas, Solórzano, Pérez, Castro, Liceaga, Procuna, Briones, Aguilar, Ramírez, Sevilla, Rivera, Bolaños, and Pastor. In Venezuela there is the Girón family. In the entire history of art, one remembers, poverty has always been a powerful, if negative, source of motivation to the artist. More artists have emerged from poverty than from affluence. But in toreo, special problems exist: there are no schools of toreo worth attending, no academies, no government support, no subsidy of any sort to the aspiring. The writer must learn tradition and, to a degree, the fundamentals of his art by reading; the torero, like the dancer, can learn little from books to serve him in the plaza.

Throughout the countries where bulls are toreados, there is no social place for the young man who wants to become a torero. Difficulties begin in the family. If the family is poor, they want the boy to work to help fill empty bellies; if the family is middle class, they want the boy to become a dentist, a lawyer, or something respectable. If there have been toreros in the family, the toreros themselves may be the most discouraging of all, with their memories of struggle, fear, sweat, and cornadas. From the outset, the boy needs unusual determination and a quality of dedication to overcome his own family. Joselito Huerta remarked that when he told his father, a poor man with many children in rural Mexico, that he wanted to be a torero, his father reluctantly agreed, saying, "If you do well, fine; if you do badly, we'll give you a wake." This may be taken as representative of the resignation with which parents agree to their offspring's taurine ambitions. The age of decision may arrive at any point between twelve and twenty. In general, if the boy does not begin early—say, by fifteen—he is not likely to survive. Some try to carry on a job or to attend a university while practicing on the side. The majority scrounge a living from relatives, friends, or, if they are lucky, they may draw a small allowance from someone in the *ambiente** anxious to act as apoderado. The latter case is more likely in Spain than in Mexico, although it remains the exception, not the rule, everywhere. Early on, the boy will learn from other novilleros that the torero does not work; with almost mystical zeal the serious young torero will refuse a job and go hungry rather than violate his calling.

The first problem for the aspirant, that of his education, looms as the most difficult and the most complex of his career; it is made all the more difficult by the fact that it is posed to him at an age when he is least able either to perceive or to solve it. As a result, one cannot assume that a specific career is typical, since typicality is ruled out in this unorganized, chaotic aspect of the fiesta. One can, however, describe the education that the aspiring novillero should receive, one which in reality he occasionally does receive if he is lucky enough to come to the attention of a competent *maestro,*† whether in or out of his own family. The following might take place between aspirant and an ex-matador de toros in the first five years of the aspirant's career—say, from age seventeen to twenty-two—or from his first serious commitment to his career to the time of his alternativa.

The place might be Madrid and environs, or Sevilla, or Mexico

---

* *Ambiente:* Atmosphere, surroundings. The entire world of toros and toreros.

† *Maestro:* A master, supreme torero.

City or Lima or Bogotá—any of the places where bulls are to-reados, where many young men every year defy family and the advice of knowing friends to hunt out the magical formula of success in the plazas. Our matador, Ayala, is a man in his fifties who has had a long, intermittently successful career, and who in turn was trained by *his* matador. He has made large sums for a few seasons, but like many matadors before the present day, he spent his earnings enjoyably as they came in; in his retirement, he lives from the margins of the ambiente, as occasional journalist, as occasional apoderado. He has taken on young lads before, only to see them fail for lack either of character or of afición. During the winter at a tienta he has seen a likely prospect: a boy of perhaps sixteen, old enough at least to have grown out of his adolescent clumsiness, well-knit, neither too short nor too tall. The boy had had a terrible time with his cow, yet in spite of repeated *volteretas*,* he had gone back each time to attempt his clumsy *muletazos*,† elbows tight to his side and bending forward from the waist.

Early in the spring, Ayala and the boy, Domingo Alameda, have a talk at a café in the city. Ayala learns that Domingo is an orphan who lives at the back of a bodega run by his uncle, who had been a banderillero but who had retired after marrying a woman whose dowry was the bodega. Domingo shares a room with four cousins; he may take his food there, but there is not really enough to go around. The uncle has told Domingo that he is a lost soul if he wants to become a torero; he has urged him to take up a trade and forget about toros. The uncle is half boozed much of the time. Ayala satisfies himself of Domingo's seriousness, of his apparent afición. He is in good health, he seems intelligent and well coordinated. Ayala warns Domingo of the hard work ahead, describes the depths of his ignorance to him, tells him that he must forget the muleta passes and the lances he has learned badly from the boys in the street, and finally tells Domingo to meet him at seven the next morning at a certain place in the park.

Domingo arrives punctually at the open place in the park near the big trees, his old cape borrowed from his uncle done up torero-style in a square of muslin. Ayala tells him to forget the cape, to leave it behind until he is told to bring it. Domingo asks why they meet in the park and not in the plaza? He has had visions of working out with the other novilleros, older boys who have fought

---

* *Voltereta:* A tossing. Also *revolcón*.

† *Muletazo:* Any pass with the muleta.

organized corridas in the provinces; he has had plans for a pair of horns mounted on a piece of board, taking his turn at practicing with the banderillas and the estoque on the *carretilla*.* Ayala tells him, sharply but kindly, "Now you know nothing. You are not ready for the plaza, and we will not go there until you know enough to keep from making a fool of yourself. From this day on, you must never go in the plaza without a sense of your own dignity. If a torero has no dignity, he has nothing. You cannot be ignorant and be dignified too."

For the next many weeks, well into the fall, Ayala and Domingo meet in the park for two or three hours, six days a week, for exercises and conversations through which Ayala prepares the boy in body and mind for a career as torero. From the outset, Ayala insists that Domingo eat good food, and when he finds that the menu at the bodega lacks meat and fruit, he gives the boy money from time to time to insure that his diet is balanced. "You must not smoke, and you may drink only a little wine with your meals. You must be like a young priest—do not go near the *putas,* and keep away from all women as long as you can. Women are not bad—clean women—but they are distracting. You must be a torero twenty-four hours in every day. You will keep away from the young homosexuals in the city, and will avoid the foreigners, particularly the Americans, who come to our country in the mistaken belief that all toreros are *maricones.*" These and many other things Ayala tells Domingo between his exercises when he pauses to take a breather, or as they are walking to Ayala's office after the morning's workout.

First thing each day, Ayala sends Domingo on a half-mile jog around the park to strengthen his legs and improve his wind. When Domingo returns from his run, Ayala has drawn a circle representing the plaza in the dust of the open place. "Here is the cuadrilla gate," he indicates with his stick; and, striding across the plaza, "here is the box of the *presidente.* Here is the toril. You will now show me how you walk in the *paseo.*"†

---

* *Carretilla:* A contraption rather like a high wheelbarrow made to simulate the toro's head and neck. A piece of cork, in Spain, or of maguey in Mexico, simulates the *cruz,* or spot where the sword should enter.

† *Paseo:* Parade. In toreo, the entrance into the plaza by the *alguaciles* (mounted deputies of the president of the corrida), the matadors, their cuadrillas, and the muleteers.

Domingo protests: he knows how to walk. *"Mierda, hombre.* If you know how to walk, you know toreo, too, and you do not need me. I am wasting my time. Tell me one thing, why does the torero wear the *taleguilla?"**

"Because they have always worn the taleguilla."

"That, too, but mainly because the torero in the plaza is not the same man he is on the street. He dresses unlike other men and he walks unlike other men from the moment he sets foot in the plaza." Ayala then explains that the torero steps off on his right foot in the paseo not for suerte, as the superstition has it, but again to remind himself that before the public and before the toro he is different from the run of men. The moment he loses consciousness of the toro, he is in danger. He spends hours dressing himself, he wears the *coleta,†* he wears the traje de luces, he walks with grace and independence in the paseo—all to establish his presence and to remind the crowd that it is not at a soccer match but at a corrida de toros. The paseo is like the prologue to a renaissance play: it alerts the public and the participants to the tone and tenor of what is to come. Each day, accordingly, the boy and the matador perform the paseo three or four times. Domingo learns to step off on the right foot, to walk as his own man, not like a soldier in step, not too slowly as at a funeral, not too fast as though he were nervous and wanted to get it all over, but with grace and pride. At the center of the ring, he learns to angle toward the president's box and to bow, not servilely like a waiter, but with the good torero's characteristic gesture of genuine respect and slight contempt for the uninitiated, the non-torero world beyond the barrera.

After the "paseo," Ayala introduces the boy to certain exercises appropriate to toreo; from the beginning the matador forbids exercises of the athlete such as push-ups, chinning, or any exercise that might overdevelop the arms or in any way bind the muscles. All the calisthenics are designed to encourage litheness, maximum movement of the torso, the neck, the back, and the long muscles of the thighs. They are stretching and loosening rather than weight-lifting exercises. Ayala demonstrates neck exercises, in which the

---

* *Taleguilla:* Trousers of the torero's *traje de luces* (suit of lights). By common usage, the entire costume.

† *Coleta:* Originally, hair braided and pinned into a small bun behind the head; since Belmonte, an artificial, buttonlike object. Cutting or removing the coleta symbolizes retirement.

neck is revolved in a circle, to right and left, not only to strengthen the neck, but also to urge the importance of always keeping the toro in view—the first law of toreo. He tells Domingo of the terrible-comic moment at Pamplona when Jaime Ostos, dedicating his toro to the singing drunks in the sun, unable to hear the warnings of his peones and of the crowd, was caught by the toro in full charge and tossed into the callejón. Domingo learns lateral movements of the torso in which he touches his legs below his kneecaps, using only the motion of the shoulder and torso; he learns to swing his shoulders in great arcs to right and left, to prepare him for the movement of the cape in the verónica and other lances. He does knee-bends to perfect balance and to strengthen his legs; waist-bends with knees stiff to make the torso supple. Sit-ups strengthen his back and stomach muscles; and to strengthen his wrists, he raises his arms above his head and pushes down toward his knees, extending and flexing his wrists. He picks up imaginary leaves, bending one knee forward and extending the other leg behind him in a straight line to give balance and to prepare for the motion of the trincherazo with the muleta.

Ayala lectures Domingo for an hour with formality and elegance on *la suerte de picar,* the picing of the toro, its rationale, its history, and its importance. The pic, he insists, is basic to all that follows in the torero's work with the toro, basic to the ganadero and basic to the entire fiesta. Without the pic, it is impossible to assess the toro's conditions, to measure its *casta,* power, bravery, codicia, or style. "The good picador—and when we go out to the tientas, I will instruct you in becoming a good picador yourself—notes carefully if the toro is fast or slow, brave or cowardly; whether he is hard and ambitious in the charge, or soft and willing to lower his head but not seriously willing to try to overthrow the horse. He will observe whether the toro tries to evade the pic, or whether he ignores the pain and pushes bravely in again and again. According to the toro's style, the picador will maneuver his horse and his vara: if the beast is brave, he will make the toro charge from a distance to see how long his power and bravery will last. And as the toro's power is reduced under the punishment, the picador will reduce the distance. But never forget that you, the matador, are in sole command. You are the director of lidia, not the picador."

As the days go by, Domingo is encouraged to run as fast backward as forward, and then to zigzag backward gracefully, without bending the upper body, as though bregando the toro. Throughout all his calisthenics, Ayala impresses upon the boy the necessity for precision and grace in all his movements. Any imprecision or laziness of movement earns him a rebuke. Finally, on their way out of the park, Domingo walks a narrow fence near the roadway again for balance and to remind himself of his physical movements in the plaza. As time goes by, the boy grows bored with the morning workouts and pleads to begin work with the cape and the muleta, but Ayala puts him off. "You still totter like an old woman when you run backward. I will tell you when to work with the cape. Can you borrow a bicycle? Ride 15 kilometers in the afternoon on the bicycle."

One morning, however, Ayala brings to the park one of his own capes and makes a present of it to the boy. It is old, faded, stained with blood and dirt, but of pure silk and nicely cut to the boy's height. His uncle's cape was both small and heavy, having been made of Mexican cotton. Ayala teaches him how to fold the cape, just as a sword-boy would do, so that it can be laid on the barrera ready for use. "You have seen toreros, good ones who should know better, take the cape in their teeth, like dogs. You will never do that as long as you are with me. To bite the cape like an animal while folding it is false *machismo*.* It is unaesthetic and I forbid you to do it. Toreo is the most manly profession possible; it is not necessary for the torero to thrust his manliness down the public's throat." Ayala instructs Domingo how to hold the cape, in the classical manner, with the ends doubled into his hands, and warns him against the modern, vulgar manner, in which the ends are not secured. The word *seguro*—assuredness, full command of one's technique—comes often into Ayala's instruction now. The Spanish manner is more seguro, for if the bull with casta catches the cape in the first lances, before he is *templado* (see footnote on page 79), then the torero is not so likely to lose the cape, and his dignity, on the toro's horn.

Domingo learns to grasp the cape with his thumbs up, the better to move his wrists. "For toreo you must develop golden wrists," Ayala tells him. "Without the wrists, you cannot properly rematar, and the torero who does not rematar, who cannot get rid of the toro, is always a dancer. He must rematar himself instead of the toro, and that is not toreo."

---

* *Machismo:* Cult of virility. *Macho* means masculine.

Before the week is out, Domingo regrets having begged for the cape, for now, each morning, Ayala stands him against a board fence in the park and makes him do hundreds of verónicas with his spine pressed against the board, all to correct his normal urge to bend his upper body forward and to *codillear*.* Ayala quotes Belmonte: " *'Suelta los brazos y torea como si no tuvieras cuerpo.'* " (Extend your arms and torear as though you had no body.)

When Domingo is not pressed against the fence sweating at the unnatural movements of his shoulders and arms, trying to imagine the charge of a tireless Murube, trying not to make his verónicas

---

* *Codillear:* A natural tendency to press the elbows (*codos*) to one's sides.

In the classical manner

like the mechanical doll he feels he is becoming, Ayala has him running backward with the cape, learning bregar, with one-handed largas, and with two-handed doubling passes and recortes. At first Domingo is silently upset that he is not permitted to get down at once to the proper business of the matador, true verónicas, the decorative lances of the quites, and above all, the muleta. He is not setting out to be a peón like his drunken uncle. He will be a matador de toros or nothing. Ayala senses the boy's unspoken rebellion, and explains that he must be able to do everything in the plaza, not merely his own work. "Do you want to be one of these toreros who knows less than his own banderilleros? When you take the alternativa, you will be called maestro. I will not let you be called maestro unless you are a maestro. Do you know that

The modern, or vulgar, manner

in the days of Cayetano Sanz and Montes, a man spent eight to ten years in the cuadrilla?"

Domingo's matador spends a lot of time with him talking apparently at random, but later in his career Domingo could see that the talk was anything but random or pointless, that Ayala had been following a plan from the first day. One Sunday evening as they are walking back from a *novillada* (a corrida of novillos) Ayala says, "Some day when you are not an ignorant boy but a man of the world and have learned English, you will read a book by the American, Hemingway. Hemingway called his book *Death in the Afternoon—Muerte en la tarde.*"

"Maestro, I already know this Hemingway. I have read a book called *El Viejo y el mar.*"

"*El Viejo y el mar* is garbage. Hemingway is a grand writer, but not in that book. Listen to me. *Death in the Afternoon* is the book of a man who knows something about the fiesta but a man who has never been in the plaza with a living animal. Such men should not write about toros. The reason is that Hemingway loves to write about death. His title refers to the death of the toro, of course. But he prefers the death of the matador, and when he writes about the death of Sánchez Mejías or my old friend Manolo Granero he enjoys himself like a *loco*. What Hemingway does not understand is that a cornada is not honorable, it is the result of a mistake. It is the matador who gives himself the cornada, not the toro. And as for death, we do not go before the toro to commit suicide, to die; we go before the toro to live. What Hemingway never writes about is the concept of distances, velocities, and positions. If he had understood such matters, he could not have been so enthusiastic about death. Nevertheless, if I live long enough I may translate his book into Castilian, although if I do no one will publish it, and if someone is so foolish as to publish it, no one will read it, for we Spanish know everything without reading books."

In the park next morning Ayala demonstrates with the cape his concept of distances. He explains that the banderillero works the toro not only to test the beast's vision and how he uses his horns but to discover the distance from which he charges. The distance, in turn, which varies with every toro, is subject to the animal's sum of bravery, strength, his eagerness to charge, his possession either of nobility or malice. The point in the charge at which the toro hooks is determined by his state of health, his skeletal structure, and by the shape of his horns. Finding the toro's distance and velocity, and observing it in all its changes throughout the lidia instructs the toro, allows for *temple*,\* and preserves the torero's life. Ayala draws a diagram in the sand, and says, "When you work the toro thus, you obviously must preserve this distance, thus:

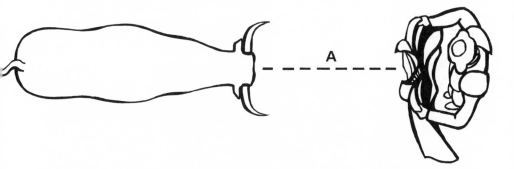

That distance *A* is the distance at which the toro can almost but not quite *cornear*,† and that is this toro's distance at this moment. The distance will probably change after the toro has been piced and has received the banderillas; it may be reduced, or it may be lengthened. And it may change again during the faena. But if you observe the toro's distances you may cut ears. And if you ignore them even for a moment you may get the horn in your belly. Or you may think of the toro's distance as the space between two cars in traffic: the first car may accelerate or it may slow down, and if

---

\* *Temple* (noun); *templar* (verb); *templado* (past participle): To adapt the movement of the lure to the speed of the toro's charge, taking into account the terrain and the distance in the execution of the suerte. When the toro is fresh, temple is subject to the speed and strength of the animal; but the true art of toreo depends upon the matador's ability to adapt his movements at the outset to the conditions of the toro, then to change and even to transform those conditions through the imposition of his personal conception and intuition of positions, speeds, and distances. Belmonte more than any other torero realized these matters, as is clear from his statement: "*Todos los toros pasan y, consecuentemente, son susceptibles de ser toreados. Lo esencial es encontrar el terreno y el sitio para colocarse y ejecutar la suerte.*" (All toros will pass, and consequently they are capable of being toreados. The essential thing is to find the terrain and the exact place in which to stand and execute the suerte.) But it should be noted that one can templar without slowing the toro's speed, and one can also pass a toro slowly without exercising temple. Without temple, the modern faena is impossible.

† *Cornear:* To hook or to catch the target with a horn.

the driver of the following car ignores the changes, unless he maintains a constant, safe interval, there will be a collision. The difference in the plaza is that one of the cars, the toro, urgently desires the collision. It is up to you as torero to direct both cars. But never forget: *Las cornadas las tiran los toros, y se las dan los toreros!*" (Literally: The toros throw the cornadas, but the toreros give the cornadas to themselves. In English: The man, not the toro, is to blame.)

At length the matador takes pity on his apprentice and begins to instruct him in the full verónica, the lance basic to all the other suertes. "When Belmonte said that you must torear as though you had no body, he was right but he was wrong, too. All toreo begins with the *cojones,* the testicles. This is the true machismo of toreo.

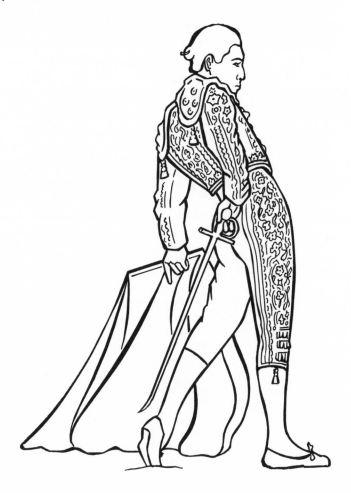

You must have cojones for valor, but more important, every lance, every pass, begins with the movement of citing, as you cite the toro with your cojones. In polite words we say the *cintura,** but we mean the cojones." Ayala then demonstrates how the first motion imparted to the cape is given by the movement of the body itself, and how that motion in turn gives the torero an extra few inches of margin that may mean the difference between a splendid lance and a cornada.

Ayala further explains that citing the toro with the testicles and hip movement rather than with the arm is not only a plastic advantage in the creation of the aesthetic effect of the suerte, but it also frees the arm to *cargar la suerte,* which may then be understood as a movement of the arm and not of the feet. Domingo does not understand fully the idea of cargar la suerte, and his matador spends a morning expounding and demonstrating his theory. Historically, before Belmonte, the toro was cited de frente, head on. It was then necessary to change the line of the toro's charge by

* *Cintura:* Waist.

The classical *cite de frente*

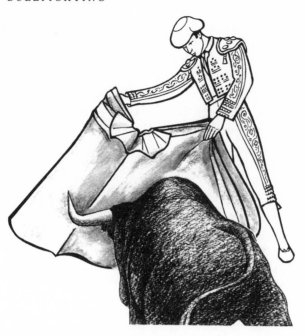

stepping into the line of attack and swinging the cape with the arms and waist movement so as literally to "send on" (cargar) the lance, and with it, of course, the animal.

Belmonte's "revolution" was to cite the toro from a three-quarter position and, later, even from a position parallel to the animal's body:

The *cite* from the three-quarter position

In the three-quarter cite, cargar la suerte in the classical manner was still a necessity, although the torero had gained an added measure of security from the horn and had often added to the plastic effect. But the difficulty and confusion arose in the cite from the parallel position. If the torero was not to lose much of the beauty of the pass, and to lose the animal as well (which was likely to take off across the plaza for having lost its target), it became most important that the new manner of cargar la suerte be observed. Ultimately, Ayala explains, cargar la suerte is a function of mando, while it makes possible the remate, by which the torero keeps control of the toro and gives himself time to turn and to cite for the next lance. "Everything in toreo is connected with something else. Without cargar la suerte you cannot rematar, and you cannot rematar without mando."

According to Pedro Romero—the Plato, Aristotle, and Aquinas of toreo—the classical rules are three: *parar, templar, mandar,* as Ayala said. But as is so often the case, these rules are gnomic; they conceal as much as they reveal. To stand your ground, to impose

The parallel *cite*

*Parar*

your own timing, and to send the animal on, hides several other processes that must be observed at the same time. Parar (stand fast) means to stand fast in a certain position in relation to a certain toro; it implies a knowledge of that animal's characteristics and a divining of its intentions. It also implies a knowledge of the animal's system of vision. Templar (literally, to soften, to temper) is impossible without knowledge of the specific animal's distances, without close observation of his behavior from the first cape-flap by the banderillero. It means divining how to *engolosinar*—to

*Templar*

*Cargar la suerte*

cajole, to lure, to seduce the toro into following the cape at your speed, not at his. It means *aguantar*, to suffer, to sustain the toro's charge and to command yourself and the toro. And mandar without rematar is to lose the animal and to have to run like a hare to start the process all over again. Therefore the rules are not merely parar, templar, and mandar, but parar, aguantar, engolosinar, cargar la suerte, and rematar. "You must learn these things with the cape, because they are difficult and unnatural, and they are more difficult with the cape because your toro has not yet been

*Rematar*

85

slowed down by the pic, nor tired out by all that takes place before the muleta. The muleta is another matter, but without good cape work, you will spoil your toro. It is because it is difficult that so many of our toreros these days are poor at the cape. They are too much in a hurry, but as for you, you will take your time," Ayala assures Domingo.

Whenever possible, which is most of the time, Ayala gets complimentary tickets from the empresarios so that he and his student can attend the corridas. Domingo at first prefers the corridas de toros and seeing the full matadors perform, but Ayala insists that the novilladas are more important, for the novilleros make more mistakes more obviously, and thus Domingo may learn all the more readily. At the corrida, sometimes high in the tendido, sometimes at the barrera, sometimes in the callejón, Ayala keeps up a running lecture to Domingo, teaching him the characteristics of the toro, the strengths and weaknesses of the men—not only of the matadors, but also of the peones and the picadors. In his middle age Ayala is no longer torerista but torista; no matador can satisfy him. Domingo, on the other hand, is an enthusiastic torerista; his favorites can do no wrong, and when even the athletes, whom he has learned to dislike, are tossed, he feels as though he himself has been tossed. Ayala's prejudice is a useful corrective. He insists that in spite of what one can know from the bloodlines of the toro, from observation at the sorteo, from any source whatsoever, each toro remains a mystery when it comes out of the toril, a mystery which the torero must penetrate by intuition and dissipate by technique. The main difference between the novillero and the full matador, he insists, is that both are confronted by the same mystery, the toro, but that the matador knows how to cover up his doubts and defects, while the novillero has not yet learned to look assured when he is not, to write his script on the wing while projecting to the crowd the impression that the script has been in his pocket all the while. Ayala insists upon the importance of the torero's recursos, saying that the most secure matadors are those who are so because they have at their command means of dealing with all manner of toros. And he repeats over and over again until Domingo is sick of hearing it, "You cannot wait for the one toro who understands you; you must be able to torear every toro that comes out of the toril. *"Cada toro tiene su lidia."* (Every toro can be dominated by proper lidia.)

Mornings in the park after they had been to a corrida, Ayala would examine Domingo on what he had seen in the plaza. "What did Sánchez do wrong in his second verónica to his first toro? You are now a master of the verónica (see plates 2, 3, & 4), so tell me."

"Maestro, I do not know. I thought it was a perfectly good lance."

"Yet he lost the toro, didn't he? A fine toro with six or seven verónicas in him, and Sánchez gave him two, let him run off, and twirled his hand for the picadors. This is what he did wrong."

Taking the cape from Domingo, Ayala demonstrates how Sánchez, from cowardice or uncertainty, had stepped *back* from the charge instead of into the toro's trajectory, thus conveying the impression of cargar la suerte but in fact sacrificing mando to the extent that he lost control of the animal altogether.

Ayala further demonstrates how the same trick is possible in the *chicuelina:**

---

* *Chicuelina:* Named for Chicuelo, Manuel Jiménez y Moreno. An adorno often used in quites in which the matador cites from the

Sánchez stepping back

87

PLATE 2.

PLATE 3.

Ayala insists upon the necessity for good manners to the toro. "You saw that carpenter, Sánchez, giving only *derechazos** in his faena. Why? Because he confuses mando, ignorance, and vulgarity. The toro favored his left horn, *bueno.* Sánchez, without respecting the toro's preference, insisted too soon on the right. That is not toreo. *Let* the toro pass on the left until he has confidence and is fixed in the muleta. Then exercise mando, and show who is truly

---

front, and turns toward the toro as it passes, enfolding the cape about him; he is then in position to cite from the opposite side.

* *Derechazo:* A right-handed pass with the muleta; it has less virtue than the natural with the left hand, because the sword extends the muleta away from the torero's body. (The torero never uses the sword in his left hand except when saluting the president at the beginning of the faena. He then doffs the *montera*—see footnote on page 130—with his right hand.)

---

The *verónica* and the *media verónica*. In Plate 2 José Julio delivers a beautiful *verónica* to a Muira toro in Seville, 1962. In Plate 3 Paco Camino shows the next phase of the *lance,* and in Plate 4 a perfect *media.*

PLATE 4.

master. You must respect the toro; he will then respect you. But if the toro senses that you fear his left horn and are fighting your own fear by avoiding his left, you are in deeper trouble and greater danger than if you allow the toro to have his way for a time. The basis of toreo lies in knowing the toro's defects and correcting them. Some defects you cannot correct, of course: defects of vision, the toro *resabiado*,* or certain other congenital defects.

"You also saw Sánchez kick the toro and stab at him with the sword to make him pass. That is bad manners, and when, as unscrupulous toreros sometimes do, they stab the toro in the flank with the sword hidden by the muleta, it is a downright abuse. If you have contempt for the toro, you do not belong in the profession. To struggle against the toro's inclination is luchar—what they call in English a 'bullfight.' We do not fight the toro, we cajole him as though he were a woman with whom we are in love. At the

---

* *Resabiado:* From *resabiar,* to contract vicious habits. Used of a toro that learns to run in on the matador or to carry out any other maneuver dangerous to the matador in the course of the lidia.

The honest *chicuelina*

same time, we cannot be dogmatic about the lidia. Sometimes a toro that charges high should be given low passes, sometimes not. You must be open and aware about it. But do not punish the toro with *trapazos;** if you must double him to show who is master, double him gently in the manner of Domingo Ortega, or give him the ayudado por alto like Manolete. Manolete almost never doubled his toros. When the torero looks as if he were tearing telephone books apart with his hands, he sacrifices all possibility of art. You must make your work look easy and gentle, even though it is almost never these things. But Sánchez is ignorant, a destroyer of telephone books."

By the end of the summer, Ayala permits Domingo to move on to work with the muleta, although he warns him that he must still give much of his time to the cape. Domingo spends an hour a day doing the verónica, the media verónica, the gaonera, and the chicuelina. And he spends half an hour practicing bregar: the

---

* *Trapazo:* 1. Any muleta pass given without art: 2. A brutal punishing pass por la cara.

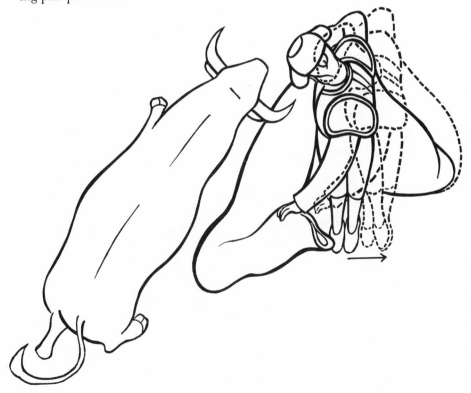

The dishonest *chicuelina* 91

matador insists that Domingo know how to defend himself; when he begins work with the muleta, he first learns *trastear*.* Ayala classifies the various suertes into those passes which are defensive in nature or used simply to move the toro from one place to another, passes por la cara (or *de castigo*) in which the toro does not pass the torero's body; passes of dominio, in which the toro does pass; and *adornos*, or *jeux d'esprit*, suertes indulged in to demonstrate full control over the animal. Like all beginning novilleros, Domingo longs to learn the adornos first, the *revolera*, the *serpentina*, the *mariposa* with the cape; the *manoletina, molinete* with the muleta, and a dozen other lances and passes he has seen in the plaza throughout the season.

But Ayala will not permit adornos and fanciness. He continues to insist upon defensive work, and upon the basic passes: the verónica above all, the natural, the derechazo, the chest pass. "First you will be a good *torero corto*† then in good time we shall make you into a *torero largo*."† His reason is based upon his

---

* *Trastear:* To work the toro with the muleta, horn to horn; used on a dangerous animal that does not pass properly, or on a toro aplomado.

† *Torero corto, largo:* A brief as opposed to a large repertory of lances and passes.

*Derechazo*

philosophy of toreo. He wants his student to have a proper mental conception soundly based in good technique. He dislikes the athletic at the expense of the aesthetic, and he regards as superficial the run-of-the-mill torero who performs adornos but cannot perform a proper verónica or a proper natural. He tries by all means open to him to convey to Domingo a conception of toreo in which the adorno is not fundamental, but rather a true *jeu,* a result of intuition, a bringing together of a mood, a particular happy relationship to a specific public, and a product of his preliminary work on a specific toro. The faena—indeed, the entire lidia—he would say, is an adventure, an improvisation which must be decided upon in a matter of seconds after the appearance of the toro in the ring. To torear each toro like every other toro: to give the half-hearted and tentative verónica, the standard chicuelina in the quite, the standard derechazos, the standard *molinetes* and

*Molinete*

*manoletinas** is to insult the animal, the public, and the self; it is like driving a bus down the same streets at the same time each day. It is the negation of toreo and the end of the fiesta. And it is the career of the great majority of contemporary novilleros, who then wonder why they have not become figuras.

Ayala's philosophy is reflected in the very muleta with which he provides Domingo. Ayala has contempt for the modern large muleta, "the size of a bed sheet," he says. His plan is to publicize Domingo as the torero of the small, classical muleta; already he is thinking of the public and of the need to distinguish his pupil from the mass of novilleros. He instructs Domingo in the classical ways of holding the *palo*:† at one third of the distance from the end in the right hand, and at midpoint in the left. "To hold the palo by the end is graceless. It is a recurso for a very dangerous

---

\* *Molinete, manoletina:* Adornos with the muleta having more in them of spectacle than of danger. Much motion after the horn has passed. See Plate 5.

† *Palo:* The wooden piece inserted in the muleta to provide a handle.

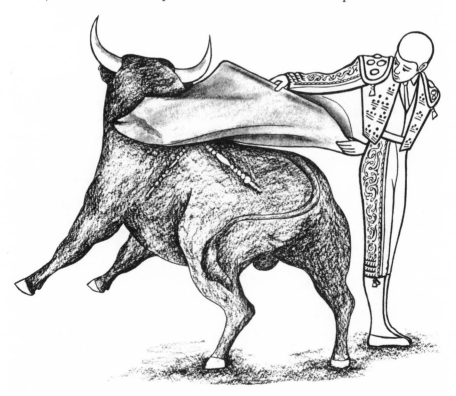

*Manoletina*

toro, one you frankly fear, but it is not a habit to cultivate," he says.

Neither will Ayala allow Domingo to use an estoque of wood or aluminum in practice. "Manolete was a magnificent torero, I can assure you," he says, "but because he used an estoque of wood, thanks to injury, or as I sometimes thought, distrust, practically all the toreros in Spain imitated him, and now many a faena is spoiled because when he is ready to kill, the matador must leave his toro standing, walk to the barrera, and exchange swords. You will be different; you will always practice with the true estoque so that your wrist will be strong and you will kill when the toro is ready."

Now in the mornings Domingo arrives with one or two of his cousins from the bodega to serve as his "toro," and for the next two weeks Ayala spends more time instructing the bull boys than he spends on Domingo. Pedro, age eleven, is a natural manso with *malicia*.* Rodrigo, a year older, prefers to be a noble, hard-

---

* *Malicia:* Malice, malignity, dirty ideas. (A term more common in Mexico than in Spain, where "sentido" is preferred.)

---

PLATE 5. Manolete completing a *manoletina* to a toro of Galache at Badajoz, 1947.

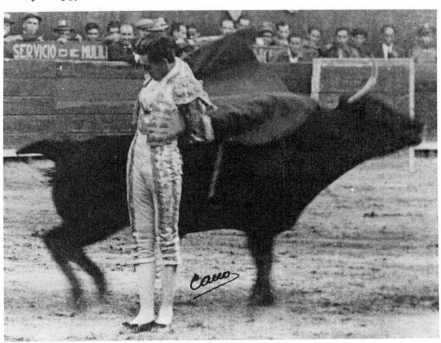

charging toro. Ayala teaches each to simulate the changing conditions of the toro throughout a corrida. The boys work hard in the autumn sun, because they like Ayala, and because he sometimes gives them tickets to the corridas, and always change from his pocket with which they buy sweet buns or cigarettes. The boys' horns are those of a five-year-old Pablo Romero thrust onto a two-foot piece of wood shaped to fit the hollow base of the horns.

One morning Ayala arrives late in the park to find Domingo practicing right-handed passes to Rodrigo *de rodillas.*\* Ayala, angry, says, "Are you a man or a dwarf? Get up on your feet. You go down on your knees to pray in the chapel, not to torear in the plaza. I will not have you be the Toulouse-Lautrec of toreo." Domingo does not understand the allusion and Ayala does not

---

\* *De rodillas:* On the knees.

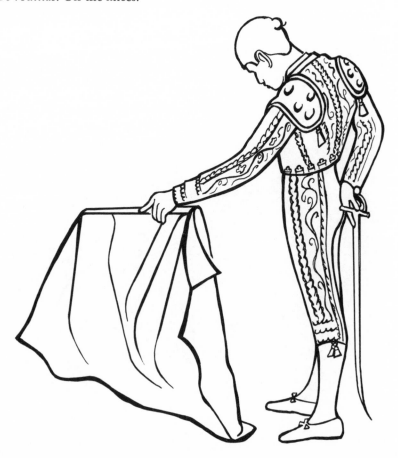

Incorrect hand position on the *palo* for the
*natural*

bother to explain. "Just so you will remember to keep off your knees, suppose you do a couple of laps around the park."

Domingo is hurt by Ayala's reproof; he had hoped to surprise the maestro with his progress. After all, did not all toreros torear de rodillas? "Not all," Ayala says, "only the second-rate." Later in the day he explains. Toreo de rodillas probably began with Francisco Montes as a recurso; he later developed the technique as an adorno. Cúchares took it over and promptly turned it into an abuse, and Gordito made it into a fundamental of his entire toreo.[1] Had the technique remained a recourse or an occasional adorno, well and good, but from the time of Cúchares it became a corruption of the classical thing, a technique for impressing the ignorant and an evasion of the torero's basic responsibility to

---

[1] Alcazar, *Tauromaquia moderna*, I, p. 232.

Incorrect hand position on the *palo* for the
*derechazo*

cargar la suerte and to dominate the animal. "It is difficult to cargar la suerte on your knees; and unless you cargar la suerte, you are not handling your toro intelligently, you are not educating him. You are merely giving him passes. And you run the risk of losing the brute altogether without the remate. If you do not cargar la suerte, you cannot properly rematar, either."

Well into the autumn Ayala drills Domingo hard in the basic passes of the faena: the natural, the derechazo, the pase de pecho, the ayudado por alto. Ayala is hard to please. He will not tolerate the slightest bending of the waist or the faintest tendency to codillear, both of which are likely to appear at the end of the morning when Domingo is tired. In the ayudado por alto, Domingo learns to stand absolutely straight, feet together, and to roll his wrists in order to raise the muleta and so force the toro to extend

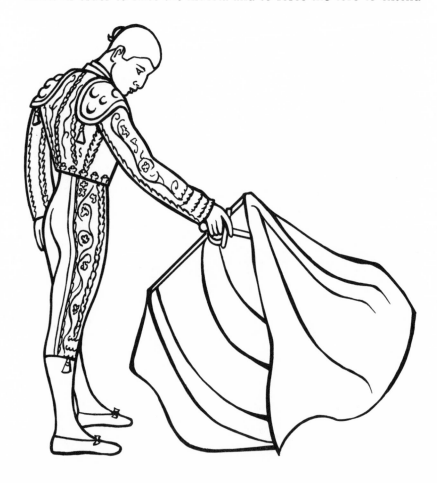

Correct hand position for the *derechazo*

and tire its neck muscles. (Plate 6.) This pass, Ayala assures him, is more aesthetic than the cruel, doubling passes and more efficient in establishing domination over the toro. "The ayudado allows you to go along with the toro. The *doblón** works against him. "Only double the toro with malicia and sentido, the toro that refuses your cooperation."

Another advantage of the ayudado por alto, Ayala says, is that the informed public will always respond more enthusiastically to a maneuver in which the toro passes the man than to work por la cara, those punishing passes in which, unlike the doblón, the toro

---

* *Doblón:* A pass which literally doubles the bull, sending him back in the direction of the line of charge; a pase de castigo, or punishing pass.

Incorrect hand position for the *derechazo*                    99

does not pass, and which are often given to difficult or dangerous animals at the beginning of the faena.

In giving his derechazo, Domingo wants to stand with his feet either together or spread too far apart. Ayala insists that comfort and balance should determine the position of his feet. He forbids *toreo a pies juntos* (with the feet joined) in the modern, decadent manner. "A corruption of gypsies," he says, "that prevents cargar la suerte, that makes the proper plastic effect between toro and man impossible, that rules out templar and mandar." Ayala works himself into a rage. *"No es toreo. Es dar parones, nada mas, aprovechando el viaje!"* (It is not toreo. It is only a wooden flapping of the muleta in the toro's face as he moves from one place to another. ["Dar parones" is untranslatable.]) The reverse defect, toreo with the feet too far apart, is unaesthetic and a threat to one's balance. (See plates 7, 8, and 9.)

Domingo spends weeks in practicing "running the hand" (*correr la mano*), and in coordinating the wrist movement with the cite, as with the cape, from the waist and testicle area. The point,

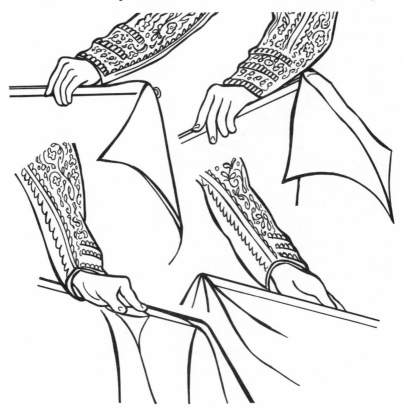

Hand and wrist movements for *correr la mano—*
running the hand

Ayala repeated insistently, is that the torero who does not run his hand must move his feet to clear the horn. Running the hand is the technique for gaining ground from the toro, and if the torero does not gain that essential ground, he must surrender some of his own.'"If you do not run your hand, you cannot get rid of the toro, and you encourage him to run in on you (*colarse*). You are asking for the cornada," Ayala says. He demonstrates to Domingo how the wrist movement with the muleta is almost exactly the same as it is with the cape, and for the same reason: for the torero's physical security, for templar, for mandar, and for rematar, which in turn makes possible the linking of passes.

In his natural, Domingo's tendency is to wave the sword about

PLATE 6.   Manolete's *ayudado por alto* to a toro of Galache, Badajoz, 1947.

PLATE 7. *"No es toreo. Es dar parones, nada más, aprovechando el viaje."* Manuel Benítez, El Cordobés, gives his wooden *derechazo*, with feet together. Compare Manolete's *derechazo*, Plate 8, and Paco Camino's, Plate 9.

PLATE 8.

PLATE 9.

with his right hand, a tendency learned in part from toreros he has seen in the plaza. Ayala insists that he keep the sword behind his back, the *muerte** away from his body. The matador who waves the sword about, Ayala says, is not only in danger of sticking himself in the calf, but either he displays nervousness or he is out to impress the ignorant by the effect of excessive motion. Or he may simply be ignorant himself of the nature of the pass, that has enough emotion for the real aficionado without the matador's addition of false emotion. Neither will Ayala permit Domingo to

---

* *Muerte:* The terminal six inches or so of the sword making up the curve, to better enable it to penetrate to the aorta.

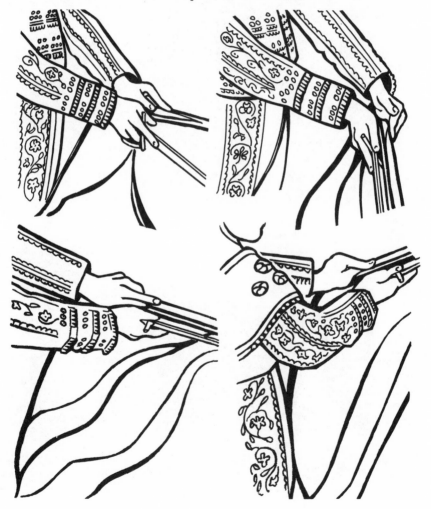

Hand positions and wrist movements in the
*ayudado por alto*

use the sword in making the natural as a semi-*ayudado;** such a procedure is to be tolerated only as a recurso in a wind, for it again conveys to the crowd a sense of nervousness and it projects a distorted plastic line. At the same time, Ayala drills Domingo in the proper position of his arm at the end of both the natural and the derechazo. The natural instinct, related to codillear, is to end the passes with the arm straight, while the proper position is to keep the arm slightly bent at the elbow. With the arm straight, there is an accompanying tendency to reduce the angle between chest and upper arm, again encouraging the toro to run in, while with the elbow bent, the torero is forced to use his wrist to rematar.

Just as he forbids the natural with the sword waving in the air, so Ayala forbids Domingo the fashionable, excessive lateral movement of the waist in both the natural and the derechazo, again as unaesthetic and falsely emotional.

As in making the verónica, Domingo learns to step forward after the natural or the derechazo in order not to lose ground to the bull before the next pass. "Sometimes, with a very noble bull you may stay in the same place, simply pivoting there for the next pass. But you must never step back, as your natural instinct tells you to do."

The *pase de pecho* (see plates 10 & 11), according to Ayala the most manly and handsome of all passes, is both a recurso which allows the torero to mandar (or send off a toro which is gaining territory on him), and a natural form of torero's punctuation in the faena. It allows both toro and torero a breather when they need it; it allows the public to see the pattern of the faena more clearly, it demonstrates mando, and it presages more to come. It is a momentary signature, a *da capo,* a couplet at the end of a stanza. Like all toreros, Domingo wants to raise his right heel in the chest pass to the right, and his left heel in the pass to the left. Ayala insists that he keep his feet firmly on the sand in all his passes, assuring him that his actual mando will be greater if he can do so, and that he will derive benefit in greater inner security, as well as conveying to the public that sense of security.

Even on wet, windy days that fall, maestro and student meet in

---

* *Ayudado:* Here, the use of the sword to "help" the motion of the muleta in the natural; in general, any pass in which both hands are used.

the park for at least a partial workout. "I do not like this any more than you, *hombre*," Ayala says, huddled in a raincoat, "but you have to learn toreo in all weathers. They do not always call off the corrida for bad weather, you know, nor can you depend on good weather to hold. A fine day in our country can turn foul in

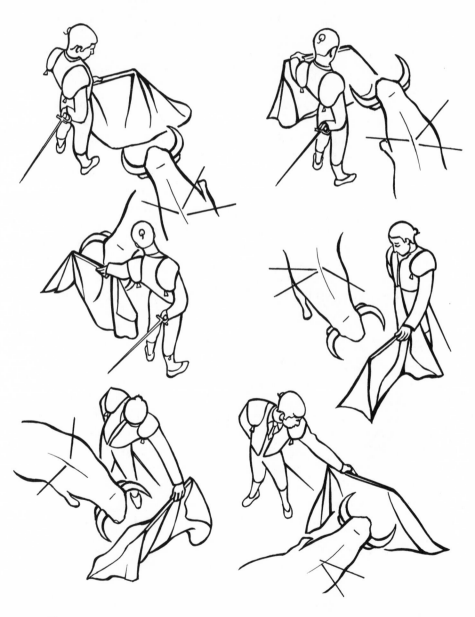

How running the hand allows the *torero* to gain ground, and to link his passes by keeping the *toro* in *suerte*

*Natural* with sword in the air

*Natural* with sword in proper position

minutes, in the middle of your faena. You must always watch the wind and the clouds. You have seen good toreros look quickly up to the top of the plaza. They are not looking for their women friends, they are looking at the pennants over the plaza to see if the wind is changing. In a bad wind, you must try to go up wind with your toro to the place in the plaza where the wind will least disturb you. Chances are that place will be at the toril, the toro's natural querencia, in which case you must change your plan." When mere water is insufficient to weigh down the muleta in a wind, Ayala says, the torero can kick dirt from the plaza onto the wet cloth to further weigh it down. As for rain, toros often like it and may charge better under a pouring sky than under a hot sun. "The crowd will be with you in rain, for it looks more dangerous than it is. You kick off your shoes, torear in stocking feet, and cut ears." Wind and rain, according to Ayala, are nothing more than a test of the torero's afición. Wind is the real enemy, not rain. A

*Pase de pecho* with heel raised

chance gust can upset the toro, and the torero's timing, and in fact cause a cornada. "To kill well in the wind is a supreme test, one you will often have to face. If you are not willing to face it, you should not become a torero." Domingo learns how heavy the cape and the muleta can be in the rain, and he learns to appreciate Ayala's philosophy of the natural.

"*El natural se llama natural porque es natural*," Ayala would say. (The natural is called the natural because it is natural.) By this he meant that historically, in the period of the brief faena and the emphasis upon the kill, the left-handed pass was virtually the only pass used, for the good reason that the matador wanted to train the toro to use his left horn, not his right. The toro that favors its right horn over its left is very dangerous to kill, obviously; thus the right-handed pass given with the sword inside and extending the muleta may feel safer to the torero but may in truth be much more dangerous ultimately. The derechazo appeared well

*Pase de pecho* with both feet firmly planted

after the natural, he explained; we do not know exactly when. It made for a more varied faena, but at the same time it represented a certain corruption in the purity of toreo. "Today," Ayala would say with scorn, "we see in the plaza novilleros and so-called matadors de toros who give entire faenas with the right hand, then have trouble killing. The great killers of the past were not afraid of the left hand; they understood that when you kill, you give the toro a pase de pecho in effect with the left hand. But if you have taught the toro to pass only to the right, of course you will have trouble with your sudden surprise. Of course he will want to veer to the right, and when he does that, *hombre,* watch out."

All depends upon the individual toro, Ayala explains. If your toro wants to favor the right side, let him do so at the beginning of the faena; go along with him and encourage him. But when he simmers down because you have been good to him, you must then insist upon the left, and educate him to your way of things. Then

---

PLATE 10.   How not to give the *pase de pecho.* This torero lacks both grace and *mando.* Note the position of his feet.

he will know you are his master, and then he will come your way like a gentleman. "These are matters you must learn in the plaza; now I can only prepare you mentally and physically for what you will meet when you are ready. And you will not be ready until you can think with your reflexes, instantaneously."

Domingo is sometimes discouraged that Ayala will not permit him to progress faster. He still will not allow him to go to the plaza with the other novilleros; he will not even permit him to practice killing. At the same time, he knows Ayala is correct, that he is not ready. Sometimes he wonders if he has the necessary courage for the profession of toreo; he does not dare to put his reservations into words, but Ayala divines what is on the boy's mind. "Of course you must have courage," he would say, "but courage is learned, like everything else. We Spanish are liars when we talk so constantly about valor and cowardice. It may even be that we are less naturally courageous than other people, since we talk about it so much. No one ever accused me of lacking valor in

---

PLATE 11. Paco Camino shows how the *pase de pecho* should be delivered. Compare Plate 10. Both men are using wooden swords, however.

the plaza, and I was known as a superior killer, good with the sword. But I was born a coward, and when I think about it, I believe all men are born cowards. Courage before the toro comes from confidence in your technique and in your ability to use your natural fear. Any man who does not fear the toro is a lying fool. Without fear, there can be no emotion. What is it that the crowd senses? It is the matador's fear and his ability to put his fear to good use through technique. The magnificence of toreo lies in the fact that the torero makes the unnatural look natural; that he dominates his own instinctive fear, and in doing so forces the toro to change his instincts to the point where the two together, man and toro, create in their confrontations certain moments of beauty that are as memorable as they are brief. But we all fear the toro, all the time. The hardest part of the profession is waiting for the next toro. He is always there with you, on Monday and Tuesday and Wednesday and Thursday, taking meals with you, sharing your wine and your nights. The next toro, which may give you a cornada and take your life, lives just here, on your shoulder, all your life as a torero. You will not know whether you have enough

*"El natural se llama natural porque es natural,"* Ayala would say

afición to become a true maestro until some toro, some day, sheds your blood and causes you pain. But I think you will survive it. If I didn't, I wouldn't be here talking to you like this."

At first Domingo derives cold comfort from such words, but later on he comes to recognize the ring of truth in them and to be grateful to Ayala for not flinging him the usual clichés about suerte, destiny, and machismo. His trust in his maestro becomes complete.

On another occasion, Ayala and Domingo had gone to a novillada in which one novillero, making his debut in the city, has been so incapacitated by fear that he was caught and gored. Ayala took up the theme of fear again. "Whoever let that boy in the plaza today with novillos is a criminal. The boy was afraid because he was not ready. He got his cornada from his apoderado, not from the novillo. But all men are afraid until they learn means to cope with their fear," he went on. "During our war I was under fire for the first time at Teruel," he said. "I, a matador de toros who had already taken the alternativa, and I assure you I was afraid, as was

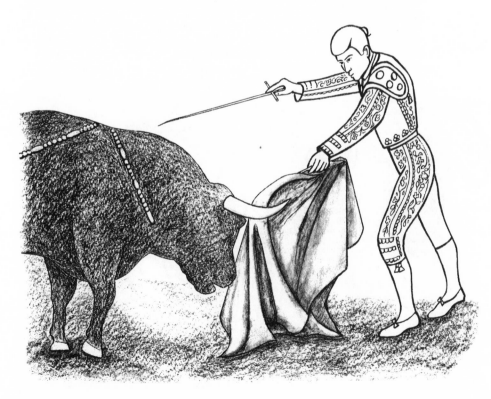

Movement of the *muleta* during the *estocada*

every man in my company. If anyone had had the idiocy to say he was not afraid, we would have torn him limb from limb. Later on in the war, in the north and before Madrid, we were still afraid, but in a different way. We learned to fear the irrationality of bullets and shells directed not at us, personally, but at a sector on a map. But as in toreo, we took some comfort from the techniques of the infantryman for avoiding getting shot, even though we retained a healthy fear of wounds and death. Compared to combat, toreo is rational, and the torero is in fuller command of the forces against him. In both combat and toreo, the waiting is the worst. And the infantryman can only hope for survival. He cannot know what the torero sometimes knows: the toro of great triumph, the toro of fame. We are not masochists, and we cannot live only with fear. We live first for the flavor of life and triumph, not of disaster and death."

CHAPTER 4

# THE
# EDUCATION OF
# A TORERO–II

B Y LATE FALL, it is clear to Ayala that Domingo has come to the
end of the first stage of his apprenticeship. The boy has learned a
good deal, and Ayala can congratulate himself that he has successfully instilled in him habits beyond habit, movements that are on
the way to becoming reflexes. At the same time, Ayala is aware of
the danger of boredom and staleness. Domingo, too, knows that he
has come to the end of a phase, reached the edge of the first
plateau, and that it is time for a change in his training. Ayala
therefore puts into action a plan he has been considering for some
time. He makes a telephone call, and the next morning he takes
the bus that winds its way through the mountain passes north of
the city to the high plain where his old friend, Galdos, owns a
ganadería.

Ayala and Galdos began together as novilleros before the Civil
War and took the alternativa within a month of each other. When
the war broke out, Ayala had fought with the loyalists, Galdos
with the revolutionaries, through an accident of geography, he
always claimed. When the two friends met after the war as ex-
enemies, the former ease between them, typical of toreros who
share a way of life, was displaced by a certain suspicion and bitter-

ness. Ayala had found himself without money and often without food, while Galdos' service on the winning side had enabled him to buy a fair-sized finca in the mountains and to bring together enough animals to start a small ganadería of fighting bulls. With the passage of years, the old bitterness was not so much forgotten as set aside in the mind by the pressure of contemporary reality. At any rate, Ayala had been able to help Galdos in selling an encierro in the capital, thus conferring *cartel** upon his ganadería, and the two men's ancient friendship had renewed itself upon a different footing. Ayala had no compunction about asking Galdos, now "Don Jaime," to take on Domingo for the winter. The matter was promptly arranged as the two men on horseback looked over the herd.

Galdos respected Ayala's judgment, and while Ayala's reserve annoyed him, it gave depth to his conviction that Ayala was onto a good thing in Domingo. Before the two men parted, Galdos hinted that he would like to buy a portion of the boy's contract. Ayala did not respond to the hint; rather, he told Galdos that he, Ayala, might be wrong about the boy's potential, and that he would appreciate his friend's own assessment of Domingo after he had time in which to observe him. Ayala had seen many a novillero come to grief through divided management. He was determined that Domingo should proceed at his own pace, and not be pushed by a combine out to make as much money as possible.

Back in the city, Ayala tells Domingo of the arrangement he has made for him. "You will live at the finca and work with the other ranch hands. You will learn to ride and to care for the toros. You will take part in the tientas in the winter, and you will learn above all to kill. It is hard work and you will receive no pay. You will use your eyes and your ears, and you will receive instruction from Don Jaime, one of the few toreros I would trust to teach you. But you will be on your own. I will not be there every day to nag you, and Don Jaime is too busy to give you as much time as I have done. It is a magnificent opportunity for any novillero and I expect you to make the most of it."

---

* *Cartel:* Program, poster. A ganadería achieves cartel by sending to a first-class plaza an encierro which is recognized by the association of breeders as possessing the necessary qualities. The term also defines a torero's fame, and particularly his drawing power. In Spanish slang, a pretty girl on the street might be said to have cartel.

Domingo knows well how great the opportunity is. He is so pleased at the prospect that he wants to roar with joy, then to weep. In his confusion, he says nothing, but his expression as Ayala talks to him is eloquent.

Ayala has next to deal with Domingo's guardian. He has known the banderillero from the old days, well enough neither to admire nor to trust him. After a talk with Domingo about the matter, Ayala goes to the uncle, proposes an arrangement giving the man a small percentage of Domingo's earnings until his majority, and empowering himself, Ayala, as the boy's only apoderado. Never having expected anything in the way of cash return for care of his nephew, the uncle now becomes greedy and wants a half interest. On a sober morning his wife convinces him of his folly, and within a week's time a formal contract drawn up by a lawyer is signed by all concerned. Ayala has the torero's contempt for lawyers, but experience has taught him the value of legal contracts over the traditional handshake and glass of cognac.

Throughout that winter and the winter following Domingo remains at Galdos' finca, from late October to April. By Christmas of his first winter he is a reasonably competent horseman, although his apprenticeship is harsh. The foreman regards him as a new hand to be broken in rather than as a novillero to be treated with circumspection. He gives Domingo the most brutish jobs about the place and works him hours longer than the other hands. After his first month of hard labor and good meals, Domingo's body is hickory-hard but stiff and unsupple. He has not had time to unwrap his cape, much less to practice with it. Ayala, paying a surprise visit one bitter day in January, finds his novillero forking frozen dung into a wagon. Ayala has a few well-chosen words with Galdos, and from that point on, Domingo's lot is mysteriously easier. Now he practices for two hours at midday, sometimes under Don Jaime's direction, and by tienta-time early in February Domingo has regained his suppleness and further perfected his style. The foreman is finally won over to Domingo's ambitions, even to the point of constructing a carretilla for him and delegating the other hands to maneuver it while Domingo practices with the banderillas and the sword in the little ring where the fighting stock is tried.

The three-day tienta is a contrast for Domingo to his previous tienta. He has the great advantage over the other novilleros of belonging to the place, and of being able to move at his ease among the full matadors who come out from the capital each day. He has the further advantage of knowing by name the cows and their offspring from his weeks on horseback; his performance with the muleta is adequate, although his cape work is still rough. One wise old cow catches him as he attempts a chicuelina, giving him his first cornada in the thigh, *leve*.* Domingo is rather proud of his wound, although ready for the tongue-lashing Ayala gives him, in keeping with his philosophy that every wound is the torero's own fault. In this instance, he says, Domingo should have known better than to attempt the chicuelina to a smart old cow that had been caped before. At the same time, Ayala is delighted at the boy's guts, while Galdos is impressed at the whole performance. Domingo is back at work in four days with a surgical dressing over his wound, but it is a month before the doctor will permit him to mount a horse.

Ayala, who had seen to it that critics from the papers were invited to the tienta, further makes sure that Domingo is mentioned, if only in a sentence, in their articles, by the judicious promise of loot to follow when Domingo begins his formal career. Ayala has less respect for critics of toreo than he has for lawyers, but he philosophically reminds himself that dealing with such people is God's punishment for his sins and for not having saved money when he was earning it. Domingo knows exactly how this beginning of his public career has come about, but seeing his name in print for the first time is no less sweet, and he is no less happy about the single sentence than he would have been by seeing his name in the headline.

During the tienta, some fourteen animals are marked for slaughter; Galdos willingly agrees that Domingo should kill them with the estoque in the little plaza, even though it means waiting for the cornada to heal. For a week of filthy weather with rain and sometimes snow flying in his face, Domingo faces the proscribed cattle at the rate of two a day. Under Ayala's supervision, he works each animal alone, running it, caping it, and giving it a complete faena before the kill. Domingo discovers a new set of sensations as he faces the animals for the kill. He learns something ultimate

---

* Cornadas, like everything else in toreo, have their own strict nomenclature: *muy grave*, or really serious; *grave*, serious but not fatal; *leve*, or *menos grave*, a cornada rather than a mere *puntazo* (wound from the tip of a horn), but one which will not create any great difficulties; *quemada* or *rayón*, a scratch.

about his own fear, and he confirms what Ayala had told him about the need to dominate that final fear which appears in the culminating meeting between man and toro, a fear different from the partial confrontation with cape and muleta. He learns the anxiety about whether or not he can deliver an honest, graceful, and efficient thrust, and the disgust with himself when he must make four, five, or more thrusts, followed by the descabello. He discovers that it is easier to kill the larger *becerros* (calves) than the small, bony, utreros once he learns to dominate his greater fear of the larger animal. Toward the end of the week, he also learns the joy of a good kill, a pleasure unlike any other in his experience.

Ayala carefully estimates the force of each animal, varying the length of Domingo's faena so that he will experience a variety of conditions, necessitating a variety of responses. Like all modern novilleros, Domingo has practiced only the kill a volapié on the carretilla. Now Ayala schools him in the kill *a un tiempo** and *recibiendo,*† and alerts him to the necessity of always being ready for the kill *aguantando*. None of Galdos' culls will allow Domingo to try killing recibiendo, but he is able to attempt with moderate success the suertes other than the volapié.

Working with the carretilla, Ayala reviews the nomenclature of the kill with Domingo, then demonstrates the errors that account for badly placed swords. Like a fencer practicing lunging at a target the size of a coin, Domingo spends hours aiming at the precise spot the size of a small fist, called variously the *cruz, rubios, agujas,* or *péndolas*‡—that point at which, if the sword is placed at the proper angle, it will cut the aorta, or in some animals, reach the heart and produce death swiftly and dramatically.

"You kill with the cape, with the banderillas, with the muleta, with the sword. But above all you kill with your own mind and your heart," Ayala would say. "The suerte de matar is not difficult in itself if you have prepared the toro properly, and if you have

---

* *A un tiempo:* When man and toro meet in simultaneous midcharge.

† *Recibiendo:* Literally, receiving; when the man remains stationary and the toro does the charging upon the sword.

‡ These terms do not translate. *Cruz,* of course, means cross. *Rubios* designates the topmost part of the morillo, or hump. *Agujas* means needles; with reference to cattle, it means bones; it is also used, more logically, of the horns. *Hoyo de las agujas,* ball of flesh between the bones. *Péndolas,* a colloquial variation of *agujas.*

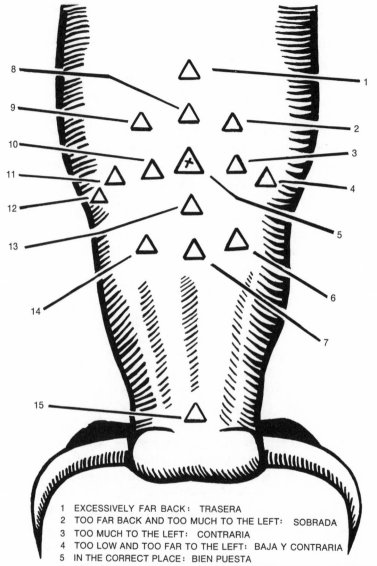

1 EXCESSIVELY FAR BACK: TRASERA
2 TOO FAR BACK AND TOO MUCH TO THE LEFT: SOBRADA
3 TOO MUCH TO THE LEFT: CONTRARIA
4 TOO LOW AND TOO FAR TO THE LEFT: BAJA Y CONTRARIA
5 IN THE CORRECT PLACE: BIEN PUESTA
6 TOO LOW ON THE NECK AND TOO MUCH TO THE LEFT: GOLLETAZO CONTRARIO
7 TOO FAR IN FRONT AND TOO LOW ON THE NECK: PESCUECERA
8 TOO FAR BACK: PASADA
9 TOO FAR BACK AND TOO FAR TO THE RIGHT: PASADA Y BAJA
10 TOO FAR TO THE RIGHT: CAIDA
11 TOO LOW: BAJA
12 EXCESSIVELY LOW: BAJONAZO
13 TOO FAR IN FRONT: DELANTERA
14 TOO LOW ON THE NECK AND TOO MUCH TO THE RIGHT: GOLLETAZO
15 DESCABELLO

Nomenclature of the *estocada*

prepared yourself properly. The *bajonazo* and the *contraria* are the result of indecision, of cowardice perhaps, of lack of resolution. You must not think of how you will place the second sword because you must not allow yourself the luxury of a second sword. If you tell yourself that you are going to kill well with the first sword, you probably will do so."

As when he instructed Domingo in the other suertes, so in the kill Ayala first demonstrates the ideal, then goes into the recourses possible in the suerte, and on to the abuses. In the perfect kill, he explains, the matador "puts the cross upon the cross": with the muleta furled in his left hand, he makes in effect a chest pass, while the sword is at right angles to the muleta, thus the matador's cross upon the cruz of the bull. At the same time, Ayala says, in the perfect kill both the matador's feet should be firmly planted in the sand at the moment the sword penetrates—a rare occurrence because of the matador's need to gain height and simultaneously to make his exit from the horn.

"You know our saying: *'Al que a la hora de matar no hace la cruz, se lo lleva el diablo.'*" (The devil takes him who does not make the cross at the moment of killing.) "You do not kill with your arm alone," Ayala says. "You kill with your heart. You must have the courage and the mental disposition to go in with your shoulder and your whole torso." Killing with the arm alone is mere butchery, he says, usually performed al cuarteo as though the matador were placing banderillas. Once in a great while, Ayala adds, you will see an aging matador, green with fear, killing *a la media vuelta*. In that recourse, the matador cites the animal's hindquarter, challenges by voice, and as the animal whirls about,

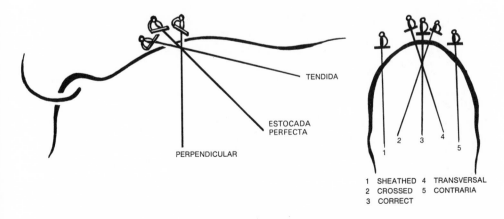

TENDIDA

ESTOCADA
PERFECTA

PERPENDICULAR

1 SHEATHED  4 TRANSVERSAL
2 CROSSED  5 CONTRARIA
3 CORRECT

More nomenclature

the matador flies by, arm outstretched, to place the sword in the neck. It is sad to see, for it requires great confidence and agility, and it is the most cowardly of all suertes de matar, unless, of course, it is used on a toro resabiado, or otherwise deficient.

"Many toreros kill badly a volapié because they stand too far from the toro. You will stand about 4 or 5 feet away, no more. It is easier to maintain your aim from 4 feet than from 8, but of course if you are cowardly, you feel more comfortable at 10 feet," Ayala answers in response to Domingo's question about terrain. Ayala forbids fakery in the form of excessive waving of the muleta. "Be sure the toro sees the muleta," he explains, "but do not cheapen the supreme suerte with false drama. The same for the sword. Some matadors are not content to raise the sword to sight it naturally in front, but produce a great swoop behind their backs. That is not only stupid—it can distract the bull—but they do it to impress the ignorant. It is gaudy and ugly and I forbid it."

"What of profiling the body before the attack?" Domingo asks. "Some toreros do so and some do not."

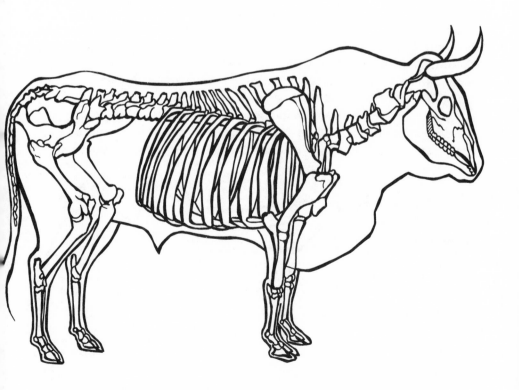

*Toro bravo:* skeletal structure

"It is a question of time. If your animal is totally aplomado, it is safe, for you reduce the size of your body in profile, and I cannot deny that it is graceful. It is not necessary, however. If your animal is nervous, or likely to attack you before you are ready to attack him—if you think you will have to take him a un tiempo—then face on is best. The important thing is to make the cross, to go in as though you mean it, and to make your exit without losing your muleta. If you hit bone and lose your muleta, you are without defense before the toro and you look foolish and undignified to the spectators. As always, you must make the difficult look easy. You must let the thing speak for itself, and it will do so, powerfully. You do not need to fake it or to embellish it."

To kill recibiendo, Ayala says, requires a sure instinct that the animal has not been overpunished, that a particular toro will charge to the voice and charge straight. It is aguantar, enduring, in its finest form, requiring courage and great self-confidence. It is the sign of the finished matador and something for every novillero to aim for. Historically, he says, it was the first form of the kill, and

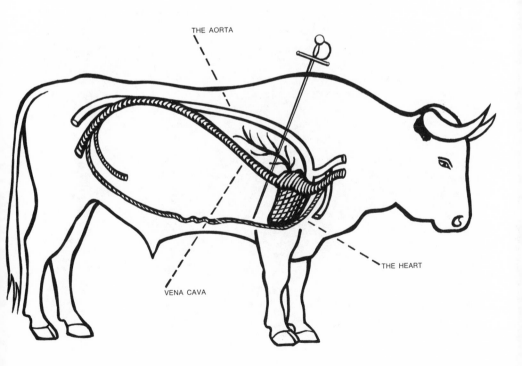

The perfect *estocada* in profile

PLATE 12.

PLATE 13.

PLATE 14.

Jaime Ostos (Plate 12) is perhaps the best living matador, in the basic sense of "swordsman." His kill, like those of Paco Camino in Plates 13 and 14, is almost perfect. The classicist would complain that the feet should not leave the ground. El Cordobés, on the other hand, shows in Plate 15 how to butcher in a cowardly manner, *al cuarteo*.

PLATE 15.

it remains the best, although it is rarely seen in the modern plaza. The length of the faena works against it, and of course a stationary target is easier to hit than a moving one; therefore the toreros lack practice and confidence in performing the suerte. "It is easy with the carretilla, though," Domingo says.

"It is easy with a 500-kilo toro," Ayala says, "if you are a genuine torero and a fine matador. And let me remind you, to kill really well, you should be able to kill with your left hand, too."

Like many novilleros and full matadors, Domingo has difficulty with the descabello. Ayala explains that the point of the recourse (and he insisted that it is a recourse, not a true suerte) is to cut the rachidian bulb at the nape of the toro's neck. To do so, the matador by maneuvering the muleta, must cause the toro to lower his head, thus uncovering the vital spot, then point the sword on a line with the animal's chin. Any other angle is likely to be ineffectual and to prolong the agony of the toro, of the torero, and of the spectators.

Ayala has Domingo practice with the descabello sword first on milk cattle, then on toros de lidia. "Never forget that the toro, even down on his knees and dying, can still kill you. The danger is that by the time you must use the descabello, you are tired, perhaps disgusted with yourself for a bad sword, or with the animal, or with the breeder, or with the crowd, or with life itself.

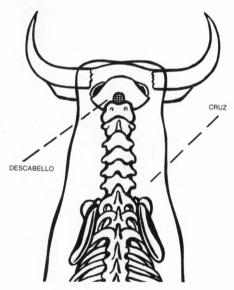

Skeleton from above showing the *cruz*

You may become careless, or lose your presence of mind, or both. Do not forget the first rule of toreo, never to lose control of yourself, no matter what the provocation."

Domingo learns the use of the puntilla, and Ayala urges him to practice with it and with the descabello whenever an animal is slaughtered at the finca. By the end of his first week as matador of calves, Domingo feels more confident than he had with the sword, yet he is aware as never before of the amount of practice before him on the carretilla. In a moment of depression he tells Ayala that he needs four hundred, not fourteen, animals to practice on. Ayala says he is correct, but that he is lucky not to be one of the many novilleros who go into the plaza for the first time without ever having killed an animal methodically, in practice.

Now the foreman and the men with whom he works call Domingo "matador," in part derisively (for some of his calves died badly), but seriously, too. They recognize him as a genuine aspirant, and over the weeks remaining their attitude to him subtly changes. For Domingo, to be called "matador" is even

The false drama of the waved sword

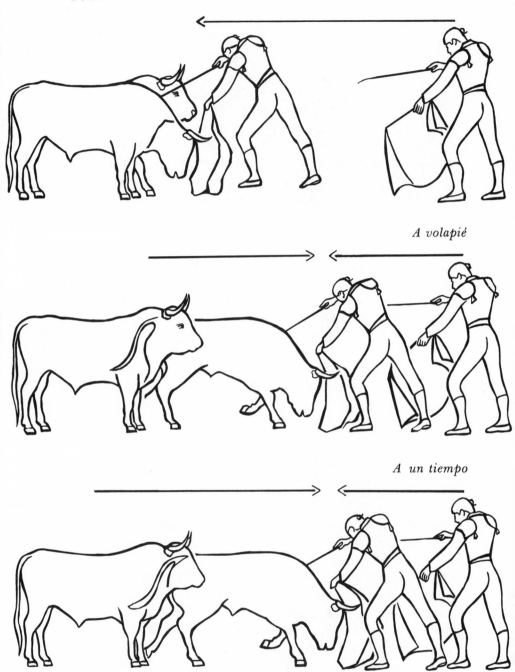

*A volapié*

*A un tiempo*

*Aguantando*

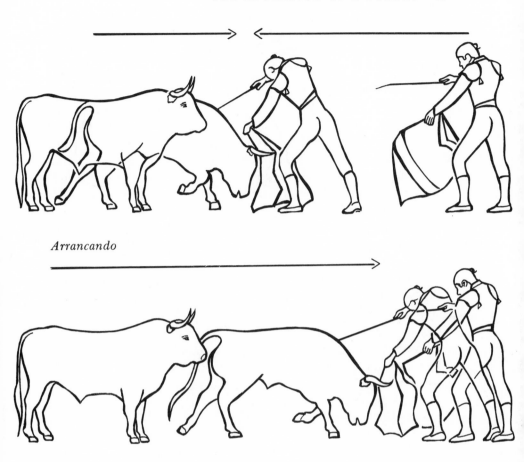

*Arrancando*

*Recibiendo*

sweeter than to see his name in the newspaper, and he resolves to let his hair grow at the back to make a proper coleta as toreros did before Belmonte introduced the artificial one. Ayala approves of the idea. "We will use that in our propaganda. Just think: a modern torero with a real coleta and a small muleta, in the old way. You will be rich and famous yet, my friend."

While Ayala is in no hurry to present Domingo before the public, he listens when Galdos says that the boy is ready to begin the long campaign. Galdos is willing to lend Ayala money to fit Domingo out, and to use his influence with the management of some of the third-class plazas in the south to whom he had sent animals on good terms when he was building up his fighting stock. Ayala hates to borrow money, but he knows that he must do so.

With a single traje de luces costing the equivalent of $225, a good *montera** costing $30, and all the other equipment in that ratio, to launch a novillero requires capital such as Ayala does not have. There would be the cuadrillas to pay off, travel expenses, and worst of all, publicity, including the bribing of certain so-called critics. Ayala himself had spent one third of his income on publicity in the comparatively innocent days before and just after the Civil War; now new techniques and new media were available to make or break the torero. The advance from Galdos would be a mere beginning in terms of the need over the three-year period that Ayala foresaw as a minimum before Domingo would be ready for the big plazas in which he might begin to come out of the red. There would always be pressure to sell the boy to the high-priced managements before he was ready, pressure in which Ayala's own poverty would be an additional force.

With Galdos' help, and using his own lines of communication, Ayala arranged five contracts in the deepest provinces, three for corridas without picadors, and two with picadors. These appearances would take them beyond Easter into May. By then Ayala would have a firmer idea of Domingo's capabilities in public, and know in which direction to concentrate his training and to further his experience. But first, to Domingo's delight, there were trips by bus to the capital to enroll him in the Union, visits to the tailor, to

---

* *Montera:* The torero's head covering, worn from the paseo to (but not including) the final tercio.

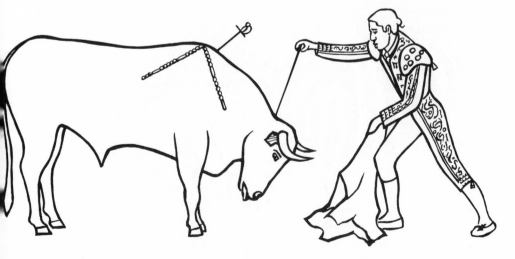

The *descabello*

the photographer, to the shirtmaker and the shoemaker for *zapatillas*.* After his harsh winter, Domingo enjoyed the sights and sounds of the city again. In particular, he liked climbing the four flights of stairs to the tailor's in Ayala's company. The tailor, a banderillero who supported his six children in the off-season by supplying trajes, capes, and muletas, was a small, muscular man who worked very fast on an old pedal-operated sewing-machine, talking all the while to Ayala about corridas they had appeared in together. He seemed to ignore Domingo, but in a month's time he produced, seemingly miraculously, two trajes, one tobacco and gold, one green and silver, "in the old way," he said, to go with Domingo's coleta of his own braided hair. When Domingo left the atelier with his professional costumes, the tailor said, "*Suerte, matador*," as though he meant it. At that moment, Domingo felt later, he entered upon his career, the moment at which he was addressed as "matador" with no trace of derision.

Now his very character and physical presence were changing. He was losing his adolescent tentativeness, and when he walked in the streets, he bore himself as though in the paseo, swinging one

* *Zapatillas:* Toreros' slippers.

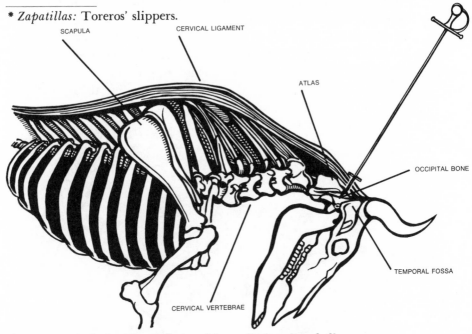

An anatomical sketch of the problem of the *descabello:* the sword is drawn as it penetrates the space between the atlas and the occipital bone to reach the medulla oblongata and the rachidian bulb, which is attached to the medulla oblongata

arm, and taking a long stride. Girls gave him the brushing, rapid glance that means interest, and were he not dedicated to his profession, he would be tempted to go back to his old neighborhood and look up the girls he had known as a boy. He gave mental derechazos to cars and chest passes to bicycles. In the old quarter of the city where the toreros' cafés and the sellers of tickets to the plaza were, Domingo would cite the percherons pulling wagons laden with wine casks, as though for the kill. He faced bulls in his dreams, and beautiful women in the barreras tossed flowers to him.

When their errands were finished, Domingo and Ayala returned together to Galdos' finca. Ayala would spend the next two weeks there, supervising Domingo's training, and in particular working on the banderillas. "It is a sign of the decadence of the fiesta that so few matadors place their own banderillas any more," Ayala explains. "You will not cut ears for placing your own banderillas, but you must learn properly if only to supervise your peones. Many a bull goes bad because of stupid placing of the sticks." And for a week, Ayala develops with complexity and finesse the many possibilities and the numerous variables at work in the relationship between toro and banderillero. "We Spanish are particularly guilty of neglect of the banderillas. The Mexicans are great banderilleros, and you must be even greater. The only trouble with the Mexicans is that they are too flashy. As in everything else in toreo, you must learn restraint and control, to repress an impulse to dazzle the crowd. It is vulgar, for one thing, and you

*Banderillas al cuarteo* to the right

are likely to overextend even a good toro, for another." Ayala reminds Domingo of the young Mexican they had seen in the fall who placed three pairs brilliantly, but who ran in figure eights before each pair so excessively that both toro and torero had little left for the faena.

The most common error, Ayala says, is the banderilleros' habit of placing the sticks only on the quarter and only on the right side. Another dangerous fault of the banderillero who is either cowardly or inept or who simply does not like the looks of a particular beast is to get the whole cuadrilla in the plaza with him to place his toro in a particular terrain. This can discompose the animal, while excessive time spent by the banderillero in lining up the animal and making false runs is time in which the toro can get to know the man's body dangerously and to prefer it to any lure. The really good toreros do not permit their cuadrillas to indulge in such maneuvers, and the greatest toreros place their own sticks in order to profit from the toro's reactions during this portion of the lidia.

As with the picador's work, so the tercio of the banderillas is a matter of lidia, Ayala said; a matter of being aware of the animal's tendency to develop a querencia, of knowing from observation of the preliminary running and cape work where best to position the toro so that the banderillas may be placed quickly and efficiently. The rule, insofar as there can be one, is to work against the querencia, the natural querencia being the toril.

Ayala made a drawing in the sand of the plaza:

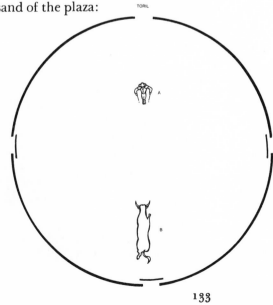

*Suerte natural*

"When the banderillero has a good animal and wants to do a good job, he places the toro at *A*, and himself at *B*."

He made a second drawing:

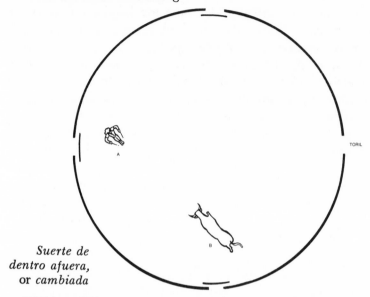

*Suerte de dentro afuera,* or *cambiada*

"With a difficult or an agitated toro, a toro not very brave or confident of itself, he will place the animal in the tablas,[1] nearer

---

[1] The portions of the actual ring are designated as follows:

The division between the medios and the tercios is imaginary, but in

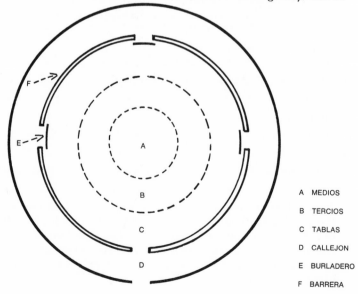

|   |   |
|---|---|
| A | MEDIOS |
| B | TERCIOS |
| C | TABLAS |
| D | CALLEJON |
| E | BURLADERO |
| F | BARRERA |

the barrera to give it confidence, to encourage it. But when you see banderilleros unable to place the sticks at all, or shooting them into the animal's loins, you can be sure that they have ignored the toro's characteristics, failed to observe his tendencies. Such an animal is virtually lost to the faena because, once discomposed, there usually is no time to win the animal back."

The work of the banderillero is a matter not of art but of *destreza,* agility, Ayala says, hence the old term, *diestro,* originally applied only to the banderillero. Now the term diestro has become a newspaperman's variant for "matador" or "torero." The basic proposition remains constant: the banderillero solves a geometric problem involving two curves, the curve of the toro's line of attack, and the tighter curve of his own approach to the toro. The animal's speed varies with its conditions, but the problem remains the same.

Domingo wants to learn to place banderillas *al quiebro,* that brave and dramatic suerte in which the torero cites the toro by voice and with the banderillas, then remains motionless while the toro attacks, moving his torso at the last moment to deflect the charge, place the banderillas, and make his exit. "It is the equivalent of killing recibiendo," Ayala says, "and like recibiendo, it is some kind of ultimate in aguantar." He demonstrated on the carretilla, and pointed out that you perform the suerte only on a bull that behaves as politely as the carretilla. By the end of the week, Domingo has learned the other common suertes: banderillas *al sesgo* (literally, "oblique"), a recourse for a manso that will not charge, or for a toro that remains aplomado after the pic; and banderillas *poder a poder* (force to force), in which the torero weaves in on the animal, straightens to approach from the front, and quarters very tightly at the final moment—again a brave and dramatic suerte.

Ayala corrects Domingo's tendency to raise his arms too high when citing, and to jump or go up on his toes when actually placing the sticks. And he explains again and again the necessity

Spain a line in white or red whitewash is painted on the sand to mark the division between tercios and tablas. The picador is not permitted to ride beyond that line into the tercios. The *burladeros,* or protective fences (*E*), are comparatively modern; originally access to and egress from the ring were over the top of barrera, via the *estribo,* or narrow wooden shelf placed about 16 inches above the sand.

for preliminary observation and the opportunity offered to correct bad tendencies and to encourage the animal. "Taste and authority," he would say. "That is what you are after in this tercio. Not flashiness and not vulgarity. If you can recognize that the tercio of the banderillas is one part of the architecture of your lidia to a particular toro, you are not likely to produce a monstrosity, like a gargoyle on a romanesque tower. Some animals permit baroque work, but others require the most classical restraint."

Domingo's ignorance of Ayala's frame of reference does not interfere with his understanding of the point. And Ayala pushes the boy's understanding in order to continue his education in a

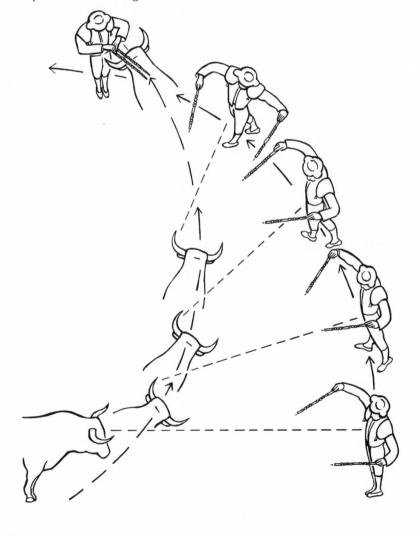

*Banderillas al cuarteo*

dimension apart from toreo. "An ignorant torero cannot be more than an athlete or clown in traje de luces," he would say, bringing Domingo a book to read, then a week later probing obliquely to discover whether Domingo had read it.

For the last ten days before his first corrida, Ayala has Domingo dress in his suit of lights during his morning practice in order to accustom him to the weight and strangeness of the costume. Galdos' servants are delighted at the spectacle, and they appear at the little plaza to shout lusty *"olés"* as Domingo places banderillas in the carretilla or gives a faena to the mounted horns. The day before he is to leave, Galdos donates a becerro for him to fight, and the event takes on the air of a small fiesta. Domingo kills with his first sword, and the foreman awards him ears and tail. "You have blooded your suit of lights," Galdos says. "Now you no longer are a virgin. *Suerte, hijo, y hasta luego.*"

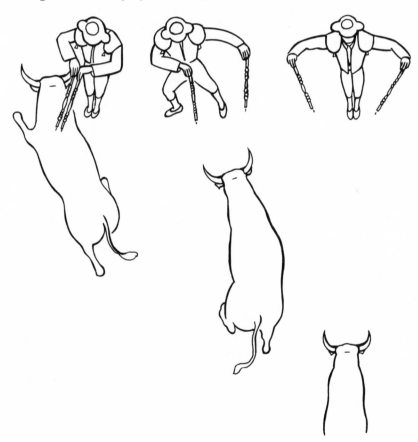

*Banderillas al quiebro*

Domingo's first corrida is an unmitigated disaster. Ayala had been assured that the animals would be becerros of good bloodlines; what he found when they reached the dusty, poverty-stricken town for the sorteo were four monsters culled from three different ganderías for defective vision, excessive horn for the full matadors, four- and five-year-olds, manso to the bone. Ayala protested loudly and profanely that it was murder to send Domingo and the other novice into the plaza with such animals without picadors. The mayor, who was to act as president, was sympathetic, but he explained that there were no horses in the town, only goats and burros, no one who had experience as a picador, and no pics. Ayala said he would act as picador himself if the mayor would produce horses, but the mayor said there was no money; they had spent all their money for the toros, of which he was proud. Furthermore, he pointed out that Ayala had signed a contract for a corrida without picadors and that as he well knew, jail awaited the torero who refused to fulfill his contract.

Domingo resolves the problem by saying that he will take on his

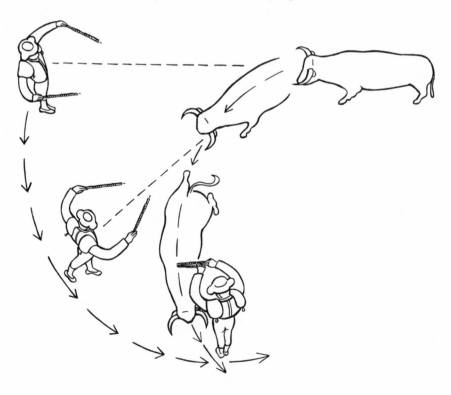

*Banderillas poder a poder*

bulls without picing; he is both frightened and fascinated by the opportunity to try himself with a full toro, after his recent experiences with the swift-moving becerros of Don Jaime. That night Domingo sleeps not at all; the room under the rafters of the local inn is hot, and he cannot stop working his animals. Ayala impresses upon him the necessity for efficient cape work, and perhaps doblones before he attempts anything of greater merit with the muleta. He reviews with Domingo the entire problem of querencias, and urges him to come to the barrera for advice if he feels he is losing control. At dawn Domingo dozes off and sleeps uneasily, dreaming wildly, until mid-morning.

Before the paseo, in the damp-smelling little chapel, Domingo discovers a fervency of religious faith in himself that he had never before been aware of. He had of course been brought up as a Roman Catholic, but his religion, like that of many of the Spanish poor in the cities, is hit-or-miss, a matter of ritual to be observed when convenient, which was most of the time. Religion was not something one thought about; one took it for granted like air and

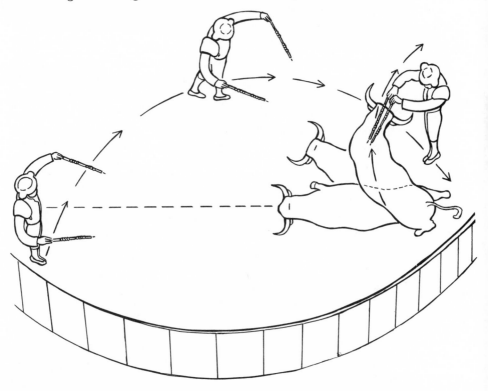

*Banderillas al sesgo*

the fact that water freezes in winter. Now he feels a terrible vulner-
ability, an enormous tenderness about his own body which he
prayed to Mary and the saints to protect, to give him bravery, and
to heal him should he be gored. The senior matador, Gitanillo de
Valencia,* who prayed nearby, was green with fear. Domingo was
somewhat reassured by the other lad's frank terror; he, after all,
was a veteran of two *capeas*.†

All the able-bodied and many of the halt of the little town are
in the plaza, filling it to the flagpoles. Drunks outnumber the
sober two to one, except for the five-man band, all five of whom
have been boozed for days. Their *pasodobles* are off-key but loud.
The day is fine and sunny, but an intermittent wind promises
trouble for the toreros. Ready for the paseo at the cuadrilla gate,
Domingo is unaware of the crowd and the noise. He is vaguely
disappointed that the banderilleros, boys of the town, are dressed
in caps and white shirts rather than in the traje de luces. But
mainly he is concentrating deep inside himself like a student
reading Spinoza rather than like a very young man about to
confront a toro de lidia.

Gitanillo, as the senior, takes the first animal, and Domingo's
agony is prolonged by having to wait and to watch the fracaso that
follows. Gitanillo, too frightened to control his legs, chooses to
meet his toro on his knees at the toril with a *larga cambiada*. The
toril is opened, Gitanillo waits, knees spread and cape on the sand,
but nothing happens, no toro appears for what seems minutes.
Gitanillo calls to the shadow, and when he seems least ready, the
animal comes out like a train to flatten the boy in the sand before
he can raise his cape. The toro stops, looks around, and determines
to go back to the chiqueros. Since the toril is closed, it chooses to
remain there, not answering to any challenge of cape or voice,
waiting defensively for its enemy to approach, at which time it
hooks violently. Gitanillo, unhurt by the collision, works with the
banderilleros for minutes slinging his cape in with one hand,

---

* "Gitanillo" means little gypsy. The affectionate diminutives often
given to toreros seem out of keeping with the dignity of the art. It is
a fact that many of the very best toreros simply use their surnames.
The nicknames, rather like those given to boxers, indicate a side of
toreo where art and popular culture meet, discussed in Chapter 6.

† *Capea:* A corrida, more or less organized, in which the toro is not
piced but is supposed by law to be killed. Domingo's first corrida is
an organized capea.

attempting to entice the animal away from the toril. At length a spectator slips over the barrera into the callejón and jabs the toro in the hindquarter with a knife. The animal bellows and takes off for the opposite side of the plaza, three men in pursuit.

Unable to bregar his toro, Gitanillo cites for a verónica, advancing a step with each attempt. One yard away, he cites again, and is thrown high in the air, as though performing a cartwheel. Domingo and all the banderilleros make the quite, and again Gitanillo is unhurt. After further inconclusive attempts with the cape, in desperation the boy goes to the barrera for his muleta, the crowd whistling and jeering all the while. After five minutes of work por la cara with the muleta, the toro is as fresh as the day before. Sweating and covered with dust and dung, Gitanillo cites for the kill, hits bone, cites again, hits bone again, and finally places a sword in the neck, while his banderillero flaps a cape from the left side. The animal circles the arena, and when no one expects it, goes down on its knees, allowing the local butcher to finish it off with the puntilla. The bravos in the crowd throw bottles, cushions, shoes, false teeth, and cigar butts while Gitanillo makes his bow to the president and retreats to the callejón to be dusted off and cleaned up.

Domingo's first beast is the smaller, some 425 kilos, and a mangy piebald in color. It comes out well but leaps into the callejón at the first wave of the banderilleros' capes. It is herded back into the ring, only to make the leap again. The animal is bronco and discomposed, and the banderilleros chase it about, unable to work it properly. "Take it now," Ayala says to Domingo. "They are making it worse. Try to get it to come to you, there in the tablas. Do not pursue it."

Domingo does as Ayala tells him, and succeeds in giving the animal two hurried verónicas, without temple. He then decides to work the animal himself, but again the beast jumps into the callejón. Again Domingo cites for a verónica, but the animal simply stands, breathing heavily and mooing. At last Domingo gives up and goes to the barrera for advice. Ayala passes him the muleta and tells him to try por altos, as many as possible, then doblones. Domingo can get the animal to charge only by leading it toward the toril; once there, he can do nothing with it. Unbidden, his banderillero capes the toro away from the toril, and Ayala gives Domingo the signal to cite for the kill. On his first trip with the sword, Domingo is caught and thrown, his taleguilla ripped from knee to thigh. Ayala himself makes the quite, assures himself that Domingo is all right, and tells him to try again. Shaken and nervous, Domingo cannot kill the animal. After his third sword, he hears his first *aviso*.\* After his fifth sword, he is ready to use the weapon on himself. The stands are in uproar, cushions are again flying down, and Domingo is utterly at a loss. He continues doggedly to line up his animal, which seems made of bone, not of flesh and hide. Domingo does not even hear the second aviso, and when the third is sounded, Ayala calls him to the fence. The indestructible toro is led into the corral by the steers, to be finished off by the butcher, and Domingo learns something about the cruelty and difficulty of the life he has undertaken. He is called every obscenity in the rich Spanish language by the drunks in the stands, and hit on the shoulder with an empty cognac bottle.

In the callejón he weeps from rage and frustration. "Do not let this bother you," Ayala says. "They are barbarians. Screw them all. Jesus Christ himself could not have fought that ox without picadors."

Gitanillo's second animal shows more casta than his first, but the novillero is unable to give it a convincing faena. He insists on derechazos when the toro is better to the left, and he dances away from the alarming spread of horn in the middle of each pass. The boy's nervousness is conveyed to the beast, which becomes more and more discomposed as the faena goes on. Even the drunks respect the animal's horns, wide, sweeping and sharp, so that when Gitanillo kills with three thrusts and uncounted descabello thrusts, he is treated to silence rather than to the uproar he expected. He mutters gypsy curses as he wipes his face with a towel, but he wishes Domingo "suerte" when the trumpet sounds for the final toro of the day.

Although this animal ambles out from the toril like the manso it basically is, it improves sufficiently for Domingo and his cuad-rilla to get some sort of display from it. It is large, powerful, and, to Domingo's eyes, the hugest beast in Spain. The toro does

---

\* *Aviso:* Twelve minutes after the matador has begun his taena the toro is supposed to be dead. If it is not, a trumpet or bugle sounds a warning, the aviso. If five more minutes elapse, the matador is given a second aviso. After three more minutes, the third and final aviso is sounded. The matador is then required under the regulations to return to the barrera, while the steers are led in to herd out the still-living toro. Avisos received are published in the records.

charge, but its charge is short and therefore dangerous. Domingo has an overpowering urge to step back in his verónicas, and to lean forward from the waist with the muleta. Ayala has to shout to him to make him aware of what he is doing. With the muleta, Domingo is unable really to dominate and control the toro. Like Gitanillo, he is unable to construct a faena; he succeeds only in giving it an ill-assorted variety of passes which bore the spectators. As he attempts a chest pass, the horn catches him in his right armpit and again he is thrown violently. When Ayala picks him up, he is half dazed, but a mouthful of water in the callejón clears his head, and he goes back, angry and frustrated, to cite for the kill. Again he has difficulty. The animal's head is high, and it takes minutes to line it up. At length the beast charges before Domingo is ready for his volapié, and to his shocked surprise he finds that he has placed a fair half-sword. His banderillero runs in, removes the sword by flinging his cape at it, and Domingo goes in twice again, flinging himself furiously over the horn, determined to kill, aviso or no aviso. The toro goes down after the third sword, vomiting blood from its lung, and Domingo has the brief satisfaction of a good descabello thrust. He hears whistles from the crowd, and unless his ears deceive him a very scattered clapping of hands. He is exhausted, and while he had felt nothing when his toros had thrown him, now his body begins to ache violently in strange places. He is dirty, thirsty, and his fine new taleguilla is held tenuously to his leg by wide stripes of tape. He isn't sure whether he wants to live or die. His purse will not quite cover his train fare, third class.

On the night train back to the capital, Domingo is sullen and silent. His body is bruised and aching, and although he wants sleep more than life, sleep will not come. "You did as well as could be done," Ayala said. "It was my fault. I should have gone to jail rather than let you torear those elephants. But that is the fiesta. Almost never is it what you expect it to be or want it to be. From now on, though, there will be no switching of toros."

Domingo can find no energy to reply, but he responds to Ayala's rare burst of sympathy by falling sound asleep, to awaken at dawn, thirsty and stiff, as the train pulls slowly into the station.

Domingo's next two engagements went better for him. The animals were the reverse of his first catastrophe—scrawny becerros with underdeveloped horns. He worked them well and killed them well, and he knew he had done adequately from Ayala's bawling him out for not showing more mando, for his tendency to tuck his elbows to his side, for rising on his toes during the chest pass. The main value of his first capeas, Domingo later decided, was his discovery of a tendency to hate the crowd, to have contempt for the rube experts in the stands, and his corresponding urge to ignore the public altogether. He talked the matter over with Ayala, who had observed the boy's disposition toward the crowd. Ayala pointed out that when the public was referred to as *"el respetable"* (the respectable) in taurine writings, the term was not used sardonically; the public was an integral part of toreo without which not only would the fiesta obviously cease to exist, but lacking which the finished torero would not find within himself the impulse to do his finest work. Later, Domingo would find spectators who were complete aficionados, who knew good work from bad, and who were as much an aid to the honest torero as the ignorant were a hindrance. The torero had to be a showman as well as a craftsman and an artist; within the limits of his own conscience, he had to play to and for the public, and genuinely respect them and educate them. The country folk were not to be blamed, for they saw only one or two corridas a year, and often the only fresh meat they had for the year was the carcass of the toro killed at their annual festivals.

Domingo's second corrida with picadors, up in the northwest province, remained memorable for him. In that corrida he gained confidence in his own ability, a confidence objectively ratified by the award of two ears from his second toro. It was a difficult corrida in that the animals for once were good, almost too good for the other two novilleros, Fuentes and Pérez. Although they were novillos, not toros, the animals were in good condition and had sufficient horn to produce the necessary sense of drama in the spectators. They had codicia and a limited nobility, although Fuentes' second and Domingo's first showed the malicious urge to run in on the torero at the last moment during a pass. Ayala, who had liked the look of the stock, took pains to line up a good cuadrilla for Domingo in the capital. He sensed that this corrida might be Domingo's opportunity to show what he could do, and that he would need every advantage.

Both Fuentes and Pérez were in their second year as novilleros. Fuentes was a cold torero, rather clumsy, but well-schooled. Pérez, a Venezuelan, seemed totally unschooled but suicidally brave to compensate for his lack of technique. Fuentes, unable to fix his first novillo in the cape, led it to the picador, who punished the animal excessively with his first pic, then when the animal charged again, missed the hump and slit open the loin, damaging nerve centers and virtually incapacitating the novillo for further lidia. Fuentes' faena was lackluster to the aplomado animal, and he killed badly. To his second, the bravest toro of the day, he was competent but cold, until the horn caught him during a natural and sent him to the infirmary with a horn wound in the scrotum. Pérez killed Fuentes' toro efficiently.

Domingo's first novillo was run beautifully by his banderilleros, with serpentine, one-handed largas; their bregar was applauded by the crowd of the provincial capital, an incident unusual in itself. Domingo was able to deliver five good verónicas and a graceful media, for which the *autoridad* (presiding judge) ordered music. It was Domingo's first experience of musical applause, and he placed his own banderillas well to more music. His novillo took three good pics, allowing each novillero a quite.* He began his faena with ayudados por alto, but then fate intervened in the form of a colossal thunder shower. Since neither Domingo nor anyone else could see more than thirty feet ahead, the president suspended the faena for the duration of the shower. Ten minutes later the sun shone again, but the sand was puddled and treacherous and the continuity of the faena was lost. Domingo was unable to recover it, and he killed with two *pinchazos*† and a full sword, to polite applause.

Pérez' second novillo, a splendid cárdeno, was too powerful for him. He lacked the technique for dominating it, and he attempted to substitute doubling passes for dominio. The novillo was infuriated and upset by the man's excessive doubling, and the lidia became mere lucha, a true bullfight which Pérez lost. In his second derechazo, the animal came on him and threw him heavily to the sand, knocking out his wind. The banderilleros made the quite,

---

* Quites are performed in precise order; in this instance, Domingo performs the first, because it is his animal. Fuentes makes the second, as the senior matador, and Pérez the third. In the senior matador's first toro, the order is simply senior, second senior (Pérez), junior (Domingo). The term "quite" is also used of any caping of the toro away from a torero who has been caught (*cogido*).

† *Pinchazo:* From *pinchar*, to prick, puncture, wound lightly. Customarily used of the poorly placed sword that hits bone, or one that penetrates only a few inches.

while the *mozos**  picked up the boy. At the barrera he recovered his breath and cleared the arena, to the applause of the crowd. He then attempted to regain lost ground by citing for a natural from 20 feet off, the muleta furled. The novillo, ignoring the muleta altogether, caught him in the upper thigh, flung him high in the air, then tried to find him on the sand for another goring. Pérez, playing dead, seemed to be pinned to the sand, but in its eagerness the animal missed the body and buried a horn in the sand next to Pérez. While Domingo threw his cape in the animal's face, a banderillero pulled the animal's tail, succeeding in their rough quite.[2] Pérez' novillo now became Domingo's to torear and kill as best he could.

At the barrera, Ayala told him to be gentle with the toro, to work the left side, not to double it, and to try perhaps seven or eight passes, then to kill it. "*Cuidado* (careful), though. If he cuts in on you, line him up and kill him at once."

Ayala is urging Domingo to a calculated risk. Normally a toro that has caught a man is dispatched at once, without any attempt at further lidia, as Pérez had killed Fuentes' novillo. Now Ayala wants Domingo to get back the spectators' sympathy. He cannot cut ears from Pérez' toro, but he can prepare the crowd to applaud his own next and last toro. The plan works nicely, and Domingo kills with a half sword and one descabello. He is warmly applauded for his work as he washes out his mouth and wipes away his sweat, waiting for his own second animal.

The novillo proves to be best he has met so far. He is able to find its rhythm, both with the cape and the muleta. His quite of gaoneras is nicely judged, and he earns *dianas*† for it. He lets the banderilleros put in the sticks upon Ayala's advice, to save his concentration and strength for the faena. "Give them a few molinetes,"‡ Ayala says. "It will be easy with this beast, and these

---

* *Mozo(s):* The badly paid and often brave ring-attendants who clean up the mess, accompany the picadors on foot, and occasionally make quites when the situation becomes desperate. Also known as "mono-sabios" (wise monkeys).

[2] The Spanish say that in toreo somebody is always saving somebody else from something.

† *Diana:* The name of a musical phrase played in applause of good work in the plaza at the judge's signal.

‡ The molinete is a muleta pass with either hand in which the torero cites as for a *cambiado,* then turns out of the pass in the direction

people like them." Domingo finds his animal still very powerful after two pics, but ayudados por alto help to reduce his strength, aided by gentle doubling passes in the manner of Domingo Ortega. He is able to get two nicely linked groups of derechazos and naturals, both punctuated by chest passes, then molinetes and two manoletinas.* His sword is a bit contraria, but in to the hilt, and handkerchiefs are waving even before he lines up the animal for the estocada. Music, three vueltas, and applause delighted him; this is what he has been after, and this is what, he began to feel, he would never experience. He insists that the ganadero take a vuelta with him, and the crowd insists that the toro's carcass also circle the plaza before the *arrastre*.† Ayala is pleased at his own strategy and at Domingo's performance, although he criticizes him for the sword just off center. Not only is the corrida written up in the papers, but Domingo also has the added pleasure of hearing his performance praised that evening on television.

Because of Domingo's success in the northwest, Ayala has little difficulty in arranging further contracts for him. In his first season, Domingo appears in eleven corridas with picadors and five without picadors. He cuts six ears and has as many disasters. Ayala estimates that each corrida means an investment of 5,000 pesetas over the 500 to 1,000 pesetas paid to Domingo. He is tempted to

---

opposite to the bull's charge. It is of course more dangerous with the left hand, since the sword is not used. The molinete is an adorno, or embellishment, given to a willing bull to impress the crowd. It is less dangerous than it may look, since the flourish takes place after the horn has passed the torero's body. Ayala would agree with Hemingway, who said that if a pass ends in "-ina," "-ete," or "-ado," it is probably a fake.

* The manoletina is another embellishment, in which a corner of the muleta is held behind the back with the left hand, the bulk of the muleta and sword in the right. As the animal charges, the man turns against the direction of the charge and the muleta flows over the bull's back. Formerly, it was called the *orteguina,* after Domingo Ortega, who took it from the nineteenth-century repertoire and refurbished it. Manolete picked it up and further refined (i.e. vulgarized) it by frequently performing it while gazing into the tendidos, a maneuver fairly safe when done to shaved horns, and safe enough to unshaved ones. See Plate 5.

† *Arrastre:* Term describing the towing out of the plaza of the bull's carcass by mules driven by the plaza attendants.

book Domingo into second- or first-class plazas, but he knows the boy is not ready, and he limits his appearances to the sum which he has borrowed from Galdos. By October, Ayala is satisfied with Domingo's first season. The boy has gained experience and confidence, and while he has been stupid on occasion and has often been uncertain with the sword, Ayala feels that another winter at the finca, a serious round of tientas, and constant practice will make a good deal of difference.

During the summer and early fall, Domingo has a room near Ayala's apartment. Each morning now he goes to the plaza to work out with the other toreros, getting up early to do his road work before the sun is high and hot, observing the other novilleros' style, their strengths and defects, and making fast friends with a handful of boys his age who are at the same stage in their careers. Ayala appears at ten o'clock or so, sometimes ignoring Domingo to gossip with the other apoderados and with the alguacil,* an old friend; at other times he puts Domingo through exacting sessions with the cape and muleta. Domingo sometimes is impressed by the bad habits of the other toreros: their fondness for the flashy and merely athletic over the pure. Ayala struggles to keep Domingo's concept of his art pure and classical, to cultivate his taste and discrimination. Ayala knows from his own career that the qualities he wants to develop in Domingo depend not only upon his work in toreo, but also upon broad general education. He recalls his own struggles to emerge from ignorance, his painful work with hired tutors, after he had taken the alternativa and could afford them, to learn French and English, to read history and literature. Like himself at nineteen, Domingo has no historical sense, little awareness of the past. Ayala knows that the entire ambiente works against his conviction, and that the literate torero is the exception, not the rule. On their way back from the plaza in the subway one day, Ayala observes the novillero with whom Domingo has been working take a comic book from inside his shirt and read it slowly, his lips moving, during the journey. When the boy gets off at his stop, Ayala says to Domingo, "You cannot read *historietas* (comic

---

* The mounted attendant who leads the paseo; the alguacil receives the key (actual or imaginary) to the toril from the presiding authority and transmits the president's commands to other participants in the corrida. Usually two alguaciles are used in Spain, one in Mexico.

books) and be a good torero. This afternoon we shall enroll you in the *Ateneo.*"*

From that time on, Domingo frequented the Ateneo whenever he was in the capital, reading slowly but intensively under Ayala's guidance. In that same period, Domingo formed a close friendship with Rafael Sabartès, a boy who had come from the capeas of his provincial town to the city to make his way in toreo. Rafael had natural talent but no instruction other than what he had gleaned from observation. Domingo had got to know him when, early one morning in the summer, he arrived at the plaza earlier than usual to practice. There he found Rafael in the medios, giving lances, and observing his own shadow carefully. When Domingo appeared, Rafael was embarrassed; later he explained that he did not like to practice before the other novilleros until he had mastered

---

* *Ateneo:* A combined library and cultural center for lectures and exhibitions found in most cities of the Spanish-speaking world, similar to the private athenaeums of nineteenth-century New England.

Sabartes and his shadow

the cape. By arriving at sunrise he could work out with his shadow the better to observe when he bent his waist or held his elbows to his sides, and to judge the speed of each pass. Domingo reassured him by quoting Ayala: "The air is the best master, because it is an idea."

The two boys would work hard through the long, hot mornings, one running the horns, the other wielding the cape or muleta. One toro would say to the matador in the middle of a natural, *"Corre la mano,"* (run your hand) and the matador might reply, "I am running my hand, are you blind?" Rafael wanted Ayala to take him on as a full student, but Ayala said he lacked the time. His true reason was that he lacked the capital to finance two novilleros. The following season, however, when he was better able to do so, Ayala became Rafael's apoderado, and two seasons later, Domingo and Rafael took the alternativa within a week of each other.

That winter Domingo again spent at Galdos' finca. Domingo, with Ayala's lukewarm support, persuaded Galdos to take on Rafael, too. Ayala and Galdos together arranged for the two novilleros to take part in many tientas throughout the country. Rafael suffered a fairly severe goring in his second tienta, but Domingo, more able and confident than ever before, came through with no more than bruises. Early in the spring, Domingo resumed his campaign, beginning in third-class plazas with small becerros, then by late May, moving up to second-class plazas. Early in June a small, anarchic Pablo Romero put him in the toreros' hospital for six weeks with a bad horn wound in the stomach. He could do nothing well for several corridas after he resumed work, not from lack of courage but from physical weakness and persistent nausea. By August he was going well again, cutting ears at the rate of one for every two novillos he killed.

Now was the time when Ayala began his publicity campaign in earnest. He was reasonably certain that Domingo would make a very good, and possibly a great, matador. The boy was killing well, controlling his animals with greater authority than ever before and making a name for himself in the provincial plazas in which he was now asked to reappear as often as his schedule would permit. Ayala's greatest problem was still lack of money, but now empresarios and well-heeled aficionados showed interest, and it was increasingly easy for him to borrow money against his protégé's future. Ayala found himself in Richelieu-like conversations with television critics, newspaper authorities, photographers, empresarios, and various shady types who made their well-paid way through the fiesta, finding money, arranging interviews, seeing that provincial corridas in which Domingo took part were reported in the city newspapers—all the activities that he despised, did rather badly, and knew to be necessary if his torero were not to disappear from view.

Life for Domingo, too, was becoming complex. Rafael, who was a lecher and could with ease have turned into a drunk, was constantly there to tempt him to the pleasures of the bed and the indulgences of the bodega. Women found Domingo much to their taste, a taste that he reciprocated. Ayala, however, was his conscience and guardian angel. Finding him hung-over and depleted one noontime in a hot, provincial hotel room, he said, "All right, matador. Which is it going to be? Toreo or the gay life? If it's the gay life you want, I'll pack my bag, leave this town, and never again in my life lift a finger in your behalf."

Domingo said nothing, but that afternoon he dedicated his first toro to Ayala, cut both its ears, and the two men were reconciled without needing to discuss the fact.

Other kinds of problem arose. A crowd of hangers-on began to gather, volunteering to do numerous odd jobs connected with a torero's daily existence, flattering the boy, eager to provide any manner of service, legitimate, illegitimate, or in between, never asking for payment but creating a subtle sense of obligation that might be paid off in drink, tickets to corridas, meals, cigarettes, and favors. Ayala looked at the crowd with contempt, got rid of the more mangy, and suffered the rest, knowing that it was a test of character that every ascendant torero had to undergo. If Domingo's head were to be turned, it would be turned and there was nothing he, Ayala, could do about it. The only answer lay in the degree of the boy's afición. If he had sufficient afición to put toreo above everything else—above the sycophants, the willing girls, the publicity, the easy money, and the corresponding physical abuse entailed—he seemed to have the potential to become a true figura, an honest torero who would not fake because he did not have to, an honor to the fiesta, a credit to himself, and a source of deep pleasure to those aficionados who hungered for just such a torero, and considered themselves lucky if they saw one or two in a lifetime. Ayala could not say these things to Domingo, but he could and did convey them through what he left unsaid, through his emphasis upon the boy's inexperience and need for constant physical and intellectual discipline, through his insistence that his ignorance be wiped out through reading and study.

After his third season, Ayala arranged for Domingo to campaign to Mexico and Venezuela during the winter. Domingo was bothered at first by the altitude in Mexico, and unaccustomed to the smaller but tricky Mexican bulls. He could do nothing in his first four corridas and was taking a beating in the Mexican press. In his fifth novillada, however, he dominated completely his two difficult Tequisquiápan novillos, working with them and improving them throughout his lidia. He provoked from the crowd in Plaza México a demonstration such as he had never heard at home, and turned in his favor the newspaper critics of the city. Before returning to Europe, he took part in the competition for the golden ear and was lucky enough to draw the only good beast of the afternoon, with which he did well enough to win the award. In Venezuela, on his way back, his "novillos" weighed almost 600 kilos and were at least six years old: he was hooted out of the plaza but was happy to be alive. The toros had been in the corrals for months, "maybe years," Ayala said, waiting for someone foolhardy or young enough to take them on.

Back in Spain, Domingo was included in two novilladas in the big *feria** of the capital in May. Although his inclusion was good business on the part of the empresa, it was regarded as an honor, too. Only the most promising novilleros were invited, those whom the empresa felt were ready for the alternativa. Domingo was more nervous than usual as he waited for May and the feria. He wanted to triumph, and he went twice to the ganadería from which his animals were to come to learn all he could about them. They were handsome, with curling black hair on their foreheads, and too much horn for comfort. When the day of his first corrida came, and his first appearance before the aficionados of the capital, he was in a serious state of nerves, compounded by sleeplessness and fear. His first novillo was a difficult manso with which he could do nothing; the silence that met his efforts was more disheartening than the cushions and bottles of the south. With his second he did better, losing an ear by needing two swords and two descabellos. By his second corrida, however, he had worked through his nervousness, and he set coldly to work forcing his animals, exposing

---

* *Feria:* Fair. Used interchangeably with "festival."

himself, nursing his toros, by turns cajoling and swearing at them. He cuts an ear from his first, and two ears from his second after a brief, brilliant faena and an estocada recibiendo which set the crowd on fire.

Ayala's greatest test occurred after that feria. The pressure upon him to have Domingo take the alternativa at once was as tempting as it was heavy. He was deeply in debt to a dozen people whom he wanted to pay off. But he knew that Domingo was not ready to compete with full matadors, and that he needed this final season at least, fighting in first-class plazas and gaining the maturity necessary to allow him not only to survive, but to triumph. Domingo accordingly fought almost a hundred corridas that season, cutting ears regularly and suffering only minor wounds. He had his own cuadrilla, now, instead of the *ad hoc,* often ill-assorted cuadrilla that the young novillero can usually afford. He bought a magnificent, twenty-year-old Rolls-Royce touring car, one of the few machines extant able to contain his gear, his cuadrilla, their gear, and himself. Ayala was able to pay off most of his debts and to give more time to Rafael, who also was coming along nicely.

Domingo's problems remained serious. He was still capable of coldness and seeming contempt toward the public when they were not with him from the outset of his lidia; and the more he learned about toros bravos, the deeper he knew his ignorance was. His instinct for the animals' ways in the plaza was good, but all too often fallible. As he was capable of believing that a basically noble animal was beyond hope, he lost many an ear that he might have cut. He continued to rely too heavily upon Ayala's judgment of a particular animal, then to ignore it when it seemed mistaken.

In his personal life, he resented the grueling round of corrida, travel, hotel, corrida, travel. He wanted time to himself, time away from the people who bore in upon him twenty hours a day. He was given to depression at the thought that he would never have the formal education he now longed for, and at the same time he disliked himself for being impatient with the men around him who had barely learned to write their own names. He wanted to travel to cities and countries where bulls were unknown, to meet exotic women and to encounter experience that was neither ritualistic, like toreo, nor fully planned, as his daily existence necessarily was. He was annoyed at the demands of relatives, who now turned up in large numbers for handouts, and with the need always to keep up a front in public. He was tempted to cut his natural coleta, which the press made too much of, but Ayala forbade it as valuable to him.

In the winter, he again went to Mexico, returning by way of New York. When he took his alternativa the following season, he could feel that he had earned it. Thousands of hours of practice, six serious cornadas, more than two hundred toros killed to his credit, grave doubts about himself and the shape of his world, fear in all its forms, the supervision of Ayala, and his own human character, shaped by whatever forces, had conspired to make him what he was—Domingo Alameda, matador de toros.

# CHAPTER 5

# CONTEMPORARY TOREO

IN CHAPTER 2 the writers made brief mention of the differences between "classical" and post-1914 toreo; throughout the narrative, we have distinguished between the diestro and the artist, between the athletic performance and that other toreo which is the product of interior vision, character, and mastery of lidia. It is now time to scrutinize these matters in detail, for what one sees in the plazas today, and how one interprets the spectacle, in part depend upon one's awareness of the relationship between past and present, between tradition and what has been called revolution. As in all the arts, effects are enhanced by the observer's knowledge of what has gone before: his knowledge of those individual artists who have enlarged the boundaries of their art, of those who were content to be journeymen practitioners, or of how the materials of the particular art might have changed. A child may enjoy a trip through a museum of fine arts, yet his pleasure would be qualitatively different from the pleasure of the child's father, who had studied art history, and who had trained himself to look at painting from many points of view: from that of craft, of ideas, of biography, of the relationships between painting and society, of cosmopolitan against provincial influences. The aficionado who ignores the history, evolution, and the aesthetics of toreo is rather in the position of the child in the art museum. His pleasure is genuine, but it is limited to an immediate, unintellectual response.

Again, we do not intend to write a history, but rather to indicate certain inevitable connections between history and the living, contemporary reality. One returns to the fact, known to every aficionado, that the basic lances are the verónica and the half verónica, and the basic muleta passes are the natural and the chest pass to the left (natural cambiada por alto), and have been so virtually since the days of Francisco Romero. Classical toreo was confined almost exclusively to the left hand because of the emphasis upon the kill. The kill was emphasized, in turn, because the large and aged toros of the eighteenth and nineteenth centuries required so much punishment from the picador that they were not fit for the muleta; thus in its origins, the faena was brief, athletic, and efficient, but not a matter of art. Verónicas and naturals were not delivered in the modern manner, low (*por abajo*), the toro's head down.* It was toreo por alto with both cape and muleta; on the basis of period art work and early photographs, the faena often

* Spanish *humillado,* from *humillar,* to lower.

"It was *toreo por alto*"

consisted of no more than doubling passes, the naturals frequently being really trastear *por la cara*.* The natural por abajo is described in the early *Tauromachias* of José Delgado (Pepe-Hillo), published at Cadiz in 1796, and of Francisco Montes (Madrid: 1836). Nevertheless, between the time of Montes' career and the late nineteenth century, the natural por abajo was rarely practiced. It was revived by Ricardo Torres (Bombita), who took the alternativa in 1899.

Modern toreo, then, is surprisingly recent. The chest pass with the right hand was the innovation of José García (Algabeño), alternativa in 1895; Rafael Gómez (El Gallo), alternativa 1902, introduced the so-called "pass of death" (ayudado por alto); the low right-hand pass (derechazo por abajo) is as recent as the career of Nicanor Villalta, who took his alternativa in 1922. To the regret of all North Americans who care about the fiesta, a braggart compatriot from Brooklyn claims to have been the first torero to give the verónica with hands lowered, in 1929.[1] As is the case with many of this person's claims, that one also is false. Tradition among toreros has it that Cayetano Sanz (1821–1891) gave the verónica with lowered hands in the course of his long career, but objective evidence is lacking. Photographic evidence is available for the fact that Gitanillo de Triana (also known as Curro Puya— his Christian and surnames were Francisco Vega de los Reyes), improving upon the verónica of Belmonte, introduced in modern times the verónica por abajo long before the North American pretender, and probably as early as 1924.[2]

One insists upon these particular lances and passes, because without them, without the revival and evolution of toreo por abajo, toreo as we know it could not exist. It is customary to explain the modern style in terms of Juan Belmonte's "innovations," and to see the rivalry between Belmonte and José Gómez (Joselito) from 1913 to 1920, the year of Joselito's mortal cornada,

---

* Trastear *por la cara*: "Working" the bull with the muleta actually in front of its face without causing it to pass; similar to bregar with the cape.

[1] Sidney Franklin, "The Modern Veronica," *Toros*, VI, No. 5 (May 1962), 5.

[2] Cossío, *Los toros*, III, pp. 978–980. Note Cossío's photographs. Also to the point is Néstor Luján, *Historia del toreo* (Barcelona, 1954), pp. 328–331. And see Vicente Vega's refutation of Franklin in a letter to *Toros*, VII, No. 3 (March 1963), 28–29.

as a great watershed in the history of toreo, a confrontation between the classical past and the exciting, although decadent, present. Joselito, according to the formula and the fact, was both the inheritor of the best of the nineteenth-century tradition, the best of Cayetano Sanz, Francisco Montes, Frascuelo, Lagartijo, Guerrita, and Bombita; he was a "long" torero, a master of the banderillas, of total lidia, and a fine killer, having adeptness at killing recibiendo. His work reflected the best of the school of Sevilla* in being florid, exciting, punctuated with adornos and *desplantes.†* At the same time, according to his passionate followers, he incorporated the best of the school of Ronda* too, in that he displayed the dignity and the sense of *oficio,‡* the restraint and the understated drama implicit in that style of toreo. Belmonte, on the other hand, also according to legend and in varying degrees to fact, capitalized upon his deficient physique to perfect a style in which he discarded classical theories of terrain to work closer to the bulls than did his predecessors, and to deliver his lances and passes with an unparalleled temple and drama.

We have already noted that the "revolution" which did in fact

---

* School of Sevilla, of Ronda: Sevilla, a city of gypsies, gives its name to that style noted for grace, fluency, fanciness, inventiveness, and even on occasion, cowardice (see the career of Rafael Gómez, "El Gallo," Joselito's brother). Ronda was the home of Francisco Romero and the Romero dynasty. Romero, as the first torero to give the art rules and classifications, also gave the name of his town, after his death, to that toreo in which the matador exhibits restraint, aguante, and complete domination. It is essentially a "short" style, basic and efficient. In modern toreo, the distinctions no longer really apply. A third school, that of Córdoba, is sometimes distinguished: it is noted for excesses of the school of Ronda amounting to *postismo,* or standing still as a post before the bull's attack. Very generally speaking, in modern toreo the Mexicans practice baroque refinements upon the style of the school of Sevilla, and the Spanish the style of the school of Ronda.

† *Desplante:* A kind of adorno, usually vulgar, in which the torero indicates his total domination of the toro by taking up a dangerous-appearing position in front of the animal's horns. Usually the desplante is a trick, for the torero will occupy the area in which the animal is blind, and often the animal is winded as well. But the desplante in which the torero touches the horn is genuine and not a trick.

‡ *Oficio:* A sense of duty to oneself and to the profession. The torero who volunteers his services without payment in a corrida for charity is displaying oficio.

occur in the years of Belmonte's career could not have been possible without genetic changes in the toros. Such changes did not occur overnight. At the same time, the revolution was both more profound and more complex than the accepted idea allows. Insofar as the revolution was a matter of craft, it involved the traditional theory of terrains, increasing awareness of the toro's system of vision, and development on the part of many toreros (other than Belmonte) of a style, or styles, of lidia which reflected an orientation of physique and character on the part of the torero himself. These are all matters that must be taken up in their order.

The classical theory of terrains (*terrenos*) is simple. It maintains that the animal will behave differently in tablas, tercios, and medios; that its preference must be observed, and will be determined by its basic conditions of bravery or cowardice, its bloodlines, and its physical condition. The second proposition follows from the first: that the toro has his area, his territory, into which the torero enters at his peril, but into which he must enter in order to provoke the charge. Before the torero can cause the toro to pass, it is essential that at some point he enter the toro's terri-

PLATE 16.   This novillero's would-be *pase de pecho* is an invitation to a *cornada*, for lack of understanding of *jurisdicción*.

tory with the target, the cape or muleta. It is possible to "work" the toro, however (bregar or trastear), por la cara, or in front of the horn, without actually causing the animal to pass; but even in

work por la cara, the torero must enter the toro's territory. As the following diagram indicates, the toro's territory might be compared to an area lit by a spotlight, while the torero's territory is the remaining dark area. The toro will not charge when the torero remains in his own territory; he will charge when the torero enters his own "lighted" area. The point at which a lance or pass begins, that point at which the torero enters the toro's territory, is called in Spanish *jurisdicción*, or jurisdiction, and the point at which the lance or pass begins is called placing the toro in jurisdicción.

In Plate 16, the torero is asking for a cornada by offering the muleta too soon, thus ignoring the all-important principle of jurisdicción.

Difficulty of interpretation occurs at the point at which one defines exactly where, with reference to the toro's system of vision, jurisdicción in fact exists. In classical toreo it was assumed that the toro uses his eyes as a human being does; that he sees best forward, and that accordingly the animal should be cited from the front. Modern veterinary research refutes the classical assumption, and it is essential to summarize certain facts that have only recently been established.

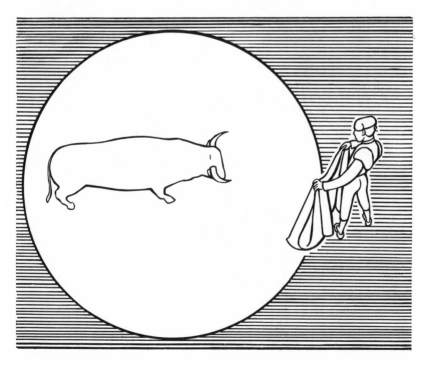

The principle of *jurisdicción*                    161

Toros are congenitally myopic, and their vision is weak and low. The eyeball is oval in shape, and the pupil is cylindrical, as in the following diagram:

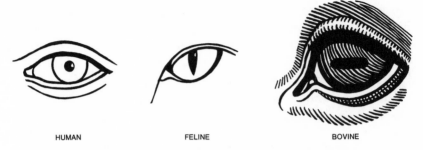

HUMAN                    FELINE                    BOVINE

Because of the horizontal plane of the pupil, the toro normally sees at the level of the eye and downward. Because the eyes are not set in a single plane but are on the lateral surfaces of the nasal bone (rather like hawsepipes on a ship or headlights on a car), the toro has a broad visual field to the side and to the rear, areas which

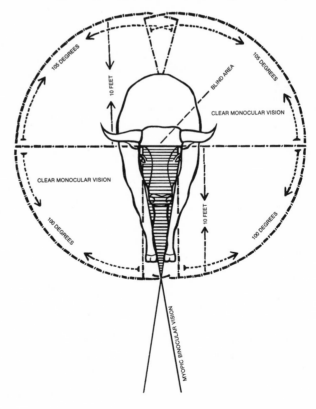

Field of binocular myopic vision

are of course perceived monocularly. Therefore, to see upward the toro must raise his head; his vision of objects to his side and to the rear is better than his vision of objects in front of him. He cannot focus easily for binocular vision because of lack of development of the ciliary muscles and lack of adaptability in the crystalline structure of the eye. As a result of continual muscular effort, vision is weak, since binocular vision requires full convergence. The great distance between the eyes creates a defect of refraction, and the degree of sphericity of the eyeball in turn contributes to myopia.

In the average angle of the monocular field, the image is more precise in the downward direction than in the horizontal. The average angle of monocular vision is 205 degrees: 100 degrees forward, and 105 degrees to the rear, with a maximum clear vision of ten feet. The toro is unable to form a clear image of objects situated at a distance. The luminous rays that such objects emit form circles of diffusion on the retina, causing vision to blur. But within the monocular field, the image is sharp and two-dimensional. Binocular vision, although blurred and limited, is three-dimensional.

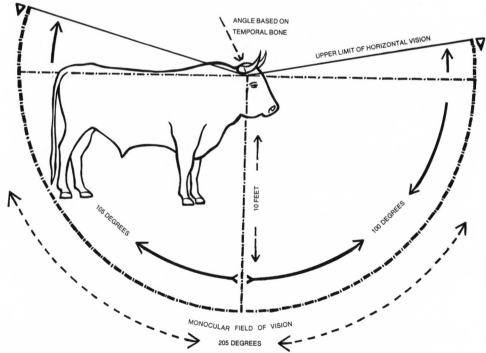

Veterinarians believe that the toro does not distinguish colors as such, but that his senses are stimulated by the wave-lengths that colors emit. The cape, accordingly, is magenta on one side and yellow on the other, and the muleta scarlet, because these colors of the spectrum have the longest wave lengths and consequently are those most likely to attract and excite the animal. Toros are stimulated to charge and free themselves of the stimuli that provoke them; not only chromatic impressions produce such provocation, but also auditory impressions and movement serve the purpose. The toro does not focus properly on objects more than ten feet away, but his ears are highly sensitive. The ears are so placed that they warn the toro of danger at considerable distances. Sharp, piercing sounds will often bring about a charge, and so the torero calls to the toro as he cites with cape or muleta or pic.

Color, movement, and sounds are the basic stimuli in the art of toreo. But within the field of vision, it is color and movement associated in dynamic activity that produce the toro's irritability and make possible the entire art. As is well known, the toro does not charge stationary objects or immobilized human beings, since immobility does not produce the necessary nervous response in the animal. Basically, the toro is a tranquil, patient animal that charges only when obliged to do so; when conflict can no longer be avoided; when he feels that to attack and fight is the only way left for him to free himself from what provokes and irritates him. At the same time, his bravery, which we have previously identified as the instinct for liberation, is a product of his system of hormones, his blood chemistry—his breeding. He is a product of many generations of selective breeding, the toro de lidia, never to be confused with the domestic animal, to which many of the above characteristics also apply.[3]

The classical torero, citing from a distance and from in front, necessarily worked por alto. The verónica was a high lance in which the man held the cape above the level of his shoulders; there had to be a good deal of cargar la suerte in order to allow the toro an exit from the target directly in front of it. Modern toreros discovered (but did not theorize upon the fact) that the toro in truth has an ocular field not like a man's but rather like the

---

[3] In addition to conversations with veterinarians, the above is also based upon C. Sanz Egaña, *Historia y bravura del toro de lidia* (Madrid, 1958).

headlights on a car, a discovery making possible work with both cape and muleta that would have seemed suicidal in the nineteenth century. Everyone by now has heard the advice given to those who had not yet seen the young Belmonte: they were warned to hurry to see him because he would not be around very long. The following diagram shows the reason:[4]

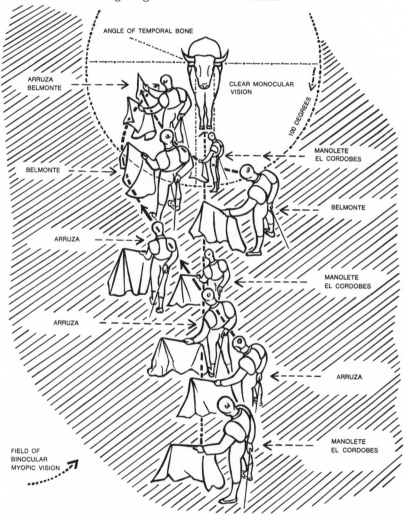

ANGLE OF TEMPORAL BONE

ARRUZA
BELMONTE

CLEAR MONOCULAR
VISION

100 DEGREES

BELMONTE

MANOLETE
EL CORDOBES

BELMONTE

ARRUZA

MANOLETE
EL CORDOBES

ARRUZA

ARRUZA

MANOLETE
EL CORDOBES

FIELD OF
BINOCULAR
MYOPIC VISION

---

[4] Walter Johnston, "The Anticone of Immunity," *Toros*, VI, No. 5 (May 1962), 7–10, is useful, although Johnston's diagram contains errors. It is important, for example, to realize that the torero's line of advance across the horns is not straight, as Johnston has it, but in the line of a curve or half moon.

It is at once obvious that a theory of terrain grounded upon the notion that a toro sees like a man will be quite different from one grounded upon the fact that a toro sees like a toro. The discovery that one could cite the opposite horn* in comparative safety and that one could actually cross the field of vision led to two contradictory results for the fiesta. On the positive side, it meant that the modern faena, in its depth and emotion, became possible. On the negative side, it meant that cape work and the tercio of the picador and the banderillero became neglected. Smaller animals meant fewer pics and fewer lances, while matadors tended to follow the easy way of Belmonte and to neglect to place their own banderillas. Everything possible was done to preserve both toro and torero for the faena. Further, the systematic working of the more-or-less blind area between the horns led to the proliferation in modern toreo of tricks as spectacular to the ignorant as they are cheap: desplantes, the larga cambiada de rodillas at the toril, the cliché of the chicuelina, and entire faenas delivered from three feet above the sand.

Belmonte's dramatic, or melodramatic, death in 1962 served to heat up old controversies and to reanimate his faction in their interpretation of the evolution of modern style. Such loyalty is admirable, characteristic of the ambiente, but possibly obscurantist in any attempt to interpret what actually occurred at the historical watershed. To challenge the attractive idea that Belmonte wrought the change single-handed is in no sense to denigrate him. Like Joselito, he has passed beyond history to myth, as so many Spanish writers have remarked. But what he did was not so much to innovate as to bring together in his remarkable personality trends and tendencies of style that had been coming inevitably for a generation. In part, his impact lay in the untranslatable term, *angel*. He possessed, like Joselito, Gaona, Sánchez Mejías, and Manolete, the quality of endowing his every movement in the plaza with meaning, the ability to project that meaning, to register the overtone of tragedy, and he possessed great suerte, good fortune, in his career. A suggestion of the meaning of angel is contained in the Roman Catholic notion of a guardian angel who looks after the devout; a personal spirit that

---

* Opposite horn: In reality, the opposite eye. We translate Spanish idiom. In giving a natural, the torero cites the toro's *right* horn, or eye, rather than the eye nearer him; vice versa for the derechazo.

sustains the individual's conscience before temptation and aids in resisting the wiles of Satan. Taurine angel,* however, is hardly a religious concept, but one having to do with the torero's effect upon the spectator.

Personality apart, what was the famous Belmonte style? Belmonte came to toreo without Joselito's training or connections, in Belmonte's case an advantage, for he was able to put in systematic practice his intuitive knowledge of the toro's vision, and to perform the classical suertes in an unclassical but moving manner. His revolution was to purify the verónica and the half verónica, the natural, and the chest pass through ignoring the classical ideas of terrain, through temple, and through *arrimarse* (working close to the horn). By working close, Belmonte was also able to link his passes more successfully than earlier toreros, and thus move toward an architectonic structure in the faena. This was doing a great deal, but Belmonte invented nothing. Rather he worked in a new way with traditional materials. Belmonte's toreo, aside from the emotion he imparted to the basic passes, remained essentially traditional. It was toreo of attack and defense. He relied upon efficient, doubling passes por la cara; passes necessarily rapid, brusque, and often rough. He was a torero of domination, mando. One report is that Belmonte's natural, regarded by many as the archetype of the pass, was really a bastard pass, closer to the chest pass than to the natural: ". . . the truth is that Belmonte did not take up the posture appropriate to [the natural], which would have been to twist the waist; to the contrary, he made the pass by advancing the left hip, and on that axis established his mando, that which, in reality, is a movement appropriate to toreo cambiado."[5] Much has been made of the fact that Joselito, the complete

---

* A related notion is contained in the term *duende,* a corny gypsy phrase to express inspiration in flamenco or in toreo. Literally it means elf, goblin, or witch, and, more sympathetically interpreted, it is the other extreme from angel. Angel is heavenly, signifying grace; duende is diabolic or tragic. Paco Camino has angel; El Cordobés has duende. According to good Mexican and Spanish aficionados, Manolete and Belmonte possessed both angel *and* duende, hence their extraordinary interest.

[5] José Alameda, *Los arquitectos del toreo moderno,* p. 95. "Toreo cambiado," that in which the bull is forced out of the line of charge by the torero's position in the moment of citing and by his use of the lure. More of this presently.

*lidiador,* natural athlete, artist, and dominator of bulls was killed by a toro, while Belmonte, who seemed by contrast to improvise, to lack the basic physical qualities, who seemed to court sudden death by working so close to the animal, lived to seventy and death by gunshot. This brings up the subsidiary but relevant point that a tossing from a toro at short range and delivered from the oblique may not be fatal, while one from long range is very likely to be grave, if not fatal. Belmonte's angel, in part, was to find comparative safety in danger; to exploit the toro's zone of immunity and to evoke a memorable psychological reaction in the process.

Again, much has been written about toreo in profile (*de perfil* or *en paralelo*) as against toreo in the classical manner, de frente, or the approach from a position immediately forward and in front of the toro's line of charge.[6] The classicists accuse modern toreo of

---

[6] For example, Gregorio Corrochano, *Teoría de las corridas de toros;* Julio de Urrutia, *Toreo paralelo* (México, 1949). In English, Walter Johnston, "Toreo profundo," *Toros,* VII, No. 12 (December 1963),

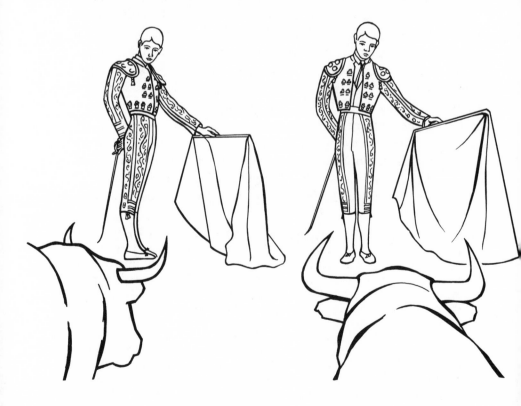

*Cite* in parallel                              *Cite de frente*

decadence, and by implication, the torero of cowardice when the toro is cited in parallel rather than de frente.

At work, apparently, in the attack upon modern toreo is a combination of what we have called earlier the conservative illusion, together with a misunderstanding of a torero's function and what goes into his conception of that function. Let us adopt, for their intelligence and efficiency, two classifications suggested by José Alameda: toreo natural and toreo cambiado.[7] These terms define concepts that are virtually in opposition; in turn, they define attitudes toward life, experience, and art which have their origin in the torero's character. Toreo natural is that style in which the matador does not force the animal to change its line of charge materially, but in which he accompanies the animal, accommodating himself to it. Toreo cambiado is that style in which the animal is taken out of the line of charge by the position of the matador's approach and by his use of the lure. Toreo natural looks

---

3ff. Mr. Johnston says that in modern toreo de perfil, "cargando la suerte has decaded [sic] into a purely decorative plasticization fortuitously resultant upon the geometry of the pass. . . ." Diction and syntax are a measure of accuracy here.

[7] *Los arquitectos,* pp. 86–88.

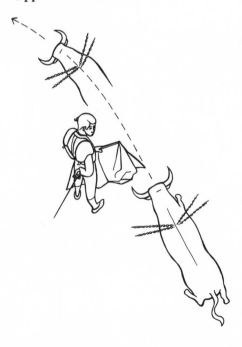

*Toreo natural*

straightforward and simple; in fact it is difficult. It requires mastery of temple and rhythm, measure. It may appear to the spectator only as a style of finesse, one which does not depend upon great mando. Again, this is a mistake. All toreo requires mando; the difference lies in the quality of drama evoked and its effect upon the spectator.

Toreo cambiado tends to be toreo *por delante;* it is a style suited to toros that do not charge well. It is forceful, even domineering, obviously reliant upon mando. The torero who favors toreo cambiado relies upon and tends to perform well those passes which are

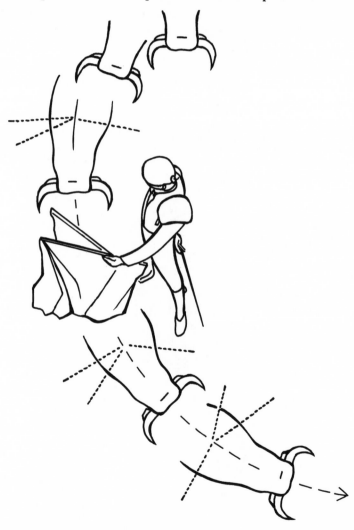

*Toreo cambiado*

cambiados, the chest pass being the most orthodox and efficient. Toreo natural is related to the technique of those toreros who do not cross the line of the toro's charge—men like Chicuelo and Manolete; toreo cambiado is related to the technique of men like Belmonte, Ortega, and Arruza, who did consistently cross the line of charge. The word "cambiado" as used here should not be confused with those passes called "cambiados" that are no more than adornos. When the torero leads the spectator to believe that he will take the toro's charge on one side and then actually takes it on the other, we say he has performed a cambiado. The word

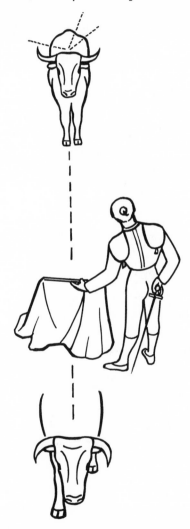

Straight lines of force

means, literally, "changed," and what has changed in the adorno is the position of the lure. But in toreo cambiado what has changed is the relationship of the hand holding the lure in relation to the horn, as opposed to that relationship in the natural. In toreo natural, the right hand cites the toro's right horn, or right side; in the natural, the left hand cites the left horn. In toreo cambiado, the right hand cites the toro's left horn and vice versa.

Belmonte realized that a problem implicit in the classical cite de frente, and the accompanying toreo por alto, was the difficulty of securing continuity between one suerte and the next. Since the toro carried his head high, he tended to lose sight of the lure, forcing the torero to begin the process all over again, by which

*Cite* from the three-quarter position

time the animal might be thirty feet away. The lines of force of this sort of toreo were essentially straight lines.

Belmonte's partial solution—and it was only partial—was to cite from a three-quarter position, and to work por abajo with the muleta, thus accommodating the lure at least in part to the actual ocular system of the animal.

As is clear from the drawing below, however, Belmonte's style was still one of straight, or slightly bent, lines. It remained for Manuel Jiménez (Chicuelo) to advance the evolution of the faena by perfecting toreo *en redondo,* or passes given in such a manner that the toro might remain in suerte—in the muleta, to describe a curve or even a full circle, rather than the straight line of the

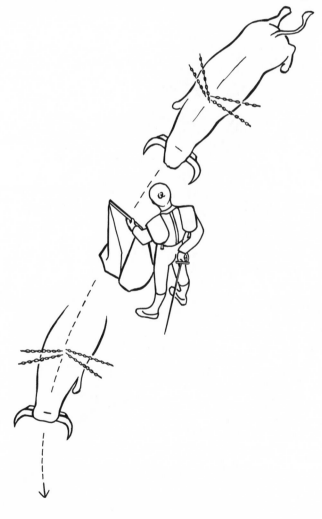

Belmonte's style produced
*toreo* of straight, or slightly bent, lines of force

classical suerte. This was to reduce what the Andalusians call
*"toreo de p'acá y p'allá"* (toreo of here and there)[8] and to make
possible continuity and profundity.

Belmonte's "revolution" was also in part the work of Domingo
Ortega, the masterful toreo of Borox, near Toledo in Castile.
Before Ortega (alternativa in 1931), difficult animals were handled in the muleta with frank punishing passes, doblandos and
brutal trincherazos por la cara in order to establish domination
and to prepare them for the sword. Such work was (and is)
frequently spectacular, although it lacks the quality of work in

---

[8] *Los arquitectos,* p. 19.

*Toreo* in profile

which the toro actually does pass. It is athletic and comparatively safe. But it is often necessary; without it, a wise toro, a manso, or a resabiado could not be fought at all. Ortega did for the punishing pass what Belmonte had done for the verónica and the natural: he transformed it from mere efficiency and brusqueness into art. He demonstrated that trastear, too, could be done slowly, gently, and efficiently, and that in the course of so doing, an "impossible" toro could be taught gentlemanly manners. It was an inspired technique for extracting any drop of good blood from an otherwise indifferent animal. Through his contribution, Ortega taught his profession that animals which previously would have been "fought" to the death could be subject to artful lidia; he extended the possibilities of the art.[9] Within the physical motion of Ortega's toreo lay concealed, of course, a conception to which he gave expression in his triumphant career and also—in a different way but equally valuably—in his two published lectures, *El arte del toreo y la bravura del toro*. Among other things, *El arte del toreo* is an explication of Ortega's own style and an attack upon toreo in profile. He writes that he has often thought that toreo needs a referee, like certain sports, and that if he were such a referee he would say to the modern torero: "Listen, my friend, what are you doing? Don't you see that is not a natural? Move away a pace or so, and give a chest pass, which is the most noble pass a man can give, and there, where you were going to stand, place the muleta. And then, when you run the muleta, do not remain rigid, because rigidity is unnatural, advance your [left] leg a bit, accompanying the movement lightly with your body, very slowly, and you will see the result: then, all the rhythm you possess will result in a sculptured grouping in motion, which is the beauty of the art of toreo. In sum, put in practice the classical rules."[10]

Without denying the validity of Ortega's conception in its context, one must emphasize that it is a defense, a defense of the three-quarter position of Belmonte and Ortega himself, and in part a revelation of hostility to toreo de perfil and all that it involves. Ortega's words of 1950 are obviously an attack upon the

---

[9] See Plate 1, in which Ortega is delivering his trincherazo, called the trincherazo de Ortega. Hemingway's contempt for Ortega, as he expressed it in *Death in the Afternoon,* speaks for that writer's dubious judgment of many aspects of toreo.

[10] *El arte del toreo* (Madrid: Revista de Occidente, 1950), p. 35.

toreo of Manolete, upon toreo natural, in favor of Ortega's style of toreo, toreo cambiado. Manolete, following Chicuelo (who was Manolete's padrino at his alternativa in 1939), practiced toreo natural; moving beyond Chicuelo, however, he too contributed to the "revolution" in his manner of citing toros. First, it should be emphasized that Manolete would have had no quarrel with Ortega about trastear, that Manolete's toreo de frente obviously owed much to the older matador. What Manolete did was to discover a new way of forcing a difficult toro, a toro *quedado,** to pass. Before Manolete, the natural began by citing from a fair distance; the torero might advance upon the toro if it did not at once answer the challenge. The pass would then either be successful, or, if not, it would end with a doubling pass, often a *chicotazo.*† Such a procedure clearly made for frustration and for the necessity to start all over again. It was necessary for the matador to revise his faena, to improvise even more hastily than as a rule he had to. Manolete's technical competence together with his knowledge of the animal's system of vision and his own great bravery enabled him to force a toro to pass, one which previously would have been taken por delante. He would cite from the side and fairly close on, moving closer and closer to the near horn until the charge. What he sacrificed was the first phase of the natural, that dramatic point at which the toro embarks upon his charge from a distance. This, it should be said loud and clear, was a sacrifice, but the gain in the number of toros genuinely toreados rather than punished outweighed the loss. Finally, Arruza and his imitators actually advanced across the zone of immunity to the opposite horn, a different sort of toreo from Manolete's, a form of toreo cambiado.

So far as the relative merits of citing from in front of the toro and citing from the side are concerned, it is useful to go to two fundamental geometric propositions stated by Alameda which are immediately apparent to anyone who has worked on toros in the plaza. First, in toreo in profile, while the toro approaches from the matador's side, it passes him entirely in front; the horn has full opportunity at the matador's vitals should any miscalculation

---

* *Quedado:* From *quedar,* to stop; identical with *parado,* stopped. Used of toros that do not charge, that are literally stopped because of poor lidia or because of their congenital nature.

† *Chicotazo:* May be made either with cape or muleta. It is a rapid, whiplike pass por abajo. In the instance cited, it is a recourse for getting rid of the toro and establishing domination.

occur. Second, in toreo de frente, the horn approaches from a forward position but passes the matador's flank.[11]

Neither technique is necessarily better than the other. To cite from the forward position has the blessing of tradition; it is exciting to observe because the toro arrives at the lure in motion, if he charges at all. To cite in profile, on the other hand, produces a different sort of excitement because the matador moves closer to the bull and very often endures moments in which no one knows whether the animal will charge the lure or the man. Both techniques have the quality that true toreo demands. They are honest; they insure the degree of fineness, bravery, and knowledge that is the basis of the art. They are different styles of toreo rather than the real thing (de frente) succeeded by a decadent trick (de perfil). Each is dangerous, if danger alone be the measure; fortunately it is not. One style is appropriate to the toro that charges openly, frankly, with sentido. The other is appropriate to the toro encountered far more often: the mansurrón, the quedado, the reluctant. That torero who can modify his style to the animal he is facing obviously has an advantage over the torero who knows only one technique and who tries automatically to put it to work on each animal he draws. As is so often the case in toreo, the technique which succeeds with a specific animal is also the more aesthetic one. That which merely bores or enrages the animal will also bore or enrage the spectators, because, among other reasons, it is unaesthetic and inefficient.

An argument similar to that over toreo in profile has been waged over the matter of whether the torero should stand with feet apart (compás abierto) in delivering a suerte or with feet together (pies juntos). Here the argument in favor of feet apart, in the classical manner, is stronger than the argument for the approach de frente. For one thing, it is easier to cargar la suerte when your feet are not joined. At least one critic says that cargando la suerte is entirely a matter of arm movement anyway,[12] but most toreros would not agree. Cargar la suerte is a simultaneous movement of arms, feet, wrists, and waist. Cargando la suerte with feet joined is not only difficult, it is often ugly as well. Toreo with feet joined is a hallmark of the school of Sevilla. It is efficient and beautiful in certain adornos, and it may be

---

[11] *Los arquitectos,* p. 53.

[12] *Los arquitectos,* ch. 9.

spectacular in the revolera and the half verónica. But with the muleta, joined feet almost always means ugliness, awkwardness, and lack of full use of both man's and animal's faculties.[13] Grace in the plaza depends upon balance. It is more difficult for a two-legged animal to balance with feet joined than when the feet are twelve or fourteen inches apart. But if the feet are too far apart, awkwardness again results. It is significant that toreros who habitually work with feet joined tend also to favor the unaesthetic practice of toreo on the knees.

Still another problem of definition and interpretation in modern toreo is that of the *pierna contraria,* or opposite leg. This is not a tactic from British cricket but one related to cargando la suerte and to the problem of keeping the toro in the lure. Here we need to return again to Belmonte's toreo, to his natural in particular. Belmonte learned that when citing de frente to a difficult toro, it was possible to move his right leg forward, advancing the muleta at the same time, then to pivot on the soles of both feet during the charge, so eliminating the classical distortion of the waist, and

---

[13] See Plate 7, in which Manuel Benítez (El Cordobés) proves the truth of our statement. See Chapter 5.

Belmonte citing *de frente*

permitting the beginnings of work por abajo. At the same time, by advancing his right leg, Belmonte was in fact discovering the three-quarter approach. Because in the natural the matador works to the toro's *left* horn, the *right* leg is the pierna contraria. This is logical but confusing. After Belmonte, the pierna contraria is referred to, by Ortega and Corrochano, among others, as the leg opposite to the direction of the charge, which of course is the *left* leg. This too is logical, because after the pivot, it is the left leg which is opposite the line of the animal's charge. The expression *"la pierna de salida"* (the leg on the side of the toro's exit) has been proposed as preferable and clearer,[14] and if there were an organized body of critical opinion in toreo would probably be adopted.

We raise this matter of the pierna contraria because the aficionado who reads Spanish will recognize the source of confusion, and he will recognize as well that the problem sums up the Belmonte' "revolutions." The question of cargando la suerte by advancing the pierna de salida is at once the mark of classical toreo as opposed to the popular idea of toreo in profile, and it is the point

---

[14] By Walter Johnston, "Toreo profundo," p. 24.

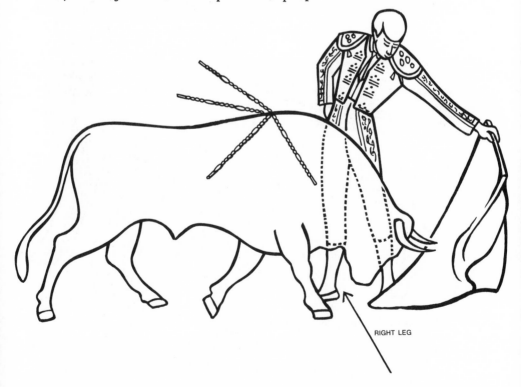

RIGHT LEG

*Pierna contraria*

over which partisans of the past take issue with partisans of the present. Another important reason for the bitterness of the quarrel is doubtless the circumstance that Manolete's career happened to span the years of the Spanish Civil War and the ensuing period of abuses in the breeding and dirty preparation of toros for the plaza. That career also coincided with unpleasant business practices that are still with us, while Manolete's impress upon the succeeding generation was such that his style was imitated, or parodied, to the point of total boredom.

The aficionado who uses his own eyes in the plaza will perceive that many of the arguments discussed are in fact what is called, in scorn, academic. Belmonte's style of delivering the natural, with the three-quarter approach and the advance of the right leg, is a form of toreo contrario. Very often the other sort of torero, one

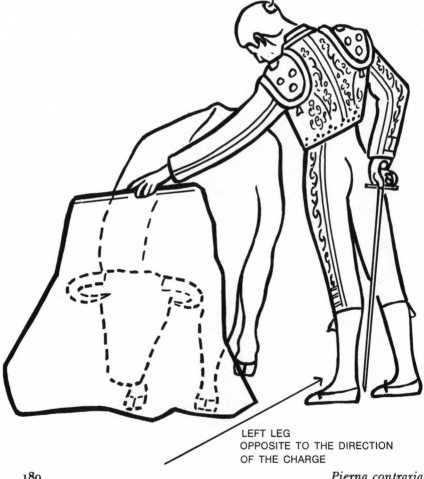

LEFT LEG
OPPOSITE TO THE DIRECTION
OF THE CHARGE

*Pierna contraria*

who is supposed to belong to the toreo natural school, will also advance the pierna contraria, thus combining the two styles. In general, however, toreo contrario tends to be toreo of great mando, to the point of oppressiveness, while toreo natural is less apparently dominating, more the toreo of suavity, grace, and temple. But to accuse the matador who cites in profile of decadence and cowardice is absurd. It reveals ignorance and reliance upon a Platonic, theoretical ideal which is rarely met in life as we know it now, and was doubtless just as rare in the life of the past.

Although the general outlines of modern toreo are those which we have drawn in terms of technique, contemporary toreo has continued to change, just as all the arts have undergone at least

Distortion of the waist

superficial changes in the past two decades. The supplanting of huge hot wars by huge cold wars, with the accompanying inevitable changes in social patterns throughout the world, for good or for evil have wrought revolutions in the audience for art. Vast numbers can now indulge in pleasures formerly reserved to the wealthy; a new class has emerged with an appetite for the accouterments of the good life. Cheap books alone have introduced millions to ideas and experience that a brief generation ago was open only to the cultural elite. In the United States, the children of parents who never did anything more cultural than go fishing for pickerel are as likely as not to evade the money-making professions of medicine and law, the traditional activities of men on the rise, to become teachers, artists, composers, or research workers. Such young people can find money with which to travel, to reflect, and to act upon their convictions, in a fulfillment of a sort of the Utopian plans of the Leibnitzian dreamers of the Enlightenment, or the most optimistic of Victorian social meliorists.

One effect of this recent historical process in the arts, particularly in toreo, has been the shattering of certain time-honored practices, a challenge to relationships between tradition and modern procedures and to classical notions of apprenticeship, all amounting to an attempt to impose a new aesthetic upon old forms. Perhaps "aesthetic" is the wrong word, for what we have seen is an anti-aesthetic, if not an abolition, of art. In music we have "concrete" compositions reproducing machine and street noises; or the music of silence, in which musicians stand there and do nothing at all. In drama we have the anti-theater of Ionesco, Beckett, Pinter, and their many imitators. William Rauschenberg has exhibited blank canvasses that have been praised as "landing places for lights and shadows" (by John Cage), canvasses that one may prefer to junk art, pop comic-strip effects and op geometry. Movies, once an honest industry, have become film, replete with pseudo-intellectual attitudes, literary trickery, and critical jargon. Even in the private arts of poetry and the novel, minor but significant instances of anti-aesthetic have turned up. The French anti-novel of Robbe-Grillet, Sarraute, Claude Mauriac and others, in which plot, character, narrative, and action are virtually eliminated in favor of description and monologue is crowned by Marc Saporta's "shuffle novel," *No. 1*, the pages of which are unbound and unnumbered, leaving the reader free to shuffle his way at his will. In poetry, anti-aesthetic for a brief period took the form of verse vulgarly called "beat." Beat verse—it never was poetry—was the fulminations of an *avant-garde* that had wandered away from the *garde* altogether, the noises of untalented people who would do anything for publicity, the gasps of a man who shouts that he is drowning when he has not so much as gone near the water.

The word "beat" has unfortunately passed into our language, and it is wryly useful in defining what has happened in toreo since 1960, for we now have beat toreo, too. Why this should be is interesting. We have seen how the Spanish Civil War and its aftermath threatened toreo, first through unavoidable abuses, then through venal and culpable ones. By the mid-fifties, the situation was under reasonable control, but not sufficiently so to induce many empresarios, certain toreros, and certain critics to return to the standards of the golden age. For lack of genuine figuras, for competition from soccer (which for a time convinced pessimists that the afición for toreo would be stolen away), and most emphatically for the influx of tourists who brought to Spain (and in a lesser degree, to Mexico) not only the usual tourists' thirst for *frisson,* but new ideas, new philosophies, an unfamiliar cosmopolitanism and an impatience with old ways, toreo was vulnerable to change. It was not the prosperous older generation of tourist that made the impact, but the new generation from France, Germany—all of Europe and America, in fact: the uncommitted wanderers, the artisans, typists, apprentices and notably the students, with some money in their pockets, intellectual larceny in their hearts, and an appetite for experience that was not to be satisfied through outlets provided by a tired and tiresome society presided over by fatigued old men. Military service was laughable; politics a filthy business leading only to mass butchery; religion an obscenity; education sometimes exciting but often aimless—a generation, in short, of great vitality, surprising objectivity, widespread curiosity, and an unsatisfied need for sensation. In Spain the empresarios, always as sensitive to change as stockbrokers, were prompt to oblige.

From the south came reports of novilleros who gave themselves idiotic sobriquets and who were doing things to their animals in apparent seriousness that formerly had been done only in charlotadas, or comic toreo. Neither the fighting stock nor the management of the third-class plazas in Spain, particularly in the south, have ever been notable for extending the possibilities of the fiesta, but now a new dimension had been added. Not only were the new novilleros citing bulls with the muleta between their legs, but the plazas were making money. They were full of people applauding the travesties and demanding more. (At the same time, five young Englishmen who called themselves the Beatles were making horrible noises in a Liverpool cellar to the accompaniment of bongo drums and electric guitars.) Unscrupulous apoderados throughout the world of toreo also put a finger up to the wind, then went out to encourage talentless, brave boys to work in burlesque of the techniques so recently refined by Cagancho, Belmonte, Manolete, and Arruza. With feet joined, elbows in, waists bent forward, novilleros came and went, often to the hospital, in a purposeful scuttling of the classical procedures of the plaza.

The lifelong aficionado was only mildly alarmed at the outbreak. After all, toreo had survived the French in Spain who abominated the spectacle; it had survived the rationalistic, anti-toreo spirit of 1898; it had survived the Civil War and the resulting abuses, and it would survive the new annoyance. What was not immediately apparent was that Spanish spectators, too, were crowding into the plazas, not to sit silently in disapproval, but to applaud with the most ignorant tourist. In Spain, too, a new generation, innocent of proper taurine education, was making itself known. It was looking for its own heroes; it was not willing to be told by its elders whom to admire and why. And if it chose anti-aesthetics to aesthetics, that was its own business. Wittingly or unwittingly, it was taking part in a subterranean movement that was, and remains, worldwide. The rebellion of the new generation is peculiarly unheroic and anti-romantic. Its gesture is not to take up arms but to lay them down; not to strike the handsome or heroic gesture but to act the clown; not to affect the grand statement, but the sort of understatement once identified only as British. And very near the surface might always be the violence of the fast motorcycle, or the reverse violence, the passive violence of self-subversion through marijuana, LSD, or heroin.

When most of the new sensations among novilleros had come and gone, one anti-torero had emerged from the heap to attain notoriety and riches of an abundance to chill the heart of the purist. Manuel Benítez, El Cordobés, was born to poverty in Córdoba in 1937. Until he was twenty he had nothing to do with toreo. In that year, hoping to make money, he attached himself to an ex-torero of no ability in the plaza but with a grand flair for publicity. Benítez' handicaps were utter lack of education, humanistic, scientific, or tauromachian, a heavy, awkward body, gracelessness to the point of grotesquerie, and an abiding inability to kill bulls. His assets were considerable bravery, even to the point of foolishness; a sense of oficio; a mop of hair and a style of wearing his suit of lights as though he had slept in it; and an open, mindless sort of youthful charm which photographed well and belied his large fund of native intelligence. His greatest asset was his first manager, whose techniques in selling his torero to the public might be studied with profit on Madison Avenue. With his awkwardness, his peculiar appearance in the plaza, his unkempt head and his sunny smile, Benítez evoked a reaction in the new public which combined the hysteria of adolescents in the thirties for Frank Sinatra, the wartime enthusiasm of the British for Winston Churchill, and the postwar uproar over the Beatles. As with the Beatles, so in the case of Benítez the relationship between excellence and reward is preposterously out of line. Nothing could be clearer than that both Beatles and Benítez are the product of social pathology, not of talent or performance. In the plaza Benítez makes only the slightest attempt with the cape; with the muleta his clumsiness is such that it appears cultivated. His feet are invariably joined and his waist movements make him look as though he will lose balance at every moment. He is able to dominate his bulls through bravery, through aguante: standing planted, no matter how awkwardly, and suffering the bull's charge. His kills are almost always disgraceful, and his ignorance of lidia is almost total.

Armed with his money-making handicaps, Benítez became the leading Spanish novillero of 1961, with sixty-seven novilladas. In 1962 he fought 109 novilladas, equaling Belmonte's record; he could have fought more, but he took time off to act, abominably, in his first film. In 1963 he took the alternativa and has continued with incomparable successes on both sides of the Atlantic. While his technique improved slightly after his alternativa, for the good reason that one cannot break quite all the rules with mature animals and live, he remains an anti-torero, a beat bullfighter who through cunning, intelligence, and clever management has imposed a debased style upon a great art, to the apparent exclusion of the real thing. Just as the television screens and air waves of Britain and the United States are filled with the horrendous wailings of would-be Beatles, so aspiring novilleros affect hair in the eyes, a slouch in the plaza, and a toothy smile, in the hope of wealth and notoriety comparable to the master's.

The fiesta will survive these excrescences, just as poetry survived beat verse. In the meantime, Benítez' seniors, contemporaries, and betters—like Ordóñez, Ostos, Camino, El Viti, Huerta, Leal, and Diego Puerta, to name but a few—are upholding the true art of toreo, disgusted though they may be with the phenomenon of a Benítez in their midst, a school of dolphins intruded upon by a blowfish. In a paradoxical sense, Benítez[15] and the beats may even be good for the fiesta, for they have made the aficionado think again about his precepts, and brought public interest to toreo, never a bad thing in itself. In fact, in the mid-sixties, while many things are wrong with the fiesta, many more things are right about it. Compared to twenty or ten years ago, it is in a state of health. Many very good, if not great, toreros are at work, and many very good novilleros are coming up. Each *temporada* (bullfighting season) sees more corridas than the preceding one; more tickets are sold, and more opportunities exist for the ever-rare, ever-evanescent afternoon on which one might have the grace and fortune to see the kind of corrida that makes one happy to be

---

[15] As of mid-temporada, 1965, one can report that Benítez' killing is improving, but that his antics are beginning to bore even his own followers. And one would predict, fervently but cautiously, that his vogue may soon pass. Technically speaking, Benítez' success must be ascribed to his awareness of the weakness of many modern toros, and the resulting necessity for the torero to initiate a charge from very close on to the horn. Apart from his posturings, Benítez is anti-academic and anti-traditional because, to give the number of muletazos (passes) he does, he cannot act in the traditional manner. He eliminates the first tiempo of the classical pass and moves abruptly into the second tiempo with a movement of waist, arm, and wrist; he then emphasizes the third tiempo with a well-timed chicotazo (whiplike movement of the muleta), which allows him to rematar, and *ligar* (link passes) if all goes well. Such a movement requires a good sense of timing, temple, and distance. The basic maneuver was developed by Manolete and Arruza; Benítez has simply refined and vulgarized their sense of the basic pass.

alive, an afternoon in which life is enriched through the violent delicacy of the unique art of toreo. For when all is said and done, toreo remains unique, *sui generis*, quite unlike any other art, however much one is tempted to draw parallels. That toreo has recently reflected the agonized social difficulties of our period is further evidence of its stature, and of its necessity to our lives. If we cannot see ourselves in the arts, we have only drab recourse to the sciences and politics.

# CHAPTER 6

# TOREO AND SOCIETY

QUESTIONS OF THE RELATIONSHIP BETWEEN ART AND SOCIETY have been raised since Plato. In the past century, with the work of men so various as Hegel, Nietzsche, Marx, Matthew Arnold, Walter Pater, Ortega y Gasset, Ezra Pound, and T. S. Eliot, questions have exploded into polemics and a bitter sort of warfare has resulted. Three main positions may be discerned in the topography of that war. First is the extreme aestheticism of Pater, which maintains that art is a rarefied pursuit indulged in by an elite for an elite, one having little or nothing to do with society; Pater's notion of art for art's sake is hedonistic and esoteric, with its base in intellectual and social snobbery. The second position is that of Marx, which goes to the opposite extreme. Crudely stated, the Marxist position is that art is the handmaiden of society, specifically of politics. It is the artist's task to place social value before all in his own interest, for only the good society—namely, the dictatorship of the proletariat—can produce good art. The third and probably most tenable position is that which rejects the extremes of Pater and Marx to insist upon an indubitably positive relationship between art and society, yet one which remains mysterious in its workings, devious in its appearances, and always susceptible to misapprehension.

It is a position worthy of closer scrutiny for its own merits and for its value in clarifying problems in modern toreo. According to the third position, any notion that art is separated from society by a barrier of sensibility or any other kind of barrier is false because it relegates art to the status of luxury and ultimately of whimsy. If the stuff of art is humanity, then all humanity is its province. If only certain pursuits of humanity are viable for art, we are returned to the dubious aesthetic of neoclassicism, which held that only "beautiful" subjects were proper subjects for the painter or writer, who was to concern himself with the average, not with the extraordinary; with the representative, not with the grotesque or the ugly. The more inclusive aesthetic not only refuses to prescribe to the artist what his material should be, but it also sees art as essential to society both in its imaginative recapitulation of human, therefore of social, values, and for the artist's ability virtually to foretell the future. This does not mean that the artist is a soothsayer, but it is to recognize his concern for reality, for truth, and his duty to deal only with the true. Art, then, exists in history, is of history, and concerns itself with history, but it stands aside from ordinary social concerns in having no ax to grind, no candidate to elect to office, no power in the political sense to wield. The artist's allegiance is to conscience, not to party or to theology. Refusing to share the usual social loyalties, the artist is often regarded as a subversive, and the role assigned to art by the practical-minded good citizen is often, paradoxically, that of the Pater-like aesthete. To the average politician, lawyer, dentist, or salesman, whatever his lip-service, art is at best an appurtenance of prosperity, and at worst subversive, inimical. Such persons may dimly apprehend the power of art over men's minds, but they distrust such power, for the artist's loyalty is unpredictable, fickle, and difficult, or impossible, to bargain for.

Philistine hostility constitutes a form of pressure upon the arts which helps, for better or worse, to add form to the outline of a particular art at a particular moment in history. And, conversely, art, according to the inclusive theory, similarly gives form to society, for whatever fundamentally influences men will take ultimately some manner of social shape. This is not to say that art will necessarily make men better, or that art has in fact usurped the place of theology in an earlier and better-ordered world. The discussion to this point is descriptive, not prescriptive.

What, then, has all this to do with the special art of toreo? To be brief, everything. Like any other significant development in human life, toreo did not develop in a void. As much as the paintings of Velázquez, Delacroix, and Goya, toreo was a response to intellectual, political, and social circumstances. Having seen the primitive origins of toreo in ritual, we need now to look at certain more recent and more objectively ascertainable facts. If we can place toreo within the intellectual and political framework that has surrounded it, and if at the same time we can relate toreo to another art that developed at the same time outside Spain, we may be able to further the cause of freeing toreo from parochial, inconsequent comment and in so doing, suggest again the contexts within which a true criticism might develop.

Although at first glance it may seem far-fetched, the history of the English novel offers some very precise parallels to the development of toreo. Modern toreo and the modern English novel appeared at the same time and for the same reasons; each art in its way satisfied similar, if not identical, orders of social reality. Samuel Richardson's *Pamela,* which we regard as the first modern novel in English for its attempts at psychological realism, was published in 1740. Henry Fielding's *History of the Adventures of Joseph Andrews* appeared in 1742. Francisco Romero invented the muleta, which made possible the entire modern art of toreo on foot, at some point between 1720 and 1740. The novel very soon proved to be a supple form, intimately bound up in society and social behavior but capable of extremes of romantic grostesquerie too. Even though the novel came into vogue in the neoclassical period of rigid adherence to well-enunciated aesthetic rules, it swiftly attracted rebels against neoclassicism. Because of the English novelist's concern with individual feeling and the contortions of the individual psyche, the novel became a weapon in the destruction of the neoclassical position. It was immensely popular. The public responded equally well to Richardson and to Fielding, different as they were; it took readily to the new vogue at the end of the eighteenth century for the "Gothic" fiction of Walpole, Lewis, and Mrs. Radcliffe. In the nineteenth century the novel became, of course, the dominant European form of art, and it remains a dominant form in our own time.

Our concern here is not so much with what happened as why it happened. Even the most conservative and pedestrian historians of the English novel have always found a cause-and-effect relationship between the rise of the novel and the rise of the middle class in the eighteenth century. Of necessity, before the spread of literacy to a wide population the arts were aristocratic. The ideals, habits, and conduct of the aristocracy were the stuff of the arts, of painting, even of the theater, with few exceptions, until trades-men, manufacturers, and those whose way of life were dependent on them made their appearance and formed an audience for the arts. The novel soon proved a chosen and favored form, and thus the tag "bourgeois" turned up early in literary history. It is significant that recent, frankly Marxist, critics such as Georg Lukács and Arnold Kettle have moved beyond tentative associa-tions between social movement and the evolution of the novel to assert loudly a continuing relationship between prose fiction and class struggle in the Marxian sense. Without having to take sides in that argument, one may agree that novelists have been promi-nent in registering the social and political conscience of their times, whether in frankly political novels such as George Eliot's *Daniel Deronda* and Disraeli's *Coningsby,* or in Fielding's social satire or Henry James's social tragedies. In the history of the English novel is contained a remarkable example of response through art to the needs of a wide public for self-definition and self-recognition; certain economic and political forces created the atmosphere for the novel, while the converse is also true, that private and ultimately public sensibility were in a fundamental sense the product of the novel.

In contrast to England, the political and intellectual history of eighteenth-century Spain offers a notoriously dreary prospect, yet that very fact is relevant to the emergence of toreo. Philip V and Ferdinand VI, the Bourbon kings, were aware of the stagnation and bureaucratic corruption by which they were surrounded, but for lack of character and ability they were unable to bring about any but nominal reform. The Inquisition, administered by worldly churchmen, blighted both political and intellectual life; at a time when the rest of Europe flourished through deep drafts of the Enlightenment, Spain was mired in obscurantism and xenopho-bia. At a time when Europe was prosperous under mercantilism, Spain's empire was being lost to economic decay, her interior economy was bankrupt, and her agriculture inadequate to feed her people. Absentee landlords exploited the masses, as did the heavy taxes and customs duties needed to pay for foreign supplies and for the long war, from 1739 to 1763, against England. A middle class, that traditional source of political and intellectual energy in modern Europe, did not exist, and the masses of the Spanish people continued to be ravaged by poverty and ignorance. With the accession of Charles III in 1759, matters improved for a time. Charles's first ministers, Aranda and Florida Blanca, aided by Campomanes and Jovellanos, made efforts to cope with the church, to reform the legal system, to introduce order into the fiscal system, and to enlarge the provincial and retrogressive intellectual outlook of the country. The reformers were suspect, however, as men under French influence, as indeed they were. Florida Blanca in particular was a student of the French *philosophes* and dedicated to leading his country from the fifteenth into the eighteenth century. His efforts, like the efforts of the handful of men who shared his views, were too few and too late. Despotism, privilege, and the extraordinary power of the Church made impossible in Spain the development of a workable political system. By the end of the century, Spain was tragically ready for her long agony, extending from the Napoleonic invasion to our own time.

In such a context, Goya's nightmare paintings look comfortable. It was within such a context that toreo developed, and it is to toreo, not to the novel or the theater, that we must look to uncover important aspects of Spain that are ignored in conventional political history. In an age of revolution, Spain, the country that most needed revolution, was forced to settle for more than a century of civil war. Denied a revolution, the people could not be denied a gesture, and their gesture amounted to a revolution in the one art available to that illiterate people, the art of toreo. We must recall that so long as the feudal system prevailed—and it prevailed in Spain far longer than elsewhere in western Europe—bulls were killed on horse with the rejón (lance). The rejoneador was an aristocrat, and toreo was an aristocratic pastime, a sport and a spectacle, but not the art it was to become. The aristocrat on horse often required his servants (peones) to cape the bull into position for his work with the lance; to this day, the banderillero is known as a peón. With the invention of the muleta, toreo on foot became the dominant form, and rejoneo regressed promptly to the elegant display of horsemanship accompanied by slight danger that it remains today. For more than a generation, however, the picador, who took over the suerte of the lance, was more highly paid than the matador on foot. Loyalty to the aristocratic form of toreo, in other words, did not disappear overnight. Of greatest importance is the fact that the matador on foot was not an aristocrat; he was a man of the people who, until well into the nineteenth century, led a wandering, poor sort of life, moving from feria to feria, having none of the social status that later was accorded him. The picador, however, soon became the buffoon of toreo. His falls before the bull's charge are called "swimming" and are too often seen as comic. By an obvious transference, the picador as buffoon is equated by a nonpolitical people with the aristocrat as buffoon, while their hot loyalties to the modern matador may be seen as a rejection of the aristocracy and its pursuits.

Denied its human rights, deprived by a peculiar history of the possibility of seizing those rights through revolution, the Spanish people took the only way open to it, rejection of the aristocracy through symbolic action. It elevated its own, the new matador who had been peón, to the status of folk hero; toreo offered apolitical politics, satisfying a need which was as urgent as it was below the level of consciousness. At the same time, the savagery of early toreo, with its hamstringings of the bull, the use of dogs, the eruption into the plaza of the spectators, may also be explained as a further outlet to suppressed revolutionary emotion.[1] Characteristically, the anti-aristocratic sentiment in toreo remained purely symbolic. The aristocracy firmly controlled the business side of toreo through ownership of the extensive lands needed for breeding toros bravos, and through ownership or management of the plazas. This in turn accounts for liberal and radical hostility to toreo, even though such sentiment is often disguised as humanitarian: the "no decent person would attend a bullfight" argument.

With the closing decades of the nineteenth century, the anti-aristocratic memories of toreo had been lost, and it was completely possible to identify toreo with social reaction. In Blasco Ibáñez' *Sangre y arena*, a full range of argument is presented, with the liberal humanitarian argument dramatically predominating. Juan Gallardo, the ex-shoemaker's apprentice, is shown first to be a proletarian hero early in his career as torero when he knows no fear. But when Gallardo makes money, buys a finca, apes the aristocracy, and falls in love, ludicrously, with an aristocrat, his virtue goes out of him. He begins to fear the bulls and to kill badly; the gentry in the shade continue to applaud him, but the working class in the sun insult him with *"Aristocrata!"* El Na-

---

[1] The remarkable violence against the clergy during the Civil War of 1936–1939 (and in earlier outbreaks, dating from the eighteenth century) may be explained by the fact that while the Spanish Church exploited the people even more egregiously than the aristocracy did, no outlet in symbolic action against the Church existed.

cional, Gallardo's loyal banderillero of confidence, emerges as a man who has lost his class and his identity through toreo. He had been a smelter in a foundry and a member of the international workers' movement, which deplored corridas *"por bárbaras y retrógradas,"*[2] and forbade participation by members. El Nacional agrees that the people need education, not corridas, and he is bitter about his own default. But the most powerful attack on toreo, apart from the career of Gallardo himself, is presented through Dr. Ruiz. Ruiz is a free-thinking intellectual whose defense of corridas is so cynical as to form an ironic attack. Reviewing the history of toreo, the good doctor finds a significant division between the pre- and post-Inquisition periods. From the time of the Cid to the Inquisition, aristocratic rejoneo was a mere intermittent diversion of knights having nothing to do with modern toreo. " 'The Spaniard with a taste for war could always find his diversion in Europe or by taking ship for the Americas. . . . The autos da fé and executions by the burning of men were spectacles so satisfying as to eliminate interest in mere games played with simple wild animals. The Inquisition gave birth to our grand national fiesta.

" 'For the day arrived,' Dr. Ruiz went on with a smile, 'when the Inquisition began to weaken. Everything in this world finally becomes exhausted. At length it died of old age, long before its suppression by revolutionary laws. . . . It lost its ambiente. People began to be ashamed of burning human beings, with all the apparatus of sermons, ridiculous vestments, abjurations, and the like. . . . At the same time, the Spanish, weary of travelling the world in search of adventure, stayed at home. Now there were no more wars in Flanders or in Italy; the conquest of America was finished together with the endless embarcation of adventurers, and that was when the art of toreo began. Permanent plazas were constructed and professional cuadrillas were formed. Lidia was subjected to rules, and the suertes of the banderillas and the estocada as we know them today came into being. The crowd found the fiesta very much to its taste. When toreo was converted into a profession, it became democratic. Knights had been supplanted by plebeians who contracted to expose their lives, and the people went into the plazas as one man, master of his fate, able to insult from the stands the same authority that inspired terror in

---

[2] "For barbarity and retrograde tendencies." *Sangre y arena*, p. 78.

the streets. The offspring of those who assisted with concentrated religious fervor at the frying of heretics and Jews dedicated themselves to witnessing with noisy applause a struggle between a man and a bull, in which the only thing that might happen from afternoon to afternoon was the death of a torero. Is that not progress?' "[3]

Blasco Ibáñez, like the men of the distinguished generation of 'ninety-eight—that group of artists who were liberals in politics, humanitarian, rationalist, anti-clerical, and cosmopolitan—was trying after the ultimate collapse of empire in the War of 1898 to force his country to come to terms with the realities of the twentieth century. That new generation, with the outstanding exception of Ortega y Gasset, tended to equate toreo with political and social stagnation. They saw it as a pastime which distracted the people from more urgent concerns, as a form of bread and circuses encouraged by an oppressive regime. And viewing it thus they were probably correct. Nevertheless, Blasco Ibáñez' portrait of Juan Gallardo contains one aspect of truth of which the author seems only partially aware himself: namely, the extent to which romanticism had affected the entire atmosphere of the fiesta.

Romanticism was undoubtedly the most powerful single movement in our history since the Renaissance. It has influenced every aspect of modern life, from our constitutions, our courts, our revolutions, and our wars to the paintings we admire, the novels we read, and the poetry we honor. So encompassing a movement has meant many things to many men. We are concerned here only with those aspects of romanticism which meant rebellion against accepted rules in art and society, the celebration of individual man as opposed to anonymous masses, the propagation of historical legends at the expense of a "scientific" or rational view of history; the elevation of inspiration in the artist at the expense of craft and tradition, and the emergence of nationalism both in aesthetics and in politics. Romantic attitudes, frequently debased, pervaded the very air of Europe and North America from the end of the eighteenth to virtually the end of the nineteenth century, very like the way in which the ideas of Freud, frequently debased, pervade the contemporary air of England and America. Romantic survivals are strong among us; just how strong is a subject for debate. Although much of romanticism at the popular level was a

---

[3] *Sangre y arena*, p. 189–190.

matter of disposition and attitude, one can and indeed must account with discipline for it and its effects upon toreo.

German philosophy[4] provided the base for an aesthetic theory that was eagerly taken up by critics and writers, an apparently innocent theory which resulted in nationalistic chauvinism and was as responsible as any single theory can be for much recent political disorder. Attempting to account for the generation of the work of art quite apart from the rules and paradigms at hand in neoclassical aesthetics, the Germans devised the metaphor of vegetable nature to express the relationship between the creator, or artist, his background, and his finished work. The work of art was said to develop in nature as a tree develops; as the tree has its own design, unique, so the poem or painting is unique, unlike any other work, subject to no rule. That "vegetable," organic theory liberated the artist from the past, insisted upon his genius, and enthroned him above all rule, human and, in extreme cases, divine. It set the scene for the artist as hero and established the pattern of the transcendental hero who, because of his unique and intimate relation to nature, was gifted to speak clearly what ordinary men could only vaguely apprehend.

Attention was centered not only on the isolated, unsocial and anti-social hero, but also upon the nature which gave him birth, and in an unholy extension of the logic of the vegetable theory of creativity, "nation" was substituted for "nature." The liberating and admirable cosmopolitanism of the Renaissance gave way to national consciousness, providing a thrusting stimulus to the emergence of nationalist emotion, and support to scrupulous and unscrupulous politicians in their various calls to arms during that turbulent period. As late as 1870, Victor Hugo responded to the outbreak of the war against Prussia with, *"Je ne sais plus mon nom, je m'appelle Patrie!"* (I no longer know my name; my name is Fatherland!) Samuel Johnson spoke for an earlier time when he said that "Patriotism is the last refuge of a scoundrel."

Romanticism came to Spain comparatively late. Its heaviest impact was in the years 1830–1845, as may be seen in the literary work of Espronceda, Larra, and a few others. This we learn from conventional literary and cultural history. In politics, romanticism

---

[4] Beginning with Leibniz' *La Monadologie*, 1714, and continuing through the work of Sulzer, Herder, Kant, Goethe, Friedrich Schlegel, and Schelling.

meant only the rise of secret societies and heroic conspirators; the ideas of Rousseau, particularly that of the social contract, were read with sympathy by liberals, but the lack of political machinery and the absence of political experience made for frustration and the isolated gesture. These are the conclusions of conventional historians, accurate so far as they go. No one seems to have noticed the obvious connections between romanticism and toreo, least of all the historians of toreo, and again one is plunged into the cultural no man's land to which toreo has always been relegated.

It is neither accident nor coincidence that toreo emerged as an art in the same years when romanticism flourished; we recall that Francisco Montes' *Tauromachia*, the first in which toreo is expounded as a true art, dates from 1836.[5] The figure of the nineteenth-century torero is identical with that of the romantic hero of fiction and poetry. Born to poverty and obscurity, he transcends his origins through his innate capacity to cope with nature, in the form of the toro; he wins popular acclaim by his exploits, which in turn absolve him from conventional social restraints. A natural aristocrat, his wealth and tastes incline him away from his background toward the aristocracy. He is expected to be as potent sexually as he is open-handed with his money. Above all, he escapes the vulgar fate of ordinary men because he is marked for violent death; not the lugubrious death in bed following debilitating illness but a glorious death on the horns of a toro. The Spanish needed neither a Wagner nor a Bizet, for they had the romantic motif of love-death in their vision of the torero. The torero achieves the fulfillment of romantic individualism and egotism. If his art is circumscribed by rule and ritual, his success depends upon his ability to improvise through inspiration, and for the romantic, inspiration is virtually all. In his speech, his bearing, above all in his dress, the romantic torero parallels the attitudes of the literary dandy. Of Baudelaire it has been said, "to the artifice of the poem corresponds the artifice of the dandy."[6] The Baudelairean technique of shock through disparity applies to the torero and his suit of lights. The poet, affecting meticulous dress while writing of necrophilia, has much in common with the effeminate

---

[5] Pepe-Hillo's *Tauromachia* (the authorship of which is dubious) dates from 1796, but it is valuable as a biographical document rather than for its aesthetics.

[6] Anthony Hartley, Introduction, *Penguin Book of French Verse*, III, (Harmondsworth, 1957), xxviii.

exquisiteness of the matador delivering the estocada to a bloodied bull. Each dramatically insists upon his separateness from routine; to the artifice of the faena corresponds the artifice of the torero. In passing, one notes that the modern more-or-less standardized suit of lights does not derive from the eighteenth century, as we so often read, but from the late romantic period.

In another context, toreo combined with a debased romantic impulse gave authority to traditional Spanish xenophobia and further support to the Spanish legend of sangre where the fiesta was concerned. We have dealt substantially with these matters in Chapter 1; suffice it to say here that without the romantic glorification of the national past and the accompanying insistence upon national identity, fanciful and nationalistic histories of toreo either would not have been written or would not have enjoyed the uncritical acceptance of so many people. Political nationalism ultimately produces Fascism and Franco. It is in the Greek sense tragic that Spain should be the one country to have had none of the political glories of romanticism in its first, fine flush, but all the horrors of a romanticism turned cancerous by scoundrels.

Romanticism may thus be seen as a movement peculiarly suited to Spanish conditions, but one which was embodied fully not in poetry or drama, as in Germany and England, not in politics, as in France and the United States, but in toreo. Because of its geographical isolation, generations of poverty and oppression, its religiosity and its national exhaustion, Spain could not find conventional outlets for its emotional energy. Only toreo was suited to its atmosphere, an art that is less intellectual than the other arts, one in which color, movement, intuition, practical knowledge, and spontaneity find release. And while toreo was Spanish and only Spanish in its origins, its inner impulses, as reflected in so universal a movement as romanticism, make it available to a far wider public than that of Spain alone. Again the history of the English novel is relevant. While English writers dominated the novel for a long time, no one, Englishmen least of all, would claim that the novel is uniquely English. Developing together, subject to similar intellectual forces, the two arts belong to all. In the arts there is no patriotism.

Traveling through Spain in about 1840, the poet Théophile Gautier went to a corrida in Madrid and made the following political observation: "Montes was with his faithful cuadrilla, a thing very important for the safety of the corrida; for, in these times of political upheaval, it very often happens that the toreros who follow Doña María Cristina [i.e., liberals] do not go to the aid of the endangered toreros who favor the Carlistas [absolutists], and vice-versa."[7] Gautier's incidental note, if true, foreshadows the Marxist venom of the Civil War in 1936, when herds of toros bravos were slaughtered, often wantonly, as a political gesture. As Jean Cau says in his admirable *Les Oreilles et la queue,* "A man of the Left makes it his duty to spit on the corrida."[8] The fact is that the astringent, puritanical side of Marxism, and of Communism in particular, is quick to denounce those arts encountered abroad which do not have obvious political purpose. Thus abstract painting is "degenerate," various writers are damned out of hand as bourgeois, and virtually any pleasure for its own sake is looked down upon as frivolous and decadent. Even so pleasure-loving a place as Cuba has under Castro put its brilliantly imaginative prostitutes in uniform and has encouraged them to play American baseball. Since Franco, toreo has been seen by the Left with its sentimental humanitarianism as a unique expression of Fascism, for its alleged emphasis upon virility, sex, blood, and death. The Left is confirmed in its view by the noises of the Jew-hating Roy Campbell, the South African poet who dabbled in toreo and wrote inaccurately about it. Again, lack of criticism is at fault for permitting toreo to seem to embody no more than Fascist motifs. But most of the Leftists who preach prudish sermons have never bothered to attend a corrida, like the British and Americans who dismiss toreo as cruel without bothering to investigate it.

Revolutionary (but not Marxist) hostility to toreo was never more fully expressed than in the decree of 1916 outlawing toreo in Mexico. The language of Venustiano Carranza, the President, is so interesting that it merits translation, literal by purpose, here:

> IN CONSIDERATION that it is the primordial duty of the entire government to assure to all individuals who make up the collectivity of the State the enjoyment of their fundamental rights, without which society could not exist, nor properly fulfill its end; and having also as a consequence the obligation to promote those uses and customs which will further the realization of that duty,

---

[7] *Voyages en Espagne,* p. 277.

[8] Jean Cau, *Les Oreilles et la queue* (Paris, 1961), p. 9. See also Jean Cau, "Izquierda y Derecha," *El Ruedo,* August 22, 1963, n.p.

whether it be to encourage the development of human personality, to procure the best adaptation of humanity to the exigencies and necessities of the epoch, or equally to accept the duty of negating and extirpating those habits and tendencies which stand as an obstacle to culture, or which condition the individual to disorder, awakening in him antisocial sentiments:

In consideration that it is our duty to bring about the civilization of the popular masses, awakening in them altruistic and elevated sentiments, and raising the moral level, all possible means will be pursued in Mexico to secure through educational institutions—and not only those which give instruction, but also instill physical, moral and aesthetic value—the adequate preparation of the individual for all social responsibility. But that work will remain truncated and incomplete, it cannot produce the desired effect, if at the same time we neglect to root out those practices which are responsible for social stagnation:

In consideration that high among those practices is the diversion of the bulls, in which without the slightest necessity the life of a man is placed in grave danger, which causes tortures, again unnecessarily, to living creatures to which morality ought to extend and which should be protected under law. In addition to that, the diversion of the bulls provokes bloodthirsty feelings which unfortunately have been a reproach to our race throughout history, an incentive to evil passions, and a means of aggravating the misery of poor families: people who, for the unhealthy pleasure of a moment remain without many days' sustenance:

For all these reasons, I have taken it upon myself to decree the following:

> *Article 1.* Corridas de toros are absolutely forbidden in the Federal District and in the Federal Territories.
>
> *Article 2.* Corridas de toros are equally forbidden in the entire Republic, until the re-establishment of constitutional governments in the various States of the Republic.
>
> *Article 3.* Authorities or individuals who may contravene the intent of this law will be punished by a fine of from 1,000 to 5,000 pesos, or imprisonment from two to six months, or both, according to the gravity of the infraction.[9]

Through the marmalade of Carranza's official prose come overtones of Rousseau, John Locke, and the American Declaration of Independence: romanticism at war with itself. Like most wars, this one was lost. Corridas continued to be held, and no less a torero than Juan Belmonte made his first Mexican tour in 1917. Carranza's attempt at suppression was not the first in Mexico; the great Juárez himself, leader of the mid-nineteenth-century Reform, had also made the attempt, in part from sentimental lib-

---

[9] Decreto número 99, *Diario Oficial*, Mexico, October 11, 1916.

eralism, in part as an anti-Spanish, anti-aristocratic gesture. Only in his native state, Oaxaca, did Juárez succeed, to the point that no corridas have been held there to this day. The willingness of Mexicans to defy law on behalf of the fiesta is testimony to anarchic social conditions, but more important, to the place that toreo holds in the Mexican consciousness. As with the prohibition of drink in the United States from 1920 to 1933, one sees that a law contrary to society's own sense of need and justice is finally not enforceable. Recent Mexican presidents have been caught in a dilemma. While they have given tacit approval to corridas by attending them on occasion, fulfillment of their promises to distribute land to the landless has resulted in the expropriation of lands belonging to bull breeders.

It is significant that under Lázaro Cárdenas (in office from 1934 to 1940), probably Mexico's finest president, a genuine rather than a sentimental liberal and a man of culture and intelligence, the rigors of the first Agrarian Code were modified to permit exemption of holdings between 300 and 50,000 hectares for fifty years, always provided that the agrarian requirements of the region were satisfied. In 1944, however, the law was reinterpreted to allow a ganadero to retain enough land to rear five hundred head of cattle. The actual amount depended upon the fertility of the land, but in no case was a single ranch to exceed 5,000 hectares (one hectare equals 2.471 acres). Anything over that amount—and it was not uncommon for ganaderías to consist of 25,000 hectares—was to be redistributed. The ganaderos agreed gracefully to the limitation, but they secured a twenty-five-year moratorium upon its enforcement, during which time they were to make the necessary transition, and upon condition that they distributed two per cent of their annual production, in cash or kind, to their landless neighbors. Some of the ganaderos observed the two per-cent agreement punctiliously, but many more did not. Thus they provided ammunition to those who favored outright expropriation, and encouragement to the various squatter movements that developed in the interim. In Mexico there are 118 recognized ganaderías. As of 1964, at least partial distribution of the lands of three ranches had begun: those of Peñuelas, Chichimeco, and Santa María de Gallardo, while four others had been listed for early disposition: those of Xajay, La Punta, Corlome, and Garabato.[10]

---

[10] *Toros*, VII, No. 2 (February 1963), p. 32; VIII, No. 3 (March 1964), p. 49; VIII, No. 10 (October/November 1964), p. 46.

Unfortunately, the redistribution of these particular lands offers an example of ideology at war with common sense. Most of the bull-breeding land in Mexico is high, barren, virtually waterless, and inaccessible. It is not suited to small holdings and intensive agriculture, the purposes intended by redistribution. The idea of redistribution itself has become a cliché, while little thought has gone to the real benefit of the campesinos involved. The obvious solution, to form cooperatives for the production of toros bravos, has never been discussed, and probably never will be, since both sides have taken up classical Left and Right positions in the dispute. In the meantime, Mexico needs the fiesta for its power to attract tourists and foreign currency.

Behind the decisions of politicians lies an even more compelling—and indeed always related—question, that of the changing relationship between toreo and the public in the various countries where toreo makes any impact upon public sensibility. Up to this point we have been concerned mainly with the traditional and ritual view of toreo and of the torero. We have sketched what traditional toreo is and how it got that way, and we have seen the art of toreo in the perspective of certain other arts, of history, and as in part a product of romanticism. What of toreo in relation to modern society? The question is complex, for modern society itself is in the process of rapid change: witness the career of Manuel Benítez. That the afición of Spain has changed is clear, but it is too soon to assess what those changes will amount to. Until the Civil War, toreo was a truly popular art in Spain. The aristocracy and the wealthy bourgeoisie were to be found on the shady side of the plaza, while tickets in the sun were within reach of the poor. All classes of society attended corridas, and knowledge of los toros was taken for granted. Now the poor are being priced out of the plazas and their places are being taken by tourists. Television, which is rapidly spreading, makes toreo in bastard form widely available, but that of course is not the same thing as attendance at the plaza. More serious, one senses that in Spain young intellectuals, students among them, have taken over the traditional liberal view that toreo is politically reactionary, and that with the suppression of toreo goes social progress.[11] Films and sport occupy more

---

[11] A straw in this wind is a letter to the editor of *El Ruedo*, December 6, 1963, from a student saying that his companions look with suspicion upon the fiesta and are unwilling to join the *peña* (fan club) of students at the Colegio Mayor San Francisco.

attention than ever before, while literacy and reading matter are more widespread than in the past. This is to say that although toreo no longer holds its monolithic position of the past, it is in no sense threatened with extinction by the new public. Spain remains the center of the world of toreo. Its bulls are the finest bred anywhere, and its toreros dominate wherever they travel. In Spain as elsewhere, and like every other art, toreo will have to make its peace with mass society, taking advantages of the opportunities and purging itself of the excrescences accompanying mass society. The dangers to toreo are the traditional ones, but their edge is sharpened by the new public: ignorance, neglect of standards through neglect of criticism, shady business practices, and the easy substitution of the mystique of sangre for knowledge. The hard core of the afición in the major Spanish plazas remains the most discriminating. They are the first to applaud honesty, to recognize the toro's conditions, to know what is happening to that toro, and to register disgust with trickery. They are as necessary to toreo as good animals and honest toreros.

The Mexican afición has definitely changed since the late 1940s. Where formerly all classes went regularly to the plaza, now the spectators are dominated by workers, and by politicians and their hangers-on who go mainly to be seen. The intellectuals ignore the toros, partly from political conviction, partly in semiconscious imitation of North American attitudes, partly in rejection of all things Spanish. To the Mexican, the Spaniard has the same low place that the French had in the Spanish mind throughout the nineteenth century, that of despoiler, shrewd businessman, and exploiter. Mexico still recognizes the Loyalist government but not Franco's. Mexican nationalism, always strong since the revolution, means the rejection of the foreign, particularly of the Spanish, tradition and the exaltation of the pre-Spanish past. Yet Spain retains a special place in the Mexican torero's mind. He longs to torear in Spain and to confirm his alternativa in Madrid. Television is having a considerable effect in Mexico, too, but again it is too early to assess that effect for good or bad. As in Spain, the afición in the smaller cities and towns is considerably more ingenuous than in Mexico City or the other large cities.

Just as the bands are larger and louder in Mexico, the crowd noisier than in Spain, so it is more exigent. The Mexicans almost never recognize a good vara on the rare occasions when they see it; almost invariably they are against having the toro piced at all.

This leads to the abuse of the under-piced toro and often to the sacrifice of a good animal in the faena. It leads to a florid style of toreo, one in which the spectators often seem to want the torero's blood and his life. One sees more and often better cape work in Mexico than in Spain; in part because Mexican toros are easier in the cape for having less casta, in part because the spectators demand more cape work, particularly in quites, and get it. One also sees more cornadas in Mexico than in Spain. This is frequently a matter of exigence on the part of the spectators, and folly on the part of the toreros, who are too often less well trained than in Spain. Plate 17 shows what happened to a torero one Sunday afternoon in March 1962. Antonio del Olivar, a very much better-than-average matador, had drawn a manso of the most difficult kind, the toro which stops in mid-charge at the lure to search for the man with his horn. Del Olivar had worked the animal with much skill, pulling from it a superb performance, and was ready for the kill. Yet he ignored his own instinct and allowed the crowd to force him to more passes and a stupid maneuver. Citing for a natural, he crossed the toro's territory completely, from one horn to the other, in the manner of Arruza. The animal still would not answer, so del Olivar turned his back slowly upon the toro, as though to cite for a pase de pecho, to the hysterical delight of the crowd, which was incapable of knowing the enormity of their demand, and perhaps of their responsibility for the inevitable cornada. Although del Olivar recovered quite promptly, he has never been the same in the plaza since that afternoon.

That Mexican incident, in its evocation of the blood of many toreros, suggests a fact known to the Greeks, that between society and its heroes there exists a paradoxical love-hatred connection. Despite society's honor and exaltation of the artist for embodying and giving voice to its own most noble aspects, society wants also, like a cruel child with a kitten, to rend and destroy that embodiment for its own nobility. In Greek legend is the figure of Dionysos as vegetable god, who had annually to be horribly murdered in order to come to life again, thus insuring fertility to the land. There is Orpheus, the god of song, who, when he had withdrawn from the crowd to meditate, was ripped to death by maenads. And there is the legend of the death of the tragedian, Euripides, whose residence at the court of Archelaus in Macedonia resulted in the jealousy of the courtiers and his death when they set savage dogs upon him. But the Aztecs themselves provide the custom most symbolic of the relationship between torero and society. Annually the Aztecs selected from among the common people a handsome young man who was pampered like a king, given every luxury and privilege for one year, when he was abruptly stripped of his privileges, his skin was flayed, and he was driven through the city, to the jeers of the populace, even as his successor was being chosen. Many an aging ex-torero, especially in Mexico, will vouch for the aptness of the parallel. If we can accept

PLATE 17. Antonio del Olivar's *cornada* of March 1962 was the result of the crowd's demands for more passes to a toro over-ready for the *estocada*.

the Warren Report's account of President Kennedy's assassination, we may recognize again something of the public need to sacrifice the unusual man, to eliminate its heroes. In still another context, there is wide public interest in gossip and biography of great men, together with ignorance, in the case of artists, of their achievements. Many people prefer to read Madame Gilot on Picasso's sexual habits (*Life with Picasso*) rather than to study his paintings; we delight in scurrility about the great, not only to bring them down to our level but to put them down beneath our level. For the torero, this terrible public need may mean his blood or his death; toreo remains close to its origins and close to our most primitive and naked selves.

Among the countries south of Mexico, toreo is practiced only in Venezuela, Peru, Colombia, Ecuador, Guatemala, and Panama. Only in Venezuela and Peru may the fiesta be said to flourish, and there it suffers from lack of fighting stock. There are perhaps three ganaderías of cartel in Peru: Las Salinas, Huando, and La Panca. Venezuelan corridas generally are made up of Mexican stock. As for Peru, we have the word of Raul de la Puente, one of the better critics of toreo in the Spanish world, to the effect that the ganaderías of Peru constantly send to the plazas "toros without *trapío* [good growths of horn], without casta, without age, and with what horns they have shaved."[12] Except in Lima, the public is uneducated in toreo and ingenuous. Anti-Spanish sentiment, misplaced humanitarianism, and absence of afición account for the lack of toreo elsewhere. Cuba had plazas de toros in the nineteenth century, but no more.

Public attitudes toward toreo in the United States cover a wide range from passionate partisanship to loathing, but for reasons which we shall presently explore, indifference is rare. Toreo has always flourished in non-industrialized countries in which the attitudes of the aristocracy and the attitudes of the agrarian peasantry combined to support the fiesta. What is surprising, perhaps, is that toreo should have any widespread attraction for a profoundly middle-class country like the United States. The man of the middle class prefers assured cash profits, personal comfort, local, parochial loyalties, and the even tenor of suburban existence to the discipline, abandon, and risks of the art of toreo, or of any other art, for that matter. Beyond age twenty-five, his diversions

---

[12] Interview in *Fiesta Española*, IV, No. 206, June 1, 1965.

are viewing television, a passive interest in professional baseball or football, and if he is unusually active, semi-sedentary sports like golf and bowling. If he thinks of the arts at all, he sees them as having nothing to do with the reality of his life; at best they are a luxury, at worst a fraud. In religion he is mildly pious or nothing. He is faithful to his wife, on the whole, not for love but because sexual adventure is messy, expensive, and scandal is bad for business. When he succumbs, he is likely to become an alcoholic, a psychiatrist's patient, or a suicide. He gives large sums to charity drives, loves his children, and assumes that they will be richer, happier, and somehow better men than he.

Having been educated to believe that discussion is good and meditation inefficient, exposed every day to television and to slick magazines, he has a ready opinion about everything, including toreo. Toreo is "bullfighting," and bullfighting is cruel to the animal, barbarous, an odd-ball sport that only backward people like the Spanish and the Mexicans could go in for. Nothing in his experience has prepared him to think of toreo as an art, any more than of garbage collecting as an art. Furthermore, he is a humanitarian, brought up in the liberal tradition. He would go to court if a teacher struck his child in school, yet he encourages his son to play football, a sport in which, year in and year out, between one hundred and one hundred and fifty players, mostly young schoolboys, are killed in America each fall. (In 1964, one torero was killed in pursuit of his profession.) He follows boxing with pleasure, although in a thirteen-month period in 1962–1963, seven boxers died from injuries in the ring. He believes in capital punishment. At his most groteque, he believes also in the politics of hydrogen bombs, feeling in his heart that America would win any war, even though a lot of people would get hurt. He cannot believe in his own death; God or Fate could not be so unkind as to incinerate him.

That American is assuredly a caricature, one which we bother to draw because only the constrictions of the caricature account for the many departures from the middle-class ethic. Fortunately, American society is open enough to permit wide departures from the Babbitt-like caricature, while the elements of truth present in the caricature serve as a goad to that large minority which provides any edge and character that the society has. Once aroused against the official blandness of American society, the dissident takes up his new position with passion. It is passion above all that he brings to toreo. The American afición must be divided into three groups: those who look to Spain and to the Mexican interior; those who live on the Mexican border; and those for whom toreo is primarily an agreeable, even glamorous, literary idea, but whose knowledge remains second-hand and literary. Obviously the number of people in group one is restricted to the few who have the money and leisure to follow the bulls abroad from season to season. Nevertheless this is an identifiable group, one whose influence is out of proportion to its size. Toreo along the Mexican border presents a special problem. It existed in the beginning to attract the tourist, therefore it developed both its own crooked business side and a kind of torero who confines himself to that well-paying circuit, almost never appearing in a plaza of cartel. Until the end of World War II, the kind of tourist who thought of Mexican border towns as places to buy cheap tequila, to find eager whores of both sexes, and to see a bullfight, in that order, predominated. Since the war, and especially in the past decade, interest in toreo along the border has developed in quantity and quality to the point where it is the gringos who are leading a crusade to eliminate abuses and to raise standards in every facet of the fiesta. More than one torero, Mexican as well as Spanish, has said privately that the new American afición is better informed than his countrymen, noting that because he starts in ignorance, the American must study, while the Latin assumes his inborn knowledge and superiority deriving from his sangre.

The literary aficionado is the person, far from uncommon, whose knowledge comes mainly from reading, often beginning with Hemingway's *Death in the Afternoon*. He is aware of toreo as an art and open to the extension of experience that toreo may embody. Given travel or residence in a country where toreo is practiced, he usually becomes a fanatical aficionado. Also within this group is the person, often a homosexual, who sees toreo as exotic and glamorous—"camp," to use the modish phrase—and the torero as his or her sexual cup of tea. Such a person is bored by toreo in its entirety, restricting his interest to the modish and chichi, in toreo as in anything else. Of greater interest is a different misreading of toreo, that of certain intellectuals who see the torero as existentialist man whose willed act is to defy death on the bull's horn, and thus to establish his identity and his existence in a meaningless universe. Although this may be an attractive idea, it omits the fact that toreros do not see toreo as a way of dying, that they are usually brought up as devout Roman Catholics, that many remain Catholic, and that their intelligence is rarely of a bookish order. The case of Juan Belmonte is to the point, the Belmonte who removed his natural coleta so that he might move in society not as a torero but like any other man, who cultivated the company of writers, but who, according to Montherlant, pretended knowledge of Valéry even though he knew no French.[13]

The increase in American interest in toreo is further indicated by a dramatic rise in the amount of time given to the subject on television and radio, principally along the Mexican border, but also as far afield as Chicago and New York. In March 1960, the Television Code Review Board ruled that corridas could be shown to the public as long as the kill was omitted. When the ruling was challenged by the American Humane Association, the Board replied that it could not "determine peremptorily that bullfighting is [a] barbaric and shocking pastime which should be barred from public view," and that the American people should have "an increased awareness of the character, values, customs and motivations of other peoples." Knowledge of toreo is extended by some thirteen "Peñas Taurinas" (clubs) in the United States, where serious discussion is carried on, trips to Mexican or Spanish plazas organized, and films shown. Books in English on toreo, whatever their quality, are readily available and widely read. Newspaper coverage, however, is sporadic, incompetent, and inevitably printed on the sports pages.

The situation in Britain is roughly the same as that in the United States. The British aficionado, man for man, is if anything keener and more intellectual about his interest than his counterpart in the United States. British interest naturally gravitates to Spain rather than to Mexico, and the accessibility of Spanish plazas means that a significant number of Britons are able to follow the Spanish temporada. In 1963, an enterprising promoter announced that he would try to arrange a series of corridas in Manchester, of all places. Needless to say, his plan came to nothing. British humane associations are even more highly organized and more vocal than they are in America, while toreo comes in for its share of attention from those opposed to the "blood sports" of stag and fox hunting. Books on toreo do well in Britain, and in general

---

[13] Henry de Montherlant, "Mi Amigo Juan Belmonte," *El Ruedo,* August 22, 1963, n.p.

interest is growing as the traditional insularity of the British diminishes in the contemporary world.

French toreo has had a peculiar history, one which has yet to be written coherently. The few French writers who have given their attention to the subject have been local patriots, eager to explicate the sports of the Camargue involving bulls, at the expense of a proper account of Spanish toreo in France. The French bull country lies in a triangle at the mouth of the Rhone, formed by Avignon to the north, Montpellier to the west, and Marseilles to the east. At the center of the base of that triangle lie the marshes of the Camargue, where the primitive European aurochs has survived with the aid of the French *manadiers* (breeders). In its pure state, the bull of the Camargue looks more like the aurochs than like the Spanish toro bravo: he is smaller and very shaggy, with large hooves, thick legs, a snub snout, and horns rising at a ninety-degree angle to his head. He lacks the developed morillo, or hump, of the Spanish bull; he is fast, often brave, and difficult to torear. Spanish toreros have to be very hungry before they will consent to take on a corrida of bulls from the Camargue; not only are the animals difficult, but they are also frequently resabios, bulls that have been caped or otherwise exposed to the sports of the region.

Those sports include the *abrivade,* or the running into a village of bulls secured by ropes, often accompanied by the rite of the *bourgine,* reminiscent of mediaeval Spanish rites, where newly born children and recently married women confront the trussed bull to insure their fertility. Confusion with Spanish toreo arises in the sport which the French call the *course de cocardes* (or *razet*), in which the athlete, unarmed with cape or muleta, attempts to snatch from between the bull's horns the rosette (*cocarde*), or divisa, of the owner. Such bulls are resabios by intent, moving from village to village and attaining much local fame. The men of the Camargue also practice the suerte, or *course,* of the trident, in which the bull's attack is deflected by a man on one knee holding a short trident, the tines of which are blunted. And in the *course landaise,* the athlete vaults the bull, either using a pole or unaided by anything but his own agility. In the latter case, the bull is often secured by lines.[14]

---

[14] Marie Mauron, *Le Taureau, ce dieu qui combat* (Paris, 1949), pp. 32, 268. Roy Campbell, *Taurine Provence* (London, 1932), pp. 31–43.

The degree of French interest in Spanish toreo is indicated by the fact that since 1865 certain breeders of the Camargue have imported Spanish cows in order to produce an animal suitable for the art of toreo.[15] Written records of the sports of the Camargue date back to 1402;[16] the earliest account of a corrida de toros in France known to the writers is that of January 17, 1701, to honor the arrival at Bayonne of Philip of Anjou, en route to assume the Spanish throne. A Spanish corrida took place at Nîmes in 1810, to celebrate Bonaparte's wedding; sporadic accounts appear dated 1819, 1825, 1827. By 1854, corridas were fairly frequent, partially because Cayetano Sanz, the great Castilian matador, had become a favorite of the French. But the historian of Spanish toreo in France must work negatively, through accounts of measures to suppress the art. Just before the French Revolution, for example, the poet Béranger denounced corridas de toros. With the passage of the *loi Grammont* in 1850, a law against maltreatment of domestic animals, the French afición began a long struggle in the courts about whether toros bravos were or were not domestic animals.[17] Entire cuadrillas of Spanish toreros were arrested, fined, and imprisoned, but increasingly the fines were nominal, no one was imprisoned, and corridas continued. Some municipalities, however, forbade the killing of bulls in public, until the mid-1950s. Now, most places where corridas "traditionally" were held allow the full Spanish art to be practiced. Today one may see corridas in Arles, Nîmes, Bordeaux, Béziers, Céret, Vic-Fezensac, Marseilles, Saint-Vincent-de-Tyrosse, Mont-de-Marsan, Bayonne, Dax, and Collioure.

Doubtless because of this history, the contemporary French afición presents a mixed bag. The French are likely to confuse sport with art, and to prefer the fancy Sevillian school with its flashiness, its many adornos, and even its trickery, to the pure form of toreo. The French are notorious among toreros for their willingness to applaud a fast kill, no matter how badly delivered. But there exists along the border a small, hard core of serious aficionados who travel regularly to northern Spanish plazas, who know the fiesta well, and who take exception to their countrymen's

---

[15] Mauron, *Le Taureau*, p. 31.

[16] *Le Taureau*, p. 271.

[17] Fernand Roux, *Affaire des courses de taureaux* (Nîmes, 1895); Timon l'Athénien (pseudonym), *Des Courses et combats de taureaux dans le Midi de la France* (Avignon, 1868).

florid and often ignorant tastes. One must agree with Jean Cau that the afición of Paris is as noisy as it is ignorant. It is in Paris, as in New York, that theories of existentialist toreo are paraded by young men who may have seen one corrida through a vinous haze, and who find it chic to improvise irresponsibly. As on the Mexican border, French toreo is good business. Tickets are dear, and the unscrupulous can make a lot of money by passing off inferior animals. The public is comparatively undemanding, and toreros, needing public applause to live, are humanly willing to accept applause and ears that they know would never have been given on home ground.

Thus in toreo as in the other arts, the traditional public has recently been inundated by a new public, to the creation of a new mode, the mass audience. Debate about the influence of the mass audience on the other arts has raged for the past fifteen years, one side taking the elitist view that the mass can only lower standards and result in the triumph of the middle-brow. Domingo Ortega has said, perhaps echoing Ortega y Gasset, "cuando la masa interviene, el arte degenera." (When the masses intervene, art degenerates.) The other, sociological side sees in the emergence of the mass audience a triumph of democracy and a challenge to artists everywhere to usher in a golden era made possible by the existence of an audience unparalleled by any period in the past. That debate is only beginning to be heard in toreo, even though toreo is more dependent upon the spectators than is any other art. Only in toreo do the spectators have a hand in the creation of the art itself, for the torero fashions his work in response to the atmosphere in the plaza. He is not merely performing another man's work, like the actor, but inventing the work and performing it simultaneously. Unless he is a saint, he is not likely to do difficult but unspectacular work to spectators who know too little about toros and toreo to respond. Toreo needs the mass in order to exist, but the mass also needs true toreo if it is not to become a mob. All talk of the mass, the public, is bound to be approximate and unsatisfactory, for the mass is composed of individual human beings, and it is finally to the individual that all art is addressed, never to a mass. The history of toreo, like the history of the other arts, shows us the intimate relationships between society and art. Art exists in and for society, while whatever matters in society finds its survival in art. Toreo, one feels certain, will survive as long as society survives, and society will survive until the mass indeed turns into a mob. This, too, we know from contemporary history.

CHAPTER 7

# THE UNDERSIDE
# OF TOREO

L YING IN HOSPITAL after receiving a cornada from a Mexican toro in the plaza at Tijuana, Antonio Ordóñez was interviewed by a reporter who asked if it were true that he had been paid more than any matador in history for his appearance in Mexico. Ordóñez answered that however much he had been paid, it was not enough. His scornful answer to an impertinent question demands the consideration of an entire side of toreo that needs to be understood before the education of the aficionado can be anything like complete. Facts are elusive here, and the reputation of the business side of toreo is downright bad, usually with justification. All artists to some degree are at the mercy of businessmen, but no one is so much at their mercy as the torero. The writer who quarrels with his publisher may go elsewhere quite freely; the torero who quarrels with an empresario may be blackballed, unless he is one of the few who has such cartel that he can dictate his own conditions. The torero does not offer a manuscript, or any other sort of finished work; he offers a promise, he offers himself and his demonstrated or potential capacity to create a work in conjunction with a wild animal. His difficulties are unique, and the business side of toreo is also unique. The problems of a businessman who contracts to bring together at one time in one plaza three matadors, their cuadrillas, the animals they are to torear, and to make all the other arrangements necessary to the fiesta (tickets, veterinarians, horses, publicity, lawyers, ganaderos, to say nothing of the public itself) may be compared to the problems of producing *Aida,* publishing a book, getting out a newspaper, staging a play, and putting on the Irish Sweepstakes all at the same time.[1] Add to this the fact that Spain and its former colonies are countries where timetables exist to be defied, exact business procedures are a joke, and inconvenient laws are often ignored, and one begins to wonder how corridas ever manage to be put on at all.

As always, one begins with the animal itself, the toro, and with the problems of the breeder. It is a rule of thumb both in Spain and in Mexico that to break even or to allow a small margin of profit in the operation of a ganadería it is necessary to sell about fifty animals a year to the plazas. In order to produce that number of animals, a herd in excess of five hundred must be maintained, at various stages of growth: of yearlings, fifty bull calves and sixty heifers; the same number of two-year-olds; of three-year-olds, fifty bulls and thirty cows; the same number of four-year-olds; five-year-olds, thirty cows; thirty six-year-old cows; twenty seven-year-old cows; ten eight-year-old cows. These absolute figures total 470, but they do not take into account losses from sickness, inclement weather, or the number of animals eliminated in the tientas, always at least ten per cent and frequently much higher. According to the Unión de Criadores de Toros de Lidia de México, of thirty-five males born to each unit of one hundred cows, twenty-four per cent will be lost for one reason or another. The remainder will not be all of absolutely first rank but will merely fulfill a minimal standard. There is no need to emphasize the rarity of really good bulls, toros *de bandera.* In 1962, a typical year in Spain, 2,300 toros bravos and 3,100 novillos were toreados, for a total of 5,400 animals. Approximately two hundred ranches provided the animals, which works out to an average of twenty-seven animals per ranch. That does not mean that all lost money; some ranches sent many more than the minimum of fifty, while others in process of growth or only partially devoted to toros bravos provided far fewer. These proportions are roughly valid for Mexico. In both countries the number of ganaderías has increased

---

[1] One hundred men are needed to operate and maintain the Maestranza in Seville; these include masons, carpenters, electricians, painters, and the like.

dramatically since 1900: there were ninety-four in Spain in that year, and two hundred in 1950—testimony to the popularity of the fiesta and to the attractions of the art of breeding toros bravos, which often is a way of life first and a business only second.

But it *is* a business, a demanding one in which there is every pressure upon the breeder to relax his standards. Even the questions of exactly what those standards ought to be and how they should be arrived at are far from simple. We have already remarked the changes in the basic toro brought about early in the century in part by toreros who wanted an animal that would be suitable for extended work with the muleta, as opposed to the old-fashioned monster which took many pics, then was summarily dispatched after the briefest faena. That particular change has become the rule, and in certain cases has even become an abuse, as obliging ganaderos, notably in Salamanca, have further reduced the armament (*trapío*) and the aggressiveness of their stock. Even taking for granted a rough community of agreement about what is desirable in the modern animal, there remains the stubborn fact that it is hazardous to predict at two years in the tienta how a particular animal will react in the plaza at the age of four or five. As is well known, testing takes place either on the open range or in small plazas constructed for the purpose at the breeding ranch. In Andalusia and in parts of Mexico, the *suerte de la garrocha** is relied upon; in Salamanca and in most of Mexico, the use in the plaza of a pic carrying a small barb is preferred. In his role as torero and ganadero combined, Domingo Ortega argues that the suerte de la garrocha is inefficient for proving bravery, because the animal's behavior on the range is almost always different from its behavior in the plaza; a querencia on the range will not imply that the same animal will take up a querencia in the plaza. According to Ortega, in some ganaderías only twenty to twenty-five per cent of the animals tested are approved for the plaza, while in others (the majority), eighty per cent and more are approved, a disparity that argues against current methods of testing. Accordingly, Ortega pleads eloquently for extending the practice of the *indulto*,†

---

* *Suerte de la garrocha:* That form of testing in which mounted men pursue the calves in order to upset them with the blunt pole, or garrocha, which they carry. In theory, the brave calves will right themselves and attack the horse, while the mansos will flee.

† *Indulto:* Literally, "pardoned." Until recently, a rarely followed procedure in which an exceptional toro, on petition to the president

since only bravery proved in the plaza can efficiently guide the breeder in his task and provide the number of seed bulls so urgently required.[2]

No complaint is more common than that the bulls are not what they used to be because of the venality of breeders. There can be no question that the horn-shaving scandal, in which a large number of breeders took an active or passive part, is responsible for the public's skepticism. The truth of the matter is more complex and more interesting than mere money-grubbing. Foot-and-mouth disease has afflicted Spain for many years, while in Mexico the prohibition of Spanish stock because of that disease (and, one should add, out of a twisted nationalism) has meant that bloodlines have not had their necessary renewal from the Spanish sources. Certain Mexican herds, Pastejé for one, have declined alarmingly in quality as a result. Second, genetic mistakes have obviously been made, partially because of the breeders' willingness to breed for suavity at the expense of casta. Such mistakes require years and taurine generations to rectify. Then there is the fact that ganaderos, on the whole, are conservative men, slow to depart from traditional ways in this most traditional form of farming. Artificial insemination, for example, is not practiced. When asked why not, one ganadero's answer was as engaging as it was unscientific: "The cow, señor, must have her pleasure of the bull, otherwise she will refuse to conceive." When one considers the amount of capital invested in breeding toros bravos (230 million pesos in Mexico alone); the number of human beings required on the ranches (12,000 in Mexico); and the importance of the fiesta to

---

by the crowd, is symbolically "killed" with a banderilla rather than actually killed in the ritual estocada. With proper treatment, such toros will recover from their wounds and be able to function as *sementales,* or seed bulls, to the theoretical improvement of the breed. Since roughly 1964, however, particularly in Mexico, *el indultismo* or *indultomanía* has arisen as an abuse. Certain toreros have discovered that they can cut symbolic ears, tails and hooves by *themselves* petitioning that the toro be pardoned; a naive public follows the torero in demanding the indulto, and all are happy: torero, public, and not least, the breeder whose merchandise is returned to him with honors. The torero is of course spared the agony, if he is a poor matador, of a messy kill, to say nothing of the danger.

[2] *El arte del toreo,* pp. 76–99.

the national economies, comparatively little scientific research is performed and almost no national planning occurs to rationalize the numerous complexities of the business. The accusation of venality also ignores the many ganaderos whose lands have been in their families for generations, and whose inherited pride is such that mere venality is out of the question. Afición, love of the thing for itself, runs high among ganaderos; unfortunately, they are also human and capable of error. With all their fallibility, the business of raising toros for the plaza is far cleaner than certain other activities connected with the fiesta.

Between the ganadero and the torero stands the shadowy figure of the empresario, as necessary to the fiesta as hinges to a door or drink to an alcoholic. He varies so much from country to country and from individual to individual that one cannot generalize about him, while the laws of libel make unwise the necessary particularization. Nevertheless, certain points must be made. Something of the nature of the empresario's business may be inferred from the following statistics for Mexico in 1962. Six hundred and ninety-four festivals were celebrated in ninety plazas; 127 corridas de toros, 167 novilladas with picadors, and 300 without picadors; and 4,858,000 spectators attended. The capital value of the plazas was 140 million pesos; matadors received 9,856,600 pesos in fees; novilleros received 1,152,500 pesos. Tourists brought into Mexico 8,750,000 pesos; fifteen per cent of them were estimated to have come for the express purpose of seeing corridas. The figures for Spain must be increased fourfold, although the percentage for tourism was without doubt significantly higher than for Mexico. Adding income from television (about 2 million pesos per year in Mexico) to the usual sources, one sees that toreo is big business indeed both in Spain and in Mexico.

In the public mind and often in reality, the empresario who must administer all this is at once financier, pirate, politician, banker, thief, philanthropist, talent scout, publicist, personnel manager, and confidence man. At his best he may be all these things at once or in turn; more often he is only the more nefarious. Almost always he is businessman first and foremost, with little time for sentimentality about the art of toreo and the glorious traditions of the fiesta. He stands to gain or to lose large sums, thus he must command either the capital or access to the capital required for a large business. In Spain, where the fiesta is far more organized in all its aspects than elsewhere, the empresario will probably have no other major interests; his career is that of empresario, and he will often have interests in more than one plaza. In fact, the danger in Spain is that of monopoly and all monopoly may imply in the way of inflating reputations of merely flashy toreros, power over the ganaderías, and choice of novices who may or may not appear. The Madrid *empresa,* for example, also controls the plazas of Valencia, San Sebastián, Gijón, Guadalajara, Alcalá de Henares, Colmenar Viejo, Fuenterrabía, and both Arles and Dax in France. And the empresa of Bilbao also controls Logroño, Salamanca, Vitoria, Burgos, Santander, Badajoz, Oviedo, Calahorra, Mérida, Almendralejo, while he organizes corridas in Toulouse, Bayonne, Mont-de-Marsan, and Orthez in France. In provincial Mexico and South America, however, often the empresario may be a fly-by-night operator, without afición, knowledge, or interest in the fiesta other than its potential for making him rich. Many a torero has been left stranded in some out-of-the-way hellhole because of the optimistic ineptness of one-shot empresarios. In the major plazas, the business side is taken care of by professionals who are more or less honest, and who perceive, however dimly, that it is to their benefit, over the long pull, to conduct their affairs honorably and efficiently.

The burden of responsibility upon the empresario is heavy. It is up to him to buy the best available encierros and to supervise the care of the animals from the time of purchase to the moment they enter the plaza. He must certify that each bull is healthy, has good vision, and has in no way been tampered with. He is responsible for presenting an encierro as advertised and is not permitted to substitute animals from one ganadería for those from another. He is not allowed, under the regulations, to kite the weight of the animals, or to pass off novillos as toros, or becerros as novillos; neither is he permitted to farm out tickets to scalpers in return for kickbacks. When an empresario indulges in some or all of these abuses in order to make money, he does so by breaking faith with the public and giving his plaza a bad name. Ultimately, he runs the risk of having to close down altogether through having estranged the public. Such abuses are common along the Mexican border, where some plazas have had to close down from time to time; in France; and in some of the lesser plazas in Spain. From 1962 to 1964, attendance fell off noticeably in many of the Mexican border plazas, in further testimony to the short-sightedness of some of the businessmen involved.

In his responsibility for the development of young toreros, the empresario has an even heavier burden. It is here that the difference between the businessman and the professional is clearest, where the presence or absence of knowledge and afición is vital. In all the arts, it is safer (i.e., more profitable) to go along with the established figures, but at the same time essential to recognize and to encourage new talent. In most countries, society itself has come to recognize this fact and to provide fellowships, grants, training schools, and patronage for the young. Even in most sports, organized effort is made to develop new talent. Toreo is the unfortunate exception, all the more unfortunate in that because of his age, the young torero is hardly ready to stand up for himself, to present himself in the proper quarters and so to become launched upon his career. Empresarios everywhere tend to be cynical, and understandably so, on the subject of the neophyte torero. The empresarios pass their lives dodging apoderados and acquaintances who want contracts for some seventeen-year-old wonder out in the provinces. And would-be toreros lacking apoderados wander the roads, taking part when possible in capeas and tientas, hoping to attract attention to themselves. They too haunt the offices of the empresarios, knowing in advance that their chances of an interview and a contract are almost non-existent. Sometimes, the provincial wonders are given their chance, only to display ignorance and ineptness and to put the public off toreo for the next month. Therefore the empresario usually depends upon a private network of friends to furnish him information about promising young men. This in turn means a life of intrigue, rumor, and suspicion. It is all too chancy and disorganized, a foolish luxury made possible by the poverty of the countries in which toreo is established. There is no lack of talent in those countries, but there is a terrible lack of opportunity for the aspirant to practice upon the living animal and to develop his talent. Many young novilleros go into the plaza in rented suits of lights without ever having had an opportunity to kill with the sword. Before mechanization, it was at least possible to practice the estocada in the abattoirs, but no longer. The development of novilleros demands time and money, money which only the empresario or the ganadero commands. For the most part they have been short-sighted and brutal in their disregard of the young.

No art or profession is so difficult from its business side as that of the neophyte torero. There is no way of knowing how many young men, each year, set out seriously to become toreros, but they number thousands, of whom only a handful have the character, stubbornness, afición, connections, and good luck to survive to appear in a novillada with picadors. And only a fraction of those will go on to some sort of career. Assuming that the aspirant has talent and has been lucky enough to embark upon a career, he will be stopped by the peculiar demands of his profession, which require that he have capital, publicity, acumen in dealing with empresarios, ability to manage a cuadrilla, and to attend while in fairly constant motion to all the requirements of a good-sized business, unless he falls into the hands of an honest manager. In Spain, apoderados tend to be retired matadors who know their way about and are prepared to earn their ten per cent efficiently. In Mexico, however, the apoderado may be an ex-banderillero, or at worst a mere hanger-on in the ambiente, a man who has failed in the profession and who lurks about waiting for a gold mine in the form of a talented novillero to mismanage. Such men lack the resources, financial and intellectual, for the wise development of a young torero; as a result they often push a lad into a career for which he is not technically ready, force him to the big plazas where the money is, collect a fast commission, drop him, and wait for the next victim. The good apoderado must combine authority with restraint, judgment of his protégé's talent, business acumen, the respect of ganaderos and empresarios, and full technical knowledge of toros and toreo. Every career has its own rhythm, and every apoderado needs to respect that rhythm. No abuse is more common than the inflation in the press of a young torero's cartel before he has the technique to fulfill the resulting public expectations of him. This is squarely the apoderado's fault. It results in false starts, or total blighting of what might often be a genuine career. The conception of "suerte" seems to be responsible for much of the trouble. "Suerte," that word heard repeatedly, day and night, wherever toreros gather, means more than "good luck." It means blessings, good bulls, fine weather, full-breasted women and willing, profit, evasion of cogidas, clear sailing, and all manner of good fortune. It is both superstitious and religious in intent, and it creates trouble because the idea of suerte tends to take the place of training, technique, craft, intelligence, and organization in every branch of toreo. It may amount to an evasion of responsibility by empresario, apoderado and torero alike. The common human failing of excusing one's own defects and failures through bad luck is nowhere so prevalent as in toreo.

Once the young torero survives his first seasons of marginal living, corridas that cost him more money than they bring in and cast on him all the afflictions of poverty; once he and his apoderado begin to make money, to attain cartel, and to be sought out, another order of abuse may take place. Juan Verde, who has been cutting ears from every kind of bull he has faced, may decide in his fourth triumphal temporada that he has the best suerte with bulls from Rancho Seco, while the bulls from Rancho Azul send him into profound depression. He therefore begins to insist that bulls from Rancho Seco must be bought for him, to the delight of Don Y, the ganadero of Rancho Seco, who in turn finds himself influenced by the preference of the matador to select those qualities of comfortable horns, gentleness, and undangerous silliness that the matador prefers, ignoring the fact that the damage to his herd will persist for years after Juan Verde has retired. And the empresarios, knowing that Juan Verde can fill their plazas, are also willing to oblige by buying as many encierros as Don Y is prepared to sell them. They might on occasion even buy an encierro from Don Y's neighbor, Don Z, and pass them off as toros from Rancho Seco. Even later in his career, Juan Verde finds that competition from certain other matadors upsets him and forces him to do things that he no longer likes to do. As long as he can fill the plazas, his apoderado is able to hint to some empresarios that those disturbing matadors be kept off the programs of Juan Verde. Such abuses are not necessarily illegal, like horn shaving, but they run contrary to the spirit of the fiesta and are corrupting to the individuals involved. Juan Verde may not himself be corrupt, but once he becomes a figura he is no longer a mere human being. He is a valuable property to his apoderado, to the empresarios, and to the ganaderías, as though he were an oil well or the latest computer. If he has a bad day in the plaza, or a bad month, he will cause many people to lose a lot of money. And if he should get a cornada and be put out of action for anything from a few days to an entire season, the losses may be disastrous. It was the money-men's greed for insured investment that brought about horn shaving in the first place, not the corruption of toreros. No braver torero than Manolete ever entered the plaza, yet Manolete faced many a shaved horn.

No one is more firmly attached in the belly hair on the underside of toreo than some of the newspapermen who set up as taurine "critics." The facts of the case are notorious, obvious, and readily demonstrable. One has only to go to a poor corrida and see with one's own eyes what happens, then read a paid report of the event. It often goes like this: Matador de toros, Juan Verde, "El Rey," is in Málaga for a corrida. He has a hangover and does not much like the animals he has drawn in the sorteo; anyway, the crowd will be mostly ignorant tourists from the beaches. It is hot. His first bull is an overfed novillo; it comes out well, but El Rey allows his banderilleros to run it into the barreras repeatedly. El Rey then stalks out and delivers two verónicas without temple from a meter and a half out, then turns the animal over to a banderillero to bregar it to the horse. The novillo-toro takes four good pics, but El Rey is not moved to make any quites. With the muleta, he gives the animal half-a-dozen severe trincherazos, three derechazos, two molinetes, then he squares off for the sword. Running in on the quarter, he puts in a low sword, and the bull slowly chokes to death in its own blood while the banderilleros buzz it with their capes. El Rey bows to mild applause from the shade and jeers from the sunny side. His second animal, a true five-year-old and well-armed, is twisted, turned, and crashed into the barrera for minutes on end by the banderilleros, to the point that the bull is too exhausted and confused to take the matador's cape. By way of his first quite of the day after the third savage pic, El Rey makes one cowardly chicuelina, stepping away as the horn passes. Again with the muleta he punishes the animal brutally and unnecessarily, dances away during his derechazos, and requires two swords and four descabello attempts before the bull obliges by expiring. El Rey is hooted and whistled out of the plaza, amidst imaginative insults to his mother.

Next day, both the Madrid and the provincial papers, including the Málaga press, will print this account, for which Juan Verde's apoderado has paid out 5,000 pesetas of the maestro's money: "Málaga, July 8. Juan Verde, 'El Rey,' the maestro from Blank, demonstrated once again today before a delighted crowd which filled the Málaga plaza to the flagpoles the domination, grace, and art for which he is so justly famous. Appearing with X and Y, who were able to do little with their enemies from the renowned ganadería of Rancho Seco, El Rey's beautiful verónicas, replete with temple, to his first adversary, like his trincheras de Ortega and his statuesque derechazos to his second, were a lesson to the neophyte and an electrifying experience to the most skeptical aficionado. Although the maestro of Blank needed but one delicately placed sword to dispatch his first animal, a mysteriously insensitive president refused him the ears that the crowd so noisily demanded. With his second animal, a dangerous manso, El Rey's work was regular, and the maestro had to accept as his reward the prolonged applause of the enthusiastic multitude."

In fairness, it should be said that the better weeklies, such as *Dígame* and *El Ruedo* are far more likely than the daily press to print an accurate account of Juan Verde's fracasos, of his waste of two good bulls, his poor lidia and his lack of oficio in his performance at Málaga. Toreros and their apoderados are frank to admit that anything from twenty-five to forty per cent of a torero's fees goes to "publicity," and publicity means not only advertising but also bribes to critics. Rumor has it that when the "critic" of a large Madrid daily retired a few years ago, full of age and pesetas, he sold his job to his young successor for 6 million pesetas. There are other critics, particularly in Mexico, who are not necessarily venal, but simply lacking in technical knowledge. They develop favorites to whose defects they are blind, and the injury to toreo is almost as bad as the injury from frank corruption. The irony of bribery in toreo is that the very men who do the bribing stand to lose most by it. It is naively cynical for any apoderado to believe that the public cannot see for itself when a torero has failed with a bull. It is safe to say that no reputation has ever been established, maintained, or saved through lying publicity. Given the organization of the profession, publicity is unfortunately necessary, but genuine criticism is even more necessary. Unless it comes about soon, toreo can only degenerate into quaint spectacle.

Journalism on toreo in English and French is pretty disgusting, too, even though the writers are not bribed. Ignorance and vulgarity combine to justify the Latin contempt for foreign aficionados. Toreo is regarded as an underhanded although glamorous sport; the few reports of corridas written invariably appear on the sports page, according to which logic baseball news should be placed among the stock quotations. Magazines like *Life, Sports Illustrated,* and *Paris-Match*—all either Luce-owned or Luce-inspired—print occasional flashy features on toreo, in which misinformation about toreros, photographs of spectacular cogidas and cornadas, and various kinds of romantic claptrap compete for the readers' attention with photographs of talking dogs, film stars, and right-wing political propaganda. We expect nothing better from those sources. But when a newspaper of the reputation and pretensions to excellence of *The New York Times* turns to toreo, the product is no better. The shameless sports writer who now and then turns out a piece on "bullfighting" takes less care than he would in reporting a cat show. Contempt combines with silliness to produce pieces for the sports page on who is or is not *número uno* in Spain, biographical vignettes, reports of deaths, preferably from cornadas, and trivial gossip. That level of attention insults the intelligence not only of the aficionado but also of the general reader, who is given a misleading idea of the entire subject.

Motifs from toreo have been used intermittently over the years by that idiot cousin of journalism, advertising, but since 1963 they have proliferated alarmingly. A single issue of *The New Yorker* in September 1963, contained no fewer than three such advertisements, for fabric, carpets, and women's stretch pants. To sell those garments, the advertiser prints a montage: in the background, a torero bregando a rather indifferent-looking toro; foreground, superimposed upon the sand of the plaza and the spectators in the tendidos, a shapely model, pubic region prominent in full center. Text: "Sportmaker's sleek and shapely stretch pants can distract the most dedicated aficionado. A brilliant Milliken blend of wool and ENKA nylon, Torero fits your figure smoothly, moves when you do, refuses to sag." Etc. This junk, which now abounds in magazines and newspapers, is often fairly funny and in itself harmless. What is alarming is that advertising agencies and the sexless people who try to set fashions for women now consider toreo chic, glamorous, and possessed of the cachet that helps them to sell merchandise. In the past whenever they have taken up something intrinsically good, they have performed a kind of intellectual defecation upon it, so alienating the many people who find that process unpleasant, not only from the merchandise, but also from the intermediate object: witness American baseball players endorsing liquids to rub in the armpits, reproductions of the Mona Lisa to sell macaroni, or that related wonder, Michelangelo's "Pietà" on view at the New York World's Fair. Toreo will hold its own against pants stretched over the pubis, just as Leonardo will hold his own against macaroni, but in the meantime both art and the public have been denigrated. This, too, belongs to the underside of toreo.

At another extreme of taurine journalism is the monthly magazine *Toros,* published in California. For all its defects of literacy—and some of its contributors write only in ungrammatical cliché—the magazine displays a concept of toreo worthy of its subject, its coverage is quite thorough, and its campaigns to correct abuses in Mexico are welcome. The reports from Spain of Angus McNab and Luis Stumer, and some of the articles by the retired matadora, Patricia McCormick, are better than anything in the Spanish press anywhere. *A la Lucha,* a monthly newssheet published by the Club Taurino of London and unfortunately not available to the general public, contains some of the best reportage and reflections upon toreo in English. In spite of its title—why "lucha"?—the editors display a philosophy of what toreo should and can be, together with a knowledge of technique that is altogether admirable.

In Spain and in Latin America, criticism and reporting of toreo is almost uniformly pedestrian. The work of Antonio Diaz-Canabate in *ABC* (Madrid) and in the weekly periodical *El Ruedo* marks an exception, as do the reports in *Exito* (Mexico City), some of the reports in *Universal* (Mexico City), and some of the work of Raúl de la Puente in *Ultima Hora* and *La Prensa* (Lima). Among Spanish periodicals, *Digame* was formerly quite reliable, although by the summer of 1965 one must report that it seemed to be falling off in quality. *El Ruedo* is as good as any, while *El Burladero* has taken the large step of ruling out toreros' paid advertising. *Fiesta Española* and the other periodicals that come and go are dominated by toreros' paid advertising and by flattering interviews with non-entities and entities.

Until the Spanish-speaking world can support many publications of the quality of the best in *Toros* and *A la Lucha,* all toreo will remain threatened by its own sulfurous underside. As it is, with empresarios thinking only, or first, of profit, with ganaderos willing to cut corners under a multiplicity of pressures, apoderados interested in toreros as business-producing things rather than as men and artists, too great a burden to uphold the fiesta is placed upon the torero alone. It is burden enough for him to maintain his sense of oficio before the toros in the plaza; he should not have to resist single-handed the massed pressures of mass society. For that, after all, is what we are talking about when we discuss the abuses of good faith in toreo. Mass society at once threatens aesthetic standards, through its ignorance of and challenge to tradition and through its sheer monetary power. In the other arts, a disciplined and almost comically aggressive body of intellectuals exists to push back the enemy by analyzing his every motive, judging his strength, gauging the caliber of his weapons, and attempting to reduce his strength through encouragement to desert. Journals of opinion are at hand, parts of the public press are sometimes available, and thus the battle is not impossibly unequal. In toreo, by contrast, no comparable resistance is yet possible, when the most essential weapon, an objective press and an informed body of criticism is not only lacking, but the men responsible have been preparing the ground for the enemy before his appearance. It is to the honor of a handful of writers in Spain and Mexico, many ganaderos, some empresarios, some apoderados, and a large number of toreros, that toreo has survived in the purity it still possesses. The future will be more difficult, for mass society, the enemy, is still forming ranks. The casual ways of the past in recruiting toreros, above all, are too wasteful to be continued. What is required are academies of toreo, endowed by the toreros' unions, the empresarios, the ganaderos, and possibly by government, in which not only toreo, but the humanities at large would be taught. Such academies, with the refusal of toreros to pay bribes, would aid substantially in eliminating the underside and in sweetening the ambiente.[3]

---

[3] Rumors in the Spanish press in the spring of 1965 had it that a Portuguese, one Luis Pinto Maeso, was on the point of getting Spanish government support for just such an academy, to be directed by Antonio Bienvenida. The writers are unable to find any substance to such rumors, however.

# CHAPTER 8

# THE BULLS
# OF FICTION

". . . GET ONE THING STRAIGHT," Pancho Camioneto emphasized. "To get to be a *torero* there's only one road: close to the horns. The cars, the clothes, the eats three times a day, the houses, the women, the applause, the friends—they're right there between the bull's withers. They're sitting there for anyone to grab, but nobody who isn't hung right gets them."

"I got the guts, you know that," answered Luis, seated now on the stirrup board that runs around the fence inside the ring.

"It's not just a question of guts, Luis. As I always say, as they all say, you got to throw some brains at the bull, not just guts. How many of us have had it at first and then messed it all up the second time around! Thousands of us—"

"Not me."

"I'm going to damn well see to it. You're either coming out a *torero* or you're coming out feet first."[1]

With sinking spirit, the aficionado will recognize this for what it is; not Mickey Spillane on American gangsters, not Jean Genêt and his homosexual fantasies, not a comic-book text on toreo, but a serious novel which won a literary prize in Mexico and was translated into American gutter language by an aficionado who should have known better. Although Spota's *The Wounds of Hunger* is less than run-of-the-mill for novels on toreo, it comes

---

[1] Luis Spota, *The Wounds of Hunger,* trans. Barnaby Conrad (Penguin Books, 1961), p. 21. (Spanish title, *Más cornadas da el hambre,* Mexico, 1949.)

close to representing all too many. The translator says in his peculiar foreword, "Let me say straight off that this is the most powerful bullfighting novel I have ever read." And he quotes with approval the demented judgment of a Mexican literary critic to the effect that Montherlant's *Les Bestiaires* (*The Matador*) is "hogwash" next to Spota's book. Further, "Hemingway's writing on the bulls is good. Spota's is better."[2] *The Wounds of Hunger* is in fact an amateurish narrative of a few months in the life of Luis Ortega, an eighteen-year-old Mexican novillero who survives the blandishments of a homosexual apoderado, quantities of hetero-sexual activity, life with a prostitute, the death by cornada of a friend, drink, marijuana, poverty, homelessness, the death of his mother, the corrupt machinations of empresarios, and his own witlessness to achieve a contract to appear in Plaza México, and by implication, to go on to fame, death, and apotheosis. Written with no distinction whatsoever and translated with even less, the novel's only attraction is for the large body of readers who enjoy vicarious sex, violence, and a view of the world as pestiferous as the bottom of a garbage pail. The novel shows how naturalism has become debased into a kind of voyeurism, while its large sale is a measure of the appetites of the mass market. To the unwary, the justification for Spota's garbage-pail view of toreo is that the writer is dealing in truth, no matter how unsavory. In fact, anyone who knows toreo, Mexico, Mexican novilleros, or literature will recognize at once that Spota's truths are false, and his conception so special as to be neurotic. Amidst the tequila, marijuana, vomit and semen, one finds nothing of the generosity, humor, sweetness, and simplicity of the Mexicans, little of the decency of many of the people of the ambiente, nor any conception of toreo beyond testicles and greed for money. Spota's passes are all given on the knees, and all his bulls are resabios. As toreo and as literature, the novel is unconscious, humorless parody of a dozen best-sellers.

Spota had been a novillero and had some interior knowledge of toreo when he wrote; one's quarrel is with his judgment and taste rather than with his knowledge. *The Corrida at San Feliu,* by Paul Scott, provokes a very different kind of quarrel. Scott knows nothing of toreo, he makes much in the novel of his central character's ignorance and dislike of the bulls, yet he places great symbolic weight upon toreo, with the result that the reader rejects his

---

[2] *The Wounds of Hunger*, p. 7.

authority in every dimension of his ambitious novel. However disappointing, the novel is a serious work concerning the life of an English writer, Edward Thornhill, his early successes in fiction, the drying up of his talent in his late middle age, his forty-year-old wife's betrayal of him, and their death in a motor accident on the night of the corrida. The narration is not straightforward, but by allusion to a story Thornhill has written, through episodes from novels he has been unable to go on with, by action, real or illusory, parallel to the central narrative which the reader must construct in his own mind. The result, which often reads like a college writing-seminar assignment to construct a novel in the manner of William Faulkner, places undue emphasis upon the culminating episode, the corrida of the title. Thornhill, who has always gone to Spain "especially not to see the bulls,"[3] has rented a villa on the Costa Brava from an aficionado, in whose library is a collection of books on toreo. Unable to write, Thornhill has idly read among them, and comes to use terms from toreo in thinking of himself in relation to his wife's betrayal; he would take up a "querencia" rather than fight his beach-boy rival, who seems to taunt him like a matador.[4] (Montherlant had used this technique brilliantly in *Chaos and Night*, of 1963.) Thornhill's attendance at the corrida is part of his resignation at his wife's betrayal, a product both of design and of chance. Once there, the author takes us painfully through six bulls, his reasonably adequate style of the previous chapters deserting him for imitation Hemingway. Of the preliminary cape work he writes, "This time Ordoñez passed it with a suave natural that turned the bull into a position from which, turning himself, he faced it at an angle of forty-five degrees and from there cited and passed it with what looked like a superb verónica cargando la suerte, which was repeated from the other side, and then again from the original side, so that for three distinct movements bull and man seemed to flow together. With each pass the crowd roared. At the end of the third cargando la suerte Ordoñez lifted one hand high and dropped the other low and as the bull came in spun round in a graceful chicuelina and so came to the remate, the finishing pass. He began to swirl the cape round, let go with his left hand, which he put behind him so that he could grasp and gather the cape as it swung up to meet him.

---

[3] Paul Scott, *The Corrida at San Feliu* (New York, Morrow, 1964), p. 4.
[4] *The Corrida,* p. 138.

The bull, coming in, was turned and fixed, the cape gone. Ordoñez walked away."[5] This peculiar sequence, with its mixture of
verónicas and adornos, its passes for lances, and its creation of a
new lance, the "cargando la suerte," is all the more chilling for
being attributed not to a fictional character but to the historical
Ordóñez. It is more than a lapse, for it deflates all the effects that
Scott has built up. The novel as a whole becomes false because of
the inexplicable carelessness of what is intended to be a high
point.

The question for us is why the art of toreo, once having
attracted as many writers as it has, should have produced so much
downright bad writing. That question needs to be answered because even the non-literary aficionado, particularly if he is not
Spanish and cannot easily get his fill of the real thing, reads some
or much of the fiction written on the subject. His conception of
toreo is necessarily influenced, and the creation of a body of
criticism, so essential to toreo, may be impeded or accelerated by
what the aficionado will accept in the related art of fiction. To
whoever has bothered to read through the fiction on toreo, it is self-
evident that novels devoted exclusively to the subject, like Spota's,
are without distinction. Certain first-rate novelists have used toreo
as a background, but that is another matter which we shall come to
presently.

Responsibility for the pedestrian work on toreo of writers in
several languages lies in the subject itself, and in the literary
traditions available. The subject of toreo may be compared to war
as a theme, and to the difficulties that war novelists have experienced. Both subjects are attractive, but both conceal traps for even
the most wary and talented of writers. War attracts because it
looks easy to frame, either grandiosely through an entire campaign, as Tolstoy did in *War and Peace,* or in miniature, through
the experience of a handful of men, as Stephen Crane did in *The
Red Badge of Courage.* War is nothing if not dramatic, serious,
and even tragic. It offers, ready-made, the possibilities of beginning, middle, and end. Despite this, few novelists have been able
to cope successfully with the subject. The very reality of war, its
historical and personal reach, creates ready-made attitudes and
situations that inhibit the play of imagination; the reader of a war
novel cannot give himself to the novelist, for he is restrained by

[5] *The Corrida,* pp. 246–247.

history itself. The drama of fact is not at all the same as the drama of fiction, thus war makes demands upon technique which few writers can satisfy. War is both literal and apocalyptic, vast in implication yet limiting to the artist in usable artifact. It enforces upon the ambitious writer an intellectual grasp of the social and historical forces that produce war, while at the same time it demands the imaginative sympathy and insight required to save the narrative from mere sociology. In our literature of war there are many runners-up: Stephen Crane, Norman Mailer, James Jones, Evelyn Waugh; the masters are few: Tolstoy, André Malraux, perhaps Ernest Hemingway.

Toreo as a subject also promises prefabricated solutions to the hard problems of structure, movement, and action. Like war, toreo is not only obviously and implicitly serious, too dramatic and too tragic, but it also invites the Spotas, men who are satisfied with obvious, mechanical people in mechanical situations. Toreo creates still another difficulty that war does not. The novelist of toreo is required to transpose the matter of one art into another, one of the most difficult things in the world to bring off. Prose fiction, after all, is not toreo, nor is it painting or music. Not even Thomas Mann, a great artist with considerable knowledge of music, could create convincingly in prose the structure, tone, form and effects in the music of his composer-hero, Adrian Leverkuhn, in *Doctor Faustus,* in all other respects a major achievement. Mann leaves us with cold, exterior description, not re-creation or evocation. Hence the novelist who would do justice to toreo needs a conception of toreo equal to that of a great torero, one founded upon full knowledge of toros, of lidia, and of the entire ambiente. Unless one is a torero, such knowledge is hard to come by, and toreros are not writers. By this one does not mean to prescribe, arrogantly, how the novelist should write, but only to emphasize the difficulties of transposing the art-form of toreo into an alien medium, the novel. Neither are we suggesting that the novel of toreo, or the war novel, forms a significant aesthetic category, any more than novels about farming or banking are such. Subject matter does not of itself create form.

Modern novels and handbooks of toreo alike tend to have lurid titles, apparently intended to terrorize the reader into attention, and to dramatize blood and death, just as alarming headlines, photographs of corpses, naked women and screaming children are designed to sell tabloid newspapers: *Blood and Sand, Glittering*

*Death, Love Lies Bleeding, The Wounds of Hunger, Death in the Afternoon, The Death of Manolete, The Gates of Fear.* Many of these novels (as well as the handbooks) have two curious grandfathers, one French and one Spanish, and an American uncle—Prosper Mérimée, Vicente Blasco Ibáñez, and Ernest Hemingway. The literary trail from Mérimée's *Carmen* (1846), through Blasco Ibáñez' *Blood and Sand* (1908), to *The Sun Also Rises* (1926) and *Death in the Afternoon* (1932) of Hemingway both accounts for the best and the worst in the contemporary novel, and reflects the history of the modern novel up to a very recent date. In the name of romanticism, Mérimée committed the first grave sin against toreo by writing *Carmen,* which through the accident of Bizet's opera, achieved a currency which the slight tale of itself never could have merited. Mérimée wrote in the full flush of French romanticism, seeking out the remote, the exotic, and the unusual. Although there is virtually nothing of genuine toreo in the narrative, *Carmen* first as opera and a long second as narrative had the dubious distinction of establising a convention and a cliché in the minds of generations to come of the "toreador" as exotic, inexplicable, doomed and damned, his only humanity his erotic attraction and his mortality. All the rest is operatic posturing, and one can only agree that Bizet chose his libretto wisely. Théophile Gautier's *Militone,* of the same period, is written in the same convention as *Carmen,* and if possible with less distinction. Neither Mérimée nor Gautier had the slightest knowledge of toreo beyond that available to any casual traveler, but both established an attitude in the minds of readers and writers, Spanish included, which retains its vitality to this day. Because the romantic view makes no demands, it is always preferred by the lazy. As we have noted before, toreo, by the important part of its nature which combines the figure of the exceptional man and his control over nature in the form of the bull, simply *is* romantic. If the writer glorifies that romantic aspect to the exclusion of the discipline and control that is equally present although not so obvious, the product can only be absurd and in the worst sense operatic. The romantic mode, appropriate to the compulsions of Herman Melville or Victor Hugo, is least suited to toreo.

Blasco Ibáñez, who approached toreo with the anti-romantic animus of naturalism, perceived the falsity of the romantic convention and set out to rectify it. A fervent admirer of Flaubert and Zola, Blasco Ibáñez would reform Spain through the pseudo sci-

ence of literary naturalism in the manner of Zola, with its preference for unpleasant subjects not previously found in art, its belief
that the novel was a kind of laboratory in which the scientist-
novelist simply observed and recorded the actions of his characters,
which actions were rigorously determined by heredity and en-
vironment. The more painful and brutal an event, the more truth
it was likely to contain, according to the naturalists, whose theory
was a rebuttal of the romantic dream of reality and a complete
rejection of romantic optimism. For the naturalist, all lovers were
syphilitics, all babies had rickets, all mothers cancer, and all wheat
fields were blighted with rust. Believing toreo to be a social evil,
Blasco Ibáñez intended to destroy it with a study of the entire
ambiente and a history of the career of a torero, Juan Gallardo, in
*Blood and Sand.* Ironically enough, Blasco Ibáñez failed in his
efforts because he failed to see the philosophical shabbiness of
naturalism as a doctrine, and he failed to see that in the writing of
the naturalists whom he admired there remained a wide streak of
the softest and most sentimental side of romanticism. The naturalists' preference for the grand subject—one which would encompass
nations, not neighborhoods—led them to the grandiose, and once
there they fell back upon the conventions already at hand, the
very conventions of romanticism which they had gone out to
destroy. For *Blood and Sand,* Blasco Ibáñez set off, notebook in
hand, to "work up" toreo, much like Flaubert "working up" the
medical details of Emma Bovary's death. Much of the detail he
industriously accumulated about the ambiente has the authority
of observed truth, and although certain details, such as Gallardo's
dressing for the corrida at the beginning of the novel, are inaccurate, they are unimportant. More important is the lack of detail
and of authority whenever Gallardo appears in the plaza before a
toro. Lacking afición, Blasco Ibáñez either did not know or did
not care about the techniques of lidia; in any event, his chosen
method, naturalism, let him down seriously at points of crisis in
the novel. But the major failure of the novel is not in such matters
but in the shift in tone and emphasis that occurs when the author
introduces Plumitas, the bandit, and doña Sol, the aristocrat with
whom Gallardo falls in love. With these characters and their
operatic background we are plunged back fifty years to *Carmen,* to
exotic, flamenco Spain—to the romantic cliché, in short. Dialogue
turns wooden, action becomes all too predictable, and the novel
breaks in two. Neither the notebook nor romantic convention has

substituted for imaginative grasp and projection, and the fragments of truth in the novel are editorial truths, as well or better incorporated in articles. Yet because of Blasco Ibáñez' subject, toreo, and the fact that he was undoubtedly a writer of some power, *Blood and Sand* has survived. It has survived, however, as an extension of romantic conventions, not as Blasco Ibáñez intended, as a denial of them. And ironically, there is sufficient power in the episodes on toreo to send the aficionado to the plaza for more, rather than to disgust him with a barbarous spectacle.

Spanish novelists of the first rank who have written about toreo, such as Benito Pérez Galdós and Pío Baroja, have done so incidentally and in passing. Galdós in *Episodios nacionales* and Baroja in *Memorias de un hombre de acción* are concerned with other matters, and toreo plays no real part in their imaginative constructions. The others, Eduardo López Bago, Joaquín López Pinillos, Alejandro Pérez Lugín, José Más, or Alberto Insúa, wrote either romantic variations upon *Carmen,* or rather uninspired, if competent, journalism slightly disguised as fiction. An exception must be made for Ramón Gómez de la Serna's *El Torero Caracho,* although this work is hardly a novel but rather an inventive fantasy, almost Joycean in its use of language. Characteristically, although Gómez de la Serna earned a small but enduring reputation through *El Torero Caracho,* the book is virtually unobtainable, nor has it been translated.

One might think that in contemporary Spain, where there are signs that writers are emerging from the long silence that accompanies wars and repressive politics, significant work in fiction on toreo might have appeared, for if not in Spain, where? Yet the only novel of any ambition of the last several years seems to be *El Torero* of Javier Martínez de Bedoya (Madrid, 1953?), a naively pretentious narrative which combines the most unfortunate influences of the nineteenth century with the most deplorable of the twentieth. Containing enough incident for six novels, *El Torero* presents the complete life histories not only of Fermín Montes, the torero of the title, but of his crooked apoderado, the three—count them, three—women who are in love with him, various toreros he is pitted against, and sundry others who have little to do with anything. The biography of the apoderado, who began life as a smuggler, is pure Mérimée of the early nineteenth century; the biography of Ivonne, the French girl who comes to play an amorous part in Montes' career, is pure *Vogue* magazine, and the horn shaving, which provides the melodramatic plot, is pure *Life*. Bedoya knows less about toreo than the greenest tourist; his torero, even though he faces animals that have been tampered with, receives never a scratch in the process of killing hundreds of them. Bedoya wisely avoids scenes in the plaza, but when he must take his toreros there, the resulting prose has the emptiness of the naturalist who has not done his homework. One would have thought that this abysmal pastiche would not have been suitable even for a bad film, but it did in fact account for the French film *Châteaux en Espagne*. Novel and film together are further evidence of the encroachment of mass society upon Spanish culture.

The most pervasive single literary influence in the fiction of toreo has not been French or Spanish, but American, in the person of Ernest Hemingway. Hemingway's work was of another order altogether from anything on the subject written in Europe, and to make sense of it one must see it in relation to certain biographical and literary facts in the career of that fascinating writer. Having served as an ambulance driver while still a young boy on the Italian front in World War I, Hemingway was appalled by war, death, and a society in which such madness was made to seem rational, where men were given medals for butchering one another. By nature and instinct floridly romantic, Hemingway was drawn to the quintessentially romantic themes of love, honor, and death. After seeing both the negative and the positive faces of war—the negative producing horror and death, the positive producing occasional acts of honor and even heroism—Hemingway went into the postwar world to search compulsively for those situations of extremity and stress in which men behave with their instincts, noble or base, rather than rationally. He wrote therefore of gangsters, boxers, soldiers, the race track, gamblers, hunters, fishermen, lovers, and, inevitably, of toreo. His formal education in a midwestern American high school was necessarily slight; he became something of an autodidact and displayed throughout his life the autodidact's suspicion and contempt for formally trained intellect. That circumstance only partially accounts for the apparent simplicity, or simple-mindedness, of most of his characters. It must be clear to us now that he was fully aware of his romanticism, suspicious of it, and determined to control it through technique. He succeeded triumphantly.

In one of his posthumously published autobiographical sketches, Hemingway writes that he swore early in his career to write only of what he knew, and to try to give only the essentials. Again he succeeded triumphantly, to the extent that he revolutionized English prose style. Beguilingly readable, the style of his best work conceals the extraordinary intellectual control that Hemingway was able to exert. That it later became mannered to the point of self-parody and that a generation of writers, attempting to imitate him, produced only superficial trickery, should not demean his achievement. He shaped the mind of his time as perhaps only one other contemporary artist, Picasso, has done.

Hemingway apprehended death and used it thematically as no one had done in English since the seventeenth century. To the American mind, and in a lesser degree to the English too, life is all, and talk or writing of death is bad manners. Religious although not pious or orthodox, Hemingway's Catholicism stood him in good stead. It may have given him his conception of dying well, even nobly; he studied death for literary purposes as Fabre studied insects. Dying well implied having lived well; it was an ultimate in tension, and it supplied him with his cherished device of that situation in which more is implied than stated. Death for Hemingway was serious in the sense that it was serious for St. John of the Cross and John Donne; a portion of Hemingway's triumph was his uncanny ability to give death the religious overtones of the great religious writers without mentioning God.

Given Hemingway's experience, character, and predilections, it was inevitable that he should have gone to toreo for a subject. At the same time, it is equally obvious that his conception of toreo from the outset was off balance through his active search for the theme of death. It is for this reason that Spanish readers are often amused by Hemingway, and sometimes contemptuous of his title, *Death in the Afternoon*. As one torero said to me (J. M.), "We do not go into the plaza to die. We go there to live, to earn our bread. Why does this Hemingway not call his book *Life in the Afternoon?*" Hemingway does not set out, like the naturalist Blasco Ibáñez, to say all about toreo, either to denigrate or to glorify it; rather he sees in toreo the possibility of projecting his obsessions with behavior under stress, and above all death. He will *use* toreo for his very special ends, and if in using it he may also abuse it, he either does not know or care. Not only his prose fiction in *The Sun Also Rises* (1926)—*Fiesta* in England—"The Undefeated" (1925), and "The Capital of the World" (1936), but also his journalism and *Death in the Afternoon* indicate his special, personal, oblique view of toreo. He is far more interested in the man, the matador, than in the bulls, in how the matador gets in trouble with the bulls, and above all in how he dies on the horns of the bull. For all its virtues and its splendid writing, *Death in the Afternoon* is foremost a fascinating necrology. Hemingway ransacked the ambiente for tales of blood, guts, and death; the professional torero's view that a cornada may be heroic, but is more likely the result of stupidity is never broached in Hemingway's writing. That view probably would not have interested him, for his center of attention was elsewhere: not on toreo roundly and fully but on those aspects of toreo, men's behavior as he interpreted it, under stress. Through discipline and intelligence magically able to evoke scene and atmosphere and to endow his view with apparent authenticity, Hemingway has often been considered a naturalist for that almost oppressive authority. He is not. His work is far too stylized and his loyalties far too uncommitted, he is too much pure artist to be forced into that ill-fitting straight jacket.

Hemingway's novel *The Sun Also Rises* is a masterpiece in small that might be considered as the only war novel in which no shot is fired but the rocket setting off the fiesta of San Fermín at Pamplona. The time is 1924; the characters are Jake Barnes, an American newspaperman based on Paris and his expatriate friends, some floating members of the minor English gentry, and the toreros at Pamplona; but the subterranean, dominant theme of the novel is the Great War and its effects upon the survivors. The sympathetic characters have either been in the war or are toreros. Their shared experience has given them a common view, a common set of values, and even a private language. Cohn, the Jewish writer, is outside the charmed circle. He behaves badly; he will not accept that he is not wanted, he is self-indulgent; he weeps shamelessly at his failure with Brett Ashley and lays about with his fists in his frustration. Jake Barnes, who is both central character and center of consciousness, upon whose mind and vision all the events of the novel are recorded, has been literally castrated by war wounds. The land he sees is waste, as much so as T. S. Eliot's *Waste Land* of 1922. Lady Brett Ashley's wound, the inverse of Barnes', is inordinate sexual appetite; she and Barnes are in love but never in bed. She travels with Michael Campbell, weakling, drunkard and bankrupt; she spends a week at San Sebastián with Cohn, whom she despises, and she lunges at Pedro Romero, the young torero, finally inducing Barnes to turn her over to Romero, to Barnes' self-disgust. Lady Brett, age 34, behaves well, however, by refusing to continue her affair with Romero, age 19, after perhaps two weeks. Although morality as such is almost never on the surface of the page, conduct, whether moral or immoral, is Hemingway's exclusive subject. The moral problems of an immoral world occupy his fullest attention, as though he were a puritan divine rather than a twentieth-century writer.

We know this not from the moralizing of either writer or characters but through the symbolical burden placed upon toreo. The fiesta at Pamplona occupies the center of the novel, just as the characters' response to toreo is a measure of their human value in the eyes of Jake Barnes:

> We often talked about bulls and bull-fighters. I had stopped at the Montoya for several years. We never talked for very long at a time. It was simply the pleasure of discovering what we each felt. Men would come in from distant towns and before they left Pamplona stop and talk for a few minutes with Montoya about bulls. These men were aficionados. Those who were aficionados could always get rooms even when the hotel was full. Montoya introduced me to some of them. They were always very polite at first, and it amused them very much that I should be an American. Somehow it was taken for granted that an American could not have aficion. He might simulate it or confuse it with excitement, but he could not really have it. When they saw that I had aficion, and there was no password, no set questions that could bring it out, rather it was a sort of oral spiritual examination with the questions always a little on the defensive and never apparent, there was this same embarrassed putting the hand on the shoulder, or a 'Buen hombre.' But nearly always there was the actual touching. It seemed as though they wanted to touch you to make it certain.[6]

This is just one of many passages in which the world of toreo, specialized, inhabited by men of a stature gained through discrimination, enclosed in its aura of knowledgeability and discipline, is equated by implication with the society of soldiers in war, who make a virtue of necessity and discover decent qualities in one another under their exposure to situations of stress. Hemingway alludes to the war only lightly and in passing, but his allusions are sufficient to keep the subject subtly in the reader's view. Of a meal the main characters take together after an argument, he writes, "It

---

[6] Ernest Hemingway, *The Sun Also Rises* (New York, 1954), p. 132.

was like certain dinners I remember from the war. There was much wine, an ignored tension, and a feeling of things coming that you could not prevent happening."[7] And later, when the fiesta is underway, Bill Gorton and Mike Campbell tell Barnes of having seen men running before the bulls in the streets:

> "The steers took them in, in the end," Mike said.
> "It took about an hour."
> "It was really about a quarter of an hour," Mike objected.
> "Oh, go to hell," Bill said. "You've been in the war. It was two hours and a-half for me."[8]

This reference to the disparity between clock time and time in combat, time in terror, serves to enhance the atmosphere of experience shared, the characters' right to a private language and private jokes; in the war veterans' exclusiveness Hemingway creates an exact counterpart of the private language and the shared tastes of the aficionados.

Hemingway's actual use of toreo in the novel is efficient; nevertheless the portrayal is flawed to the degree that the structure of the work is undermined. Despite the extent of his talent, Hemingway felt obliged to insist upon his expertise, whether he was writing of fishing, shooting, boxing, or toreo, a habit that has set many a reader's teeth on edge. His expertise in toreo, assuredly greater than that of many aficionados, was in fact not so overpowering as he would give the reader to believe. At this point in his afición, he seemed to favor the cape over the muleta; his descriptions of cape work are impeccable, both in terms of the toros' conditions and in terms of lidia. He described effects, but he prepared us for the effects through his precision in observing and recording technique. The faenas are another matter:

> During Romero's first bull his hurt face had been very noticeable. Everything he did showed it. *All the concentration of the awkwardly delicate working with the bull* that could not see well brought it out. The fight with Cohn had not touched his spirit, but his face had been smashed and his body hurt. He was wiping all that out now. *Each thing that he did with this bull* wiped that out a little cleaner. *It was a good bull, a big bull, and with horns, and it turned and re-charged easily and surely.* He was what Romero wanted in bulls.
> *When he had finished his work with the muleta* and was ready

---

[7] *The Sun Also Rises*, p. 146.
[8] *The Sun Also Rises*, p. 200.

to kill, the crowd made him go on. They did not want the bull killed yet, they did not want it to be over. Romero went on. *It was like a course in bull-fighting. All the passes he linked up, all completed, all slow, templed and smooth. There were no tricks and no mystifications. There was no brusqueness.* And each pass as it reached the summit gave you a sudden ache inside. The crowd did not want it ever to be finished.[9]

From the italicized passages, those which have to do with the actual faena, it is clear that Hemingway is concentrating upon effect, not on the thing itself. Any authority present is the authority of emotion, which in turn is linked to the theme of the narrative as a whole: the relationship between Brett, Barnes, Cohn, and Pedro Romero. Hemingway skillfully creates the illusion of a faena, but he does not create the faena. In itself this is not a flaw, although the expertise of "Take it from me, reader, and I know, it was a great faena," may annoy. The illusion is at odds with what happens when Hemingway does become specific, as in his description of Romero killing a un tiempo: "The bull charged as Romero charged. Romero's left hand dropped the muleta over the bull's muzzle to blind him, his left shoulder went forward between the horns as the sword went in. . . ."[10] Had Hemingway known what he pretended to know, he would have been aware that the last thing a matador wants at the moment described is to "blind" the bull. He wants the bull to follow the muleta smoothly, as he has educated the animal to do throughout his entire lidia; only if the bull *follows* the cloth can the matador make his exit. But to blind the bull during the estocada is to ask for a horn in the stomach. It is Hemingway himself who asks for this sort of niggling criticism through his knowingness, through his affectation of specific, professional language and detail.

A more serious flaw is the introduction of Juan Belmonte into the narrative (and one remembers Lorenzo Garza in Spota's, and Ordóñez in Scott's). It is a flaw because the writer's fictional reality, so carefully constructed, is violated rudely by the comparison with historical reality in the person of the historical individual. The several pages on Belmonte are no more than an editorial attack upon him, an essay that violates the fictional illusion and has the unfortunate effect of showing off Heming-

---

[9] *The Sun Also Rises,* pp. 219–220.
[10] *The Sun Also Rises,* p. 218.

way's knowingness through his café gossip assassination of an extraordinary torero.

Which novel, however, is not flawed? Like the perfect corrida, the perfect novel is an ideal rarely or perhaps never completely realized in the real world. Through toreo, Hemingway in *The Sun Also Rises* is able to project a view of the world that has enduring validity. His theme, the disintegration of values accomplished by war and all that makes war possible, is too large, shattering, abstract, and unwieldy to confront directly. Writers like Hermann Broch in *The Sleepwalkers* who have confronted it directly, have come to grief. "Pure" toreo and the almost virginal purity and decency of Pedro Romero offer the possibility of a rounded, comprehensible analogue to Hemingway's interior vision of one side of humanity, while Brett Ashley's virtual rape of Romero provides a dramatic analogue to what has happened to Barnes, and to many young men in all our wars. Toreo is at the center of the work, but it is not the central subject; it is related to the novel as an architectural plan is related to the finished building. Toreo gave Hemingway the uncluttered, apparent yet not obvious symbolic frame that he needed, and it suggested a technique only the shadow of which his imitators were to apprehend. The force and essence of his work remain his alone, for like any writer of his excellence he is inimitable.

Superficially Hemingway looks imitable, and imitations abound. Numerous unimaginative writers have reproduced the short sentences, the diction, and the apparent mindlessness of the characters, unaware that these and other devices conceal while they reveal themes that are neither mindless nor unimaginative. His ability was to convey the results of thought through action and through sensuous processes. Where he achieved tension, his imitators achieve only melodrama and violence. In spite of appearances, he is one of the most intellectual of writers. Subtract from his work the tension between thought, however unregistered on the page, and action, and all that remains is mannerism. It is then a short way from Lady Brett's Muratti cigarettes, Barnes' menus, his Valdepeñas and Château Margaux wines to the resounding vulgarity of Ian Fleming's James Bond, with his Chesterfields and his specially ground breakfast coffee. So in the fiction of toreo, cheap vulgarity in dialogue replaces Hemingway's witty obscenity; film scenarios in the guise of fiction replace his symbolic narrative.

Between his fiction on toreo and *Death in the Afternoon,*

Hemingway hypnotized virtually every subsequent novelist of toreo. Belden, the narrator of *Love Lies Bleeding,* by Peter Viertel, is all too clearly modeled upon the figure of Jake Barnes. He too is a veteran of war, he is world-weary, afflicted with a blighted love affair in the recent past, and presented as unable to love rather than incapable of love. He glumly recounts the return from retirement of Juan Ramon Vasquez, master torero, and his rivalry with the rising star of Ortega, who is cast in the role of the young man predestined to supplant Vasquez in public favor. Vasquez is burdened with much money, too many seasons in the plaza, a pregnant wife, two mistresses, and a dying father. The father inevitably dies, the maestro inevitably gets two grave cornadas from his rivalry with Ortega, and Belden inevitably leaves Spain in the bitter, elegiac manner of Barnes leaving Pamplona. Both the ambiente and the scenes in the plaza are done well, but they are neither dramatic nor imaginative; they never get beyond inspired reportage, nor does the work as a whole. Belden's disenchantment, like Vasquez' problems, is merely described; it is never imaginatively constructed. Early on, one realizes that Viertel has gone beyond Hemingway's first novel for his model to the embarrassing journalism of "The Dangerous Summer." Vasquez and Ortega are all too recognizably Dominguín and Ordóñez, and Viertel has not pretended to recast his models for the purposes of fiction. Thus we are left with the uneasy feeling that results from the mixture of fiction with nonfiction, like mixing Scotch whisky with Pepsi-Cola. Floridly overwritten and often ungrammatical, the novel also shows the influence of Hemingway's late, self-parodying style: Vasquez tells Belden of having tried to help an *espontáneo*\* in the plaza, only to find that the boy was too terrified to face the bull again. ". . . he had lost the blind momentum of his courage and was faced with the big fear every torero feels, every artist: the fear of not being able to perform,

---

\**Espontáneo:* Literally "Spontaneous one"; that is, not on the cartel. Usually an untrained youth who leaps into the plaza with a homemade muleta to attempt passes before he is either knocked down by the bull or carried away by the cuadrilla. A stupid performance all around, for it may unsettle a good bull, and more important, teach him the difference between man and lure. At least one torero has been killed because of the work of an espontáneo. With the exception of Manuel Benitez, virtually no torero has begun his career as an espontáneo.

which is bigger than the fear of the cornada. He was afraid of being made to look ridiculous, which is the same thing you face when you try to write. That is when you can tell if a man has valor, when a man is able to face the responsibility of his profession, of his art, if you like. For you write with your cojones, too. With your mind, of course, and with passion when you are lucky. But mostly you write with your cojones, always, every day, even when you have to force yourself to do it, on the days when you write with duende, and on the days when you find you have left your duende behind you in bed when you got up. That is why it is easy to do a thing once, one book, or one afternoon with the bulls. But to do it for many years, day after day, that is what is difficult, that is the proving of a man."[11] In his early, good work, Hemingway was able to suggest virility without having to write essays; Viertel's imitation of bad Hemingway is at best boring and at worst disastrous. For all its length, *Love Lies Bleeding* is finally without a subject. Toreo is presumably the subject, but toreo is overshadowed by the pall of unsubstantiated emotion that everyone is said to feel but which the reader cannot share. We never know what is eating Belden, while in a different sense we know all too well about Vasquez, for we have met him in life, if not in *Life*. In *The Sun Also Rises*, the compelling, interior subject, the uneasy disorder of the postwar world, is fully created through character, scene, and atmosphere; but in Hemingway's imitators, and particularly in Viertel's novel, the subject never emerges from its journalistic trappings.

Hemingway's aging novillero, Manuel Garcia of "The Undefeated," is his fullest fictional portrait of a matador. Manuel is described as illiterate, without cartel, very able, brave, and unlucky. He works so close to his bulls that he makes even Zurito, the old picador, uncomfortable. Needing money, Manuel begs a place as substitute on an evening program, following a charlotada. His brave and noble work goes unappreciated by the spectators, who have come to see comedy, and he receives a cornada because he has tried to kill well. Zurito wants to cut his coleta and so force him to retire, but even on the operating table Manuel resists. On the surface, Manuel is one of Hemingway's gallery of unthinking noble savages: "He knew all about bulls. He did not have to think

---

[11] Peter Viertel, *Love Lies Bleeding* (New York: Doubleday, 1964), p. 117.

about them. He just did the right thing. His eyes noted things and his body performed the necessary measures without thought. If he thought about it, he would be gone."[12] That apparent view of humanity as athletic, instinctual, illiterate, unthinking, and un-educated suggests the celebration of the simple-minded slob and the denigration of thought itself. What in fact gives "The Unde-feated" and much of Hemingway's other fiction its power is the writer's own control and placement of detail, his ability, in the case of Manuel, to suggest delicacy, honesty, and performance which is not athletic, but the essence of art. Hemingway would seem to deny the first precept of toreros, in Paco Camino's words, *"Que tenga mucha cabeza en la plaza."*[13] In fact, Hemingway is portraying precisely through Manuel a quality of toreo which is difficult to put into words, because it is not literary: the marriage in the great torero of duty to the self, to the animal, and to toreo, resulting in dignity and satisfaction in a degree known only to the artist.

Only the crude outlines of such a conception come through in Hemingway's imitators, and Manuel Garcia has had strange prog-eny, among them Tom Lea's Luis Bello, of *The Brave Bulls,* and Spota's Luis Ortega. Luis Bello is a doom-laden, illiterate, un-thinking creature of bravery, sexual lust, and mere instinct, with no more preparation beyond bravery for a career in toreo than a mentally deficient farmhand's. The Mexican ambiente described is inhabited by swine out to swindle toreros, and by willing women seemingly invented to register contempt for that sex. Lea's knowledge of toreo is adequate, but his melodramatic conception gets in the way of his portraits of bulls as of people. Where Hemingway achieved a fine tension through careful balance of many conflicting elements, Lea and Spota give us only cheap brutality and violence for its own sake. The final indignity is Lea's parody of some of Hemingway's mannerisms in language. Where Hemingway amused himself by translating certain Spanish phrases literally, Lea translates commonplaces like *"Como no?"* into "How not?"; the bull is a "package," in imitation of the Spanish cliché, *"bulto,"* and many more too tedious to dwell on.

---

[12] Ernest Hemingway, "The Undefeated," in *The Fifth Column and the First Forty-Nine Stories* (New York, 1938), p. 358.

[13] "That one have 'much head' in the plaza." In an interview with J. M., January 1962.

In France, Hemingway's influence is apparent in Joseph Peyré's novel, *Sang et lumière* (*Glittering Death* in English), of 1935. Again we have a Jake Barnes-like narrator, one José, a business-man who comes to Spain to meet the matador Ricardo Garcia and to tell us of his emergence from retirement, of his rivalries with the young, of the exigence of the public, of Garcia's wife in hospital with tuberculosis, and of his mistress, who may or may not be taking drugs. José, too, has the familiar world-weariness, cause unspecified; Garcia has been badly hurt by the bulls and does not want to face them again. He does so because he needs money for his ill-advised business ventures and for his expensive mistress. He allows an unscrupulous apoderado to arrange for his reappearance, and his death in the plaza, bravely, is predictable. Hemingway's mark upon Peyré is not, fortunately, a matter of language, but of conception and of atmosphere. Seediness, corruption, and an at-tempt at naturalistic honesty make up the atmosphere of the novel. The conception of toreo, however, is deficient. Unlike Hemingway, the author does not know quite what to do with his torero when he is in the plaza. We are told that Garcia is remem-bered by the public for something called "the immortal quite," but even that quite remains visually vague. Nevertheless, the novel has value, not because of toreo but in spite of it. The time is 1934, and the unrest in Madrid and in the countryside preceding the outbreak of the war in 1936 are rendered with considerable power. Because of his genuine abilities apart from the subject of toreo, Peyré demonstrates vividly the difficulties of toreo for the novel, the peculiar demands it makes even upon the writer who possesses imagination.

France does not need Hemingway, for she has Henry de Mon-therlant, a writer who has been called with a certain accuracy "the French Hemingway." Athlete, *aficionado práctico,** dramatist, poet, and novelist of fine talent, Montherlant has written two novels of toreo, one in extreme youth, the other in his age. *Les Bestiaires* (1926) was begun when Montherlant was fifteen; *Le Chaos et la nuit* was published in 1963, when Montherlant was

---

* *Aficionado práctico:* The aficionado whose afición is so great that he confronts living animals, usually becerros or novillos, often bought from his own pocket, at every opportunity. Fairly common among the Spanish and Mexican middle classes, although groups of work-ing men too will often save up their money for an annual novillada.

sixty-seven.[14] The two novels are as different as youth and age; each in its way is impressive, and each is of first importance to the genre of fiction on toreo. Montherlant resembles Hemingway in two significant ways. He knows that his basic impulse is romantic, he is suspicious of it, and he therefore exerts icy control over it; secondly, he uses toreo symbolically for other purposes, even when, as in *The Matador,* he seems to confront it head-on. There all resemblance ceases, for where Hemingway seems to celebrate the unthinking, ordinary, or sub-ordinary man of action, Montherlant presents the man of action who is also a man of contemplation, highly intellectual, both elitist and aristocratic, and individual to the point of eccentricity. Although Montherlant is not particularly interested in photographic naturalism, his writing on toreo has a dimension of validity lacking in Hemingway's. It is the difference between writing from experience of the living toro in the plaza, and writing from observation, however intelligent, unfleshed by immediate experience.

A writer incapable of cliché, Montherlant invents characters who are always difficult, quirky, inconsistent, even perverse. His point of view is always oblique, complex, and finally anarchic, in society and in art. He will deliberately destroy the dramatic structure of his narrative rather than fulfill his readers' conventional expectations. Years before Brecht and the cult of the absurd in fiction and theater, Montherlant discovered for himself the technique of the anti-dramatic, through which the writer forces his reader away from emotion to an intellectual consideration of the work (see Brecht's theory of *Verfremdung*). On the surface, *The Matador* is a conventional, romantic novel of education (*Bildung—* that typically romantic genre), an account of a seventeen-year-old Parisian boy's infatuation with toreo, picturesque Spain, and a lovely Spanish girl—purest Mérimée, but only on the surface. Through brilliant technique Montherlant succeeds where many have failed, in making his adolescent, Alban de Bricoule, interesting to us. Montherlant does so by his intrusions upon the narrative, by obliqueness of construction, and by superimposing upon his recital of the boy's thoughts and actions allusions to his thoughts and actions as a mature man in the years to follow.

---

[14] Both have been translated adequately into English: *Les Bestiaires* as *The Matador,* trans. Peter Wiles (London: Bestseller Library, 1960); *Chaos and Night* (New York: Macmillan, 1964).

Fascinated by bulls and already a veteran of becerradas at Burgos, Alban persuades his recently widowed mother to finance his school holiday in Spain. In Madrid he meets the Duke de la Cuesta, ganadero of Isla Menor, near Seville, and father of Soledad, one of the few interesting Spanish girls in all fiction. At first Alban despises Soledad and finds her ugly, but invited to Isla Menor for the tientas, he changes his opinion after Soledad offers him unexpected praise for having dominated a savage horse and performed well with the cape. He comes to recognize her sensuality and to speculate upon her physical availability to him. Then, seeing her in a room from a distance, "He suddenly fell passionately in love with her wrists."[15] Soledad teases him on, seeming to promise herself to Alban if he will face Mal Angel, a particularly ugly novillo of her father's, in a benefit performance. Alban agrees, but only after a characteristic passage of candor in which he tells the girl that he fears the novillo, he is neither old enough nor experienced enough to master it, adding, "You're asking me to risk my life, and I'm asking myself whether you're worth it."[16] Soledad has said that any Spaniard would instantly have agreed to face any toro for her; the struggle between the two immediately transcends the romantic pattern to take on a dimension of sexual strife that we know in English from the work of D. H. Lawrence. Where Lawrence made a cult and a career of it, however, Montherlant keeps the exchange within a convincingly human perspective, while he mounts an attack upon romanticism which is based upon a valid concept of toreo.

Montherlant further shatters the romantic pattern by causing Alban to decide, almost humorously, that he *will* face the novillo, but that he will have nothing further to do with Soledad; he recognizes that she is moved by egotism, not by him as a distinct human being. A different romantic pattern now emerges; Alban genuinely fears the novillo, to the point that he almost invents a telegram to call him home so that he will not have to appear in the plaza. He succeeds in mastering his nerves, and on the day, after an utter fracaso with his first novillo, he succeeds admirably with Mal Angel, then returns joyfully to Paris, to mother, and to school, like the schoolboy he is. Even though toreo is more central to this narrative than to *The Sun Also Rises*, Montherlant is always using

---

[15] *The Matador,* p. 76.
[16] *The Matador,* p. 128.

it to develop his major themes, sexuality and religion. The novel in fact becomes a brilliant failure because of the burden of idea Montherlant imposes upon it. He combs anthropology and comparative religion for connections between bulls and religion; Alban is a Catholic, but one who honors Christ for his legendary derivation from Mithra, the sun god whose rites involved the sacrifice of bulls. But only rarely is such matter worked into the novel proper, as when Alban, about to begin his faena to Mal Angel, decides to dedicate the animal to "the sun," meaning the spectators sitting on the sunny side of the plaza. The phrase makes him think of Mithra, and he dedicates instead to the sun, our astral body, to Mithra—to the mystification of the public.

Despite Freud and before Jean Cocteau, who in *Le Corrida du premier mai* (1957) borrowed shamelessly from Montherlant, the latter explored in *The Matador* every conceivable connection between toreo and sexuality. Alban's afición is equated from the outset with the raging lust of adolescence; the toro's horns are compared to the male sexual organ; killing with the sword is identified with sexual release, as against the frustration of the simulated kill of the Camargue; Alban can master Mal Angel because he loves him, while he had no love for his first novillo of the benefit. "Like a poet hammering at inspiration, like a composer improvising his way towards a theme, like a man in bed moulding his beloved, with long groping caresses, to the shape he wishes her to assume," so Alban in his faena to Mal Angel.[17] Montherlant's view of humanity, finally savage, almost horrifying, is brilliantly developed in this novel, through the symbols that toreo provides. However imperfect and off balance, scornful and perverse, it was an extraordinary work for so young a writer.

*Chaos and Night,* written more than three decades later, contains all the virtues and none of the defects of *The Matador*. It is a rare example of a late work bearing out all signs of promise in an early one, of development in the fullest sense. *Chaos and Night* is a pitiless account of the last few months in the life of Celestino Marcilla, age 67, Madrileño by birth, anarchist in politics, ex-captain in the Loyalist forces, an exile in Paris for twenty years after the victory of Franco. A widower, he lives with his daughter, Pascualita, writes political articles that are rarely printed, has a few Spanish friends only, since he has refused to learn French. He

---

[17] *The Matador,* p. 200.

is in splendid health. Domineering, imperious, argumentative, he estranges his friends, and in his isolation faces for the first time the reality of his own death. Celestino has sworn never to return to Spain while Franco was in power, but the death of his sister in Madrid, together with his suspicion of his brother-in-law, tempts him to return to look after his inheritance. Having faced toros as an amateur in his youth, he longs to see one corrida before his death. During his service with the anarchist troops he has killed men in cold blood, therefore his return to Spain is dangerous. His visa comes through promptly, and he sets out with Pascualita, as a man walking into an ambush, yet he is detained neither at the border nor in Madrid. Pascualita enjoys Madrid and her new-found relatives; Celestino sees them as Fascists and brutally insults Pascualita, his last link with the living. He goes about the city like a sleepwalker or a mental case, fearing arrest, convinced that the bloodshed of the Civil War was pointless. He will return at once to Paris to die alone, without his daughter, but first he must see his corrida. He does attend, in the snow, an impossible *fracaso*. The toreros are butchers, one toro emerges backward into the plaza, Celestino does not even know the nomenclature of the lances and passes of the new toreo. He briefly falls asleep; he is more estranged than ever from the living. He returns to his hotel after the third toro, still fearing arrest, and there dies, calling against his will on God, Who does not exist for him. No sooner is he dead than the police arrive to arrest him. On his body they find the marks of Christ's Passion, the stigmata. Celestino is buried in sacred ground under the inscription "LAUS DEO."

Such an account cannot give any true impression of the power, the restraint, the terror of the novel, effects which in part relate to Montherlant's subtle use of toreo. The portrait of Celestino is that of a brave, obsessed man, done in by his own defects and strengths, his own human inhumanity. That humanity is presented by allusions to the one code of behavior which has retained validity for Celestino, that of the plaza. As he faces death, he derives life from his memories of toreo; he conducts himself with conscious images of the torero in the plaza before him. Yet toreo is not sentimentally equated with death, but with life. "As a young man he had said to himself, life is a toro de lidia. Now he reflected that rather it was man who was the toro. It was man himself who was being toreado in this plaza, in hundreds of plazas, every Sunday. One killed the wild animal instead of the man. It would surely be better to kill the man, as had in fact happened on both sides during the war, when one's political adversary was toreado according to all the rules to his death in a city arena or a village marketplace. Unfortunately that could not happen in peacetime. Then the toro took upon himself, within the confines of the quarter hour of the lidia, all human destiny. And men came to observe, respectable and in safety, that which they wanted to do to other men. Spain simulated the passion of the man, under the guise of the passion of the beast, just as the Church pretended to simulate the passion of a god, in the guise of the passion of a man."[18] These bleak reflections of Celestino at the corrida give some notion of how Montherlant uses toreo to encompass his central themes of death, politics, and religion. We move from the immediate scene through a reinforced view of the character Celestino to a vision of an entire world, but always dramatically and convincingly, never through the mere essays of *The Matador*. We are prepared for the ultimate scenes of the novel and their transcendental meaning, however, by the humor and pathos of Celestino, still in Paris, anticipating joyfully his return to Spain to see a corrida, and going out into the boulevard to cape passing cars with his raincoat, only to be cursed at by a driver whom he has taken too closely in his verónica. Just as the actual corrida is a fracaso, creating in our minds a reversal, so the entire technique of the book is based upon reversal. Celestino, pigheaded, selfish, out of touch, is in fact correct in his error, Christlike in his atheism, human, again, in his inhumanity. *Chaos and Night* is an ambitious novel in that Montherlant has been able to include all the dimensions of our world, philosophical, political, theological, and social, within his single, brief, deceptively simple narrative. It is without doubt a masterpiece in itself, and one which cannot fail to influence one's conception of toreo because of the writer's success in creating a texture which indicates powerfully those relationships which are at the root of all art: life and death, sensibility and intelligence, human failings and the seed of tragedy implicit in all human activity. Montherlant's novel is tragic in the very sense that great toreo is tragic, and one cannot avoid the fact that here, almost

---

[18] Henry de Montherlant, *Le Chaos et la nuit* (Paris: Gallimard, 1963), p. 250. J. M.'s translation. It should be noted that in his other fiction, Montherlant frequently uses terms from toreo both metaphorically and to establish character.

uniquely, one art has flowed to the other and returned again, to the enhancement of both, and of us.

The bulls of fiction prove to be as difficult to dominate as the bulls of fact. Writers who are moved to use the easy glamor of toreo invariably fail, for they are lured into a dimension of reality that does not easily lend itself to the peculiar reality of fiction. The problem is perhaps clearer in painting. It is no accident that few painters have been drawn to toreo, any more than to sunsets. Goya and Picasso have succeeded, just as Hemingway and Montherlant have, from their ability to impose stylization upon the material without distorting or violating it. But the innocent who would photograph either the sunset or the corrida can only fail because of the intransigence of the subject, its quality of writhing vitality and constantly changing meaning that makes such inordinate, extra-literary demands before it may be fully comprehended, much less reduced to the confines of a different art. From Spota to Montherlant, we have attempted only to indicate what some of those difficulties are, and in so doing, to gain still another vantage point upon toreo.

CHAPTER 9

# CONVERSATIONS WITH CARLOS:

## A NON-COLLABORATIVE CODA BY J. M.

C ARLOS, MY MATADOR, was a remarkable man. He had spent twenty years in the plazas, written poetry, and had toured Spain with Manolete. Long retired after an uneven career—he had not courted empresarios and had organized the toreros' union in Mexico—he lived by journalism. He knew everyone in the ambiente, and he was training me for my first public corrida. We spent hours together every morning for almost a year, but I was never once bored in his company. Monday through Saturday I would pick him up at his apartment at six in the morning, then we would drive to Plaza México or to El Toreo and work out until eleven or twelve. On Sundays we would meet in time for the sorteo at noon, have a glass of beer and a sandwich, attend the dressing of one of the toreros, and go to the corrida. Sometimes we would sit together in the barreras, at other times Carlos would connive a photographer's pass to the callejón for me. I would then take Carlos' camera, although I hated photography, and shoot an occasional shot just to keep Carlos honest. Carlos' idea of what my education in toreo should be was as elaborate as Castiglione's in *The Courtier*. Education meant not only a cruel amount of early-morning work on the dry horns and the carretilla; it also meant waiting around for a chance to cape the novillos that the rejoneadors were practicing on, wangling invitations to ganaderías, and observing corridas from the callejón.

Education meant reading at night, although I had already done a good deal of that. My time with Carlos and all the people in the ambiente he introduced me to made me think of the things that never got into books. One Sunday afternoon in March we went to see the matador L—— who was dressing for his toros. I thought of all the novels that included such a scene and how none of them really came off. L—— was twenty-nine and had been a torero since he was seventeen, a full matador at twenty. He was elegant, cold, and maybe a bit lazy. He earned less than many others of his cartel because the public made him buy so many toros. Everyone knew he had married a wealthy woman, so when he had a bad day—and he had his full share—they took it for granted that he would present an extra toro. He was both humorous and a little bitter about all the extra animals he had not only to pay for but also torear. On this Sunday we took the elevator to L——'s suite in the expensive-cheap hotel near the plaza, and found the usual small group of men: L——'s brother, who was also his apoderado; the mozo de espadas, a short, gnarled man of sixty-five at least; and six or seven others—two young novilleros, a magazine writer, and tag-end relations of L—— who wanted tickets to the corrida and reflected glory. As always, the atmosphere was a cross between that of a barbershop and the chapel of a funeral parlor. The rooms smelled like a barbershop, of shaving soap, steam, and hair oil. L——'s new suit of lights, scarlet and gold, was laid out precisely on a chair, but his street clothes were strewn about among newspapers and magazines, and the bed was unmade. On a feminine vanity table near the bed was the ritual miniature triptych of the Virgin of Guadalupe, with various saints' medals pinned to the velvet stuff on which the image of the Virgin was mounted. A television set was on, but the sound was not. Only Carlos spoke in his normal voice, loud and clear; the others spoke low, several decibels below their normal pitch, and this too was ritual, out of deference to the torero, to the occasion, to L——'s possible mood. When L—— came out of the shower, they would let him set the tone of the hour, and if he were talkative or inclined to joke, the voices would rise.

At length the hissing of the shower stopped, and L—— appeared, dressed only in a scapular and in the scars, in varying hues of red and blue, on his calves, inner thighs, and abdomen. What was missing in the novels, I thought, was the increasing abstraction of the torero from the rest of us in the hour of his dressing. He at once acknowledged us and did not acknowledge us. His total cleanliness, his nudity, and then his slow assumption of the suit of lights, the taleguilla so tight that two men were needed to lift him so that he squeezed slowly with all his weight into the garment, all combined with his increasing concentration upon the toros of the afternoon to set him apart from us. I knew him quite well—we had worked out in the plaza together only two days before, when he had invited me to his dressing—yet, when he joked about whether I still wanted to torear, it was as though some stranger were making the joke. He smoked a cigarette and had the mozo offer us brandy and whisky, but increasingly he moved away from us, rather like troops climbing into landing craft for an invasion, I thought, except that he was just one trooper, alone, with quite other motivations than those of invading troops. The matador's frame of mind before a corrida will differ from man to man and from day to day, but the psychic withdrawal, the removal of an important part of the self from his surroundings, is always apparent, always almost tangible, and to me, memorable. That particular Sunday, L—— was colder than ever, and he had to buy another toro.

The next day I asked Carlos about this, whether as a gringo who had not grown up with the toros I was reading things in, romanticizing perhaps, or whether he felt the same about it. Some things have personal truth, others public truth. "You're absolutely right," Carlos said. "Before a corrida, the torero is not in an ordinary, human situation, and he cannot react like an ordinary human being, although he will usually try."

"Because of fear?"

"Fear is just part of it. All have some fear, and some have a great deal of fear. It is many things. There is the public, and nobody understands the public. You may have the best toro in the world, you may work miracles with him, but unless the public is with you, it is no use. Some days the public is kind, warm, and indulgent; other days they are cruel, they want your blood—particularly our Mexican public. The relationship between the torero and the public is like a marriage. Marriage is never the same, year in and year out, but it changes with the changing conditions of life. Only the professionals know this. When he has had a good Sunday or two, the young novillero is like a bridegroom, and he thinks his bride will always be the same, loving and responsive. But she changes; she must change because she is a human being. If the torero feels an inner security in his technique, and if he can dominate his panic, the public will usually go along with him. But if he depends on suerte instead of technique, the public will know that, and they will put horns on him by transferring their love to the next torero who seems to have the security he lacks. I have seen toreros, not young novilleros but mature professionals, so bothered by fear, not of the toros but of the public, that they were like somnambulists before the paseo. You would talk to them and they could not hear you. I have seen one go into the plaza at my side with a cigarette between his lips. I had to reach over and take it away. These are some of the reasons a torero seems to move away from you before the corrida."

"Then why is everybody forever wishing everybody else 'suerte'?"

"Suerte is very complicated. Never forget that toreo is an art in which chance has a great deal to do with success or failure. You know and everyone knows that if you draw a toro with bad vision, or a manso perdido that will not take the vara, you may lose contracts or you may end up in the hospital. Nevertheless, the good torero is the one who does everything in his power to get away from suerte, from chance. By studying bloodlines and knowing the ganaderías he may reduce the area of suerte in the sorteo. And by learning the techniques appropriate to varying conditions in his animals, he reduces the area of suerte still further. The torero must foresee everything in the plaza: the condition of the sand, the wind, the changing conditions of the toro during his lidia. But if a man falls in a bad patch of sand, or if his muleta blows during a pass, that is not mala suerte, that is his own stupidity. Like the commander of a ship at sea, he has to foresee trouble in order to cope with it in time. The torero who blames suerte for his errors can never learn from them. Egoism comes into it, too. If your ego is so great that you cannot criticize yourself, that you must blame suerte, you can never become a maestro except in the cafés."

"But doesn't suerte also have something to do with religion?" This had bothered me, for while every torero went through the ritual of prayer and traveled with his portable image of the Virgin, the only one I had ever met who seemed genuinely religious was Juan García, Mondeño, who proved it by retiring from toreo to become a Dominican monk.[1]

"Call it superstition, not religion. When a man plays with forces he cannot dominate, he becomes superstitious. When his technique fails, it is easy to charge his failure up to a supernatural force. But I repeat, on the whole, the man who has the greatest ability will have suerte. If he has valor and intelligence, and if he has also the agility and the physical fitness to apply them, he will create his own suerte. He won't need superstition."

"That's clear enough, but you haven't said anything about religion. Put it another way. In *Chaos and Night*, Montherlant has one of his characters say, 'No country except Russia has done so much for atheism as we Spanish.' When I read that, I thought it had something to do with toreo, and I still do."

"It is an uncomfortable question, one that I do not like. To me it is like this. In Mexico and in Spain, too, we are religious but we are without religion. I speak now of toreros, and of men who have had some education, some training. We are religious because we are surrounded by religion from birth. It is in the air we breathe, and we cannot expel it because we live in poor countries where most of the people have nothing but religion to distinguish them from the animals. But how can we honor our church, which has dirtied itself in politics? That may be what Montherlant is talking about. As for the toreros, with their Macarenas and Guadalupes and their holy medals, they are in part religious and in part superstitious. When you begin as a novillero, you pray before the corrida just as you take up smoking cigars and drinking brandy; it is part of the life, part of being a torero. Later on, you pray because it has become a habit and because you are a little superstitious too, and you want all the help you can get from whatever source. Still later when you have been with the toros for many temporadas, you give it up, because you know that you are alone

---

[1] It may prove something about the pull of toreo over religion to note that as of late winter, 1966, Juan García has left the monastery of Candeluega and is in training to resume his career as torero.

and that no one can torear for you, not the Macarena nor the Guadalupe, only yourself. By then it is probably time to retire anyway."

"Why?"

"Because of the solitude."

Carlos' almost casual use of that single word, "solitude," set off in my mind a series of associations that illuminated a murky aspect of toreo that I had been struggling with for years. The problem for me, as for many people I knew who were not born in a country where toreo is taken for granted, was how to make rational and logical to the skeptic the place of toreo in the modern world, not as a mere survival of a picturesque, barbaric rite, nor as an art open only to those of Latin "sangre." No one I had read in Spanish bothered with the problem, because Spanish writers could not or did not see it as a problem. Writers in English and French who tried to go beneath the surface always ended up in a jungle of Freudian penises and protuberances, the funniest example being Jean Cocteau's idea of the matador either as a female figure, or somehow bisexual, in *La Corrida du premier mai*. When I gave Carlos that book to read, he returned it saying, *"Bonita basura"* (pretty garbage). Only Jean Cau among the French came close to the heart of the matter, but he did not face up to it squarely because in *Les Oreilles et la queue* he was writing reportage, not aesthetics. The best books in English—Hemingway's, John Marks' *To the Bullfight,* or Kenneth Tynan's *Bull Fever*—did not face up to my problem, either. Hemingway saw toreo as an art, but a decadent one which in any event he was not interested in discussing beyond the limits of the thing itself. Marks wrote that "clearly the bullfight is an anachronism, which in an age adrift, like our own, must spell anathema." This was unsatisfying because Marks began by making a case for toreo as an art; to me an art by definition cannot be anachronistic; if an activity becomes so, it cannot be an art. Although Kenneth Tynan's instincts are critical and aesthetic, in his book he was busy recording impressions rather than constructing arguments. And he shared Marks' notion of the Spanishness of it all, an idea which to me was patently false, if not dangerous.

Carlos' word, "solitude," was electrifying because it was also André Malraux's key concept, Malraux, the very great novelist whose work defines our time to us as no other's, whose ideas have influenced not only a generation of writers, among whom Albert

Camus is the outstanding figure, but in whose work the one philosophy that has had any attraction for our generation, that of existentialism, is prefigured (or has seemed so to many readers). From *The Conquerors,* his first novel of 1928, through *The Royal Way* (1930), *Man's Fate* (1933), *Days of Wrath* (1935), *Man's Hope* (1937), to *The Walnut Trees of Altenburg* (1943), he has written marvelous variations upon a single theme, man's necessity to engage the enemies of humanity, and in so doing to discover his own dignity, his solitude, and his death. That theme necessarily took him to revolution—in China and in Spain—to a study of the various political solutions at hand, and to our two World Wars. Himself a man of action, active in the Chinese revolution of the 1920s, leader of a bomber squadron with the Loyalists in Spain, colonel in the French Resistance, Malraux's work might seem to register only a personal view of recent history, but that is far from the case. Rather he is a tragedian whose experience has given him a view of humanity both exalted and bleak; his heroes—and he gives us true heroes—pursue paths to knowledge which inevitably lead them to death. They are not struck down senselessly, but like Katov, in *Man's Fate,* who, condemned to die, gives his cyanide pellets to two comrades, they choose death consciously and intellectually, just as they have chosen their activities in life, politics, revolution, or war, which would very likely lead to death. Choice is nevertheless determined; the context of individual heroism is never simple. In *The Walnut Trees of Altenburg,* what Malraux means by "solitude" is most fully defined, the context of choice most fully presented: "We know that we have not chosen to be born, that we will not choose to die. That we have not chosen our parents. That we can do nothing against time. That between each of us and universal life there is . . . a sort of gulf. When I say that each man experiences powerfully the presence of destiny, I mean that he experiences—and almost always tragically, at least in certain moments—the world's indifference." Malraux's work is tragic rather than merely existentialist, however, because of the honor he pays to the attempts of his heroes to deny their solitude, their apprehension of "the world's indifference," whether through eroticism, as in *The Royal Way,* political brotherhood, as in *Man's Fate,* or in a missionary conviction of rectitude beyond political dogma, as in *Man's Hope.* His heroes are heroic because they act, and they are tragic because in their action lies knowledge of death. But knowledge of death is knowledge of man.

Here, it seemed to me, was the connection between the art of toreo and the modern world. At the same time, Malraux's conception of isolation and death offered further reason to distrust the attraction of toreo for a man like Hemingway. Superficially Malraux and Hemingway were similar writers, men of action who reproduced their experience in fiction, romantics attracted to the highly romantic themes of social uproar, love, and death. In actuality they differed as classic from romantic. In Hemingway's treatment of death in toreo, there is often something gothic, grotesque, almost obscene; he was a man using material for its own sake, wanting to startle and appall us with the gruesomeness of it all, and so to impress us with the depth and intensity of his personal experience. Along the way, he either lost sight of toreo, or he distorted it into something quite else, using it for his own ends. Malraux, on the other hand, always provides a context that is verifiable in the "real" world, available to us all. Because of his intellectual power, his insights are historically verifiable in terms of aesthetics and in terms of human life beyond the confines of his particular setting. Hemingway said in effect that the connection between toreo and man is death in all its horror. Malraux corrected Hemingway, for me, by suggesting that the connection is life lived in the consciously chosen presence of death, which is a very different matter. The power and deep passion of the fiesta, its capacity to make the spectator drunk with joy, then peculiarly depressed when it is over lies far beyond the visual effects of men and bulls which induce those emotions, and beyond any residue in us of response to a primitive, tragic ritual of fertility and seasonal sacrifice. Toreo has the power to move us so forcefully because, in addition to these things, it also plays back to us the modern, secular apprehension of ourselves in relation to one another, to the social forces we should like to control, and to our apprehension of death itself. Unless we are open to a tragic understanding of life, we can only see toreo as sport and spectacle. But if we attach any value to individual heroic effort, to the illusion of control over terrible forces, if we are capable of recognizing the analogy between toreo and tragic impulse, then we are capable of afición.

Here again was something that did not get into the novels of toreo, with their sculptured faenas and men and bulls flowing into one; the separateness, the solitude of the man, not only as he dresses for the corrida, where it is unmistakable, but in his entire life as a torero. Just as the suit of lights marks him off in the plaza from the run of men, so in his own mind he is marked off always, for his thoughts and preconceptions are conditioned by the art he serves, by the re-enactment he repeats of the basic human condition. Every writer on toreo, regardless of his competence, has remarked that toreros age fast, and that their faces go haggard because of their fear. The torero's fear is real enough, but it is different from our usual fears—fear of the unknown, of humiliation, of failure, of violence, of mutilation, of death. The closest thing to it I knew was fear before combat, but that was different, too, because there was always the comforting sense of having been coerced. Somebody out there, the admiral or the enemy or society was to blame, and if my precious blood were shed, it was on them. Indignation removes pain. The difference in toreo lies in the element of choice. Only the torero chooses quite freely to risk wounds or death, but choice is a kind of balm, too, for to choose is to begin to master fear. As Carlos said, fear is just a part of it, in toreo as in combat. It is the torero's sense of apartness, his solitude, the burden of his symbolic role, his frequent confrontations with the elemental that etches lines in his face and ages him.

Not that toreros go about the world as self-conscious bearers of other men's burdens, Christ-figures seeking a crucifixion. It was only the rare half-dozen true maestros who indicated both in and out of the plaza that they knew, consciously and intellectually, that particular burden. And then I thought of what Carlos had said repeatedly about la técnica, technique. After weeks of fundamentals with cape and muleta, he said, "All the rules are relative. Toros have a sure instinct for what is going on, for who is master. Great toreros know this, sense it, and respond accordingly. Technique is a media, a way, not an end in itself. What is the torero's purpose? It is to create beauty, using the qualities and the defects of the toro to do so. Only the technique that succeeds in this end is the proper technique. In each lance, each pass, the great torero invents his technique. The merely competent torero, and most are merely competent, has enough technique to get by on, to come through, but he does not have the instinct for the particular toro which tells him how to modify his standard work so as to bring out the best in the animal. He wants to shine before the public, but at the toro's expense.

"The artist begins where the technician leaves off. The artist knows that if the toro looks good because of the torero's accurate instinct for what it will answer to, he will look even better because of his accommodation to the toro's conditions."

"Fine. But what is a maestro, then, if not that?" I asked.

"A maestro is the torero who is not content with instinct or invention or mere beauty, although he must include all these things, of course. A maestro goes beyond beauty to create tragedy, to project tragedy to the most drunken, stupid *villamelón** in the tendidos. When you see a torero whose performance causes you pain, makes you want to leave your wife and children, abandon cigarettes, drink, and God, and reminds you of your own death, then you are seeing a maestro. You may go to corridas all your life and never see this, but if you are lucky enough to see it just once, you know what toreo is about, why men become toreros and why, even when they have no talent, they come back again and again."

"Pretty words, Carlos, but what is this famous tragedy a maestro projects? How does he do it? You're losing me in words—a snow job." I spent some time trying to translate "snow job" into Spanish, but it was impossible.

Carlos paced back and forth, flexing the blade of my practice sword. "Tragedy is in consciousness," he said finally. "In the torero's of course, but also in the toro's consciousness. And it is in the setting. Remember, when the animal comes out of the toril, no one—neither the ganadero, nor the toreros, nor the toro itself—knows its qualities. The first moment in which the peones run the toro is a wonderful moment, a moment of discovery, of revelation. The torero and the toro are two friends, not 'enemies' as the critics always write in the newspapers, one of whom must leave the plaza dead. It is the power of elemental strength in the animal against the intelligence, intuition, and character of the man. In the toro is concentrated centuries of breeding for this moment, this action and death. The noble toro has *bravura,* enthusiasm for life, and his appearance in the ring is an explosion of happiness, of willingness to fight and to live. The luminous moment of tragedy arises when he realizes that unless he can destroy the very ring in which he is confined, he must die. Throughout the tercios of the lidia, his instinct for his own death becomes increasingly apparent, cruelly so, until the magical moment when he says, in effect, to the matador, '*Mátame*'—kill me.

---

* *Villamelón:* A term of contempt to describe the pseudo-aficionado who attends the corrida rarely, but who shouts bad advice to the torero when he does attend. He always has a loud voice.

"That moment when the matador, alone in the plaza, first engages the toro is no less luminous. He goes out to the toro to keep a pact of life with death; of life, mind you. His situation is that he may emerge from the pact with glory, or with a cornada; he may create a fracaso and leave the plaza with his confidence undermined and his personality confounded, or serenely and triumphantly. In that moment he is writer, director, and actor who must give the form, structure, and resolution to the tragedy. At the same time he needs the mathematical precision of the scientist, for there can be no errors, no rehearsals. All must be decided in fractions of seconds, yet nothing he does must appear mechanical. The maestro's engagement with the animal is an act of love, an act in which he establishes his identity. The purpose of his lidia is to provoke the toro in order to invite danger and create his art. Each lance, each pass is an adventure, heroic and aesthetic. He must have the concentration necessary to divine each movement of the toro during each phase of each movement, to gauge the animal's strength, and always to treat the toro so that it can give its best. Lidia is not a matter of giving pretty passes, but of building a totality, fulfilling an interior concept of what is possible with the particular animal. And all the while, the torero must dominate himself, his own instincts of panic and fear, and so express his desire not only to live, but to live with *grandeza*—grandeur—and nobility, as well as projecting the toro's desire to die bravely.

"Consciously to act, not just to suffer; to create plastic beauty out of the meeting of life and death. That is worth our while, isn't it?" Carlos smiled so as to indicate he knew he had got carried away, but he didn't mind, and I certainly didn't, either.

In the weeks that followed, I came back to this subject with Carlos time and again. I was reassured to know that a torero with twenty years in the plazas behind him could not only have such a concept, but get it out. It supported my own rather literary views and instincts, which until then I distrusted for being literary and perhaps fancy. Above all, Carlos' view seemed to confirm my thoughts about Malraux. As an experiment I gave him *Man's Fate* to read, and I was delighted when, without any prompting from me, he said there was more about toreo in it than in Cossío or any other book on the subject.

To his three classifications of toreros as technicians, artists, and masters, Carlos added an unofficial fourth, *pobrecitos*—which might be translated either as "poor bastards" or "lost souls," depending on your mood—the numerous company of youngsters who went into the plazas without adequate training, or perhaps without any training whatsoever, armed only with guts and ambition, who were tossed and trampled unmercifully by the inferior cattle they usually faced. I knew some of these novilleros from my workouts in the plaza, where they put in a lot of their time, practicing desultorily and talking a great deal. Their conception of toreo, when they had a conception, was athletic and venal. They had gravitated to toreo as others to soccer or boxing, and they hoped, somehow, some day, to make a lot of money. They were affable, engaging, and generous with cigarettes and their few pesos; how they lived was never clear. They never worked, or read so much as a newspaper, or lost their temper. Time had no meaning for them. One stands out in memory for a trick he had learned in his native Yucatan. He could *banderillar con la boca*—with a banderilla between his teeth, he would quarter in on the toro and place it neatly with a powerful movement of his back and neck—a grotesque and spectacular stunt. Unfortunately he could do nothing with the cape or muleta. Pobrecitos indeed.

The technicians make up the great mass of toreros. They are the men with sufficient training and knowledge to do a creditable job with perhaps half their animals, but whose instinct is flashy and athletic. They spend more time on their knees than on their feet; they know all the tricks to make their work look more dangerous than it is. They deliver breathtaking "passes of death" (ayudados por alto) to toros on their way to a querencia. They lurch into the animal after the horn passes to smear their taleguilla with blood, and they hold the palo at its extreme end to keep a maximum distance between themselves and the toro, while at the same time they lure the animal with the opposite end of the palo rather than centering the toro in the cloth. They petition the president to change the tercio after an animal has had one severe pic in order to keep the crowd with them, thus depriving themselves and the spectators of the opportunity to judge the toro's true bravery, or else to take advantage of the gesture in foreknowledge that a wise president will deny it. They are masters of the last-moment step back from the horn and of the safer estocadas. In spite of their tricks, their work is monotonous, for their style is a pastiche of the style of Manolete, Arruza, or more lately, El Cordobés—whoever currently is making the most money. Within limits they give the same faena to every toro they face, with a *teléfono** or some other such vulgarity occasionally thrown in. Their cuadrillas often punish their animals cruelly, and their sense of lidia remains underdeveloped. Because they are athletes, they fade fast, embittered, never comprehending what has happened to them. Some become banderilleros, others become car salesmen or politicians. Then they are not pleasant men to know.

Unpleasant toreros are a rare exception. I was constantly surprised and pleased at the frankness, generosity, and lack of pretension among working toreros. Pettiness, bitchiness, the operatic airs and the indulgent neuroticism that pervades the other arts is unknown among toreros, who conspicuously do not speak badly of one another. Only in the merchant marine had I encountered a similar atmosphere of openness and lack of falsity. Toreros, like sailors, know their job and are at ease with themselves. You cannot be a fake either at sea or in the ring with a toro; fakes go elsewhere to lead their lives. Jealousies and animosities of course exist among toreros, but they do not poison the atmosphere as they may do among, say, professors or lawyers. The torero's characteristic courtliness and openness in part relates to the sense of fraternity men feel with others who are leading unusual lives and facing unusual problems; in part to manners, to the Spanish idea of *señorio* and pundonor.

Señorio is hard to translate. It means both gentlemanliness and *noblesse oblige,* consciousness that one's position entails recognition of others, awareness that every man occupies space in the world, has problems, virtues and vices, and that until he serves notice by word or deed to the contrary, he is a man of good will. Pundonor is all this plus honor, oficio, duty to self, to one's companions, and to one's·calling. These aristocratic attitudes are assumed without any embarrassment by men of most humble background, making toreo one of the great democratic confraternities. I learned some of this to my shame one day at El Toreo, early in my career as aspirant. I was standing with Carlos, talking, my cape folded over the barrera near us. Someone had bought a cow to practice on, and when the cow was released, the plaza became an unorganized capea, with fifteen or twenty people

---

*Teléfono:* A vulgar, ugly desplante in which the torero places an elbow on the toro's forehead and his hand on his own head, simulating, presumably, communication. Arruza was fond of it.

flapping capes at the animal. A novillero whom I did not know came running to the barrera, helped himself to my cape, and went out to deliver a verónica to the cow. The wise old cow sliced her horn through the cape, trampled it, and ripped it almost in two. When the cow had been killed, the stranger returned to the barrera, folded the cape over it with a *"gracias,"* and walked away. I asked Carlos what the hell the man was doing with my cape in the first place, and why he had said nothing about having it repaired, at least. Carlos was shocked at my selfishness. He said that in the ambiente everyone was generous and that no torero would think of making an issue of such an incident. According to Carlos, the novillero was sparing my feelings by neither explaining nor apologizing for having destroyed my cape. Carlos' interpretation seemed oriental at the time; regret for my anger came later.

On another occasion early in our acquaintance, however, Carlos indicated that the generous old ways were passing or gone. That afternoon we had seen the fine young Spanish matador, C——, cut ears from both his toros. Carlos wanted me to meet him, and he wanted to talk to C——'s apoderado, an old friend from Madrid whom he had not seen for years. The hotel suite was blue with cigar smoke, and pulsating with human beings and their talk when we arrived, less than an hour after the corrida. In theory everyone was there to congratulate C——on his triumph, but in fact most of the men in the suite were there on business of one kind or another. Novilleros and their apoderados came because of a rumor that the empresario was on his way; some wanted interviews with C——, some looked to be selling things, and some just wanted a free drink. C——, kneeling on the bed in pajamas, was speaking furiously into the telephone. In that din he could not possibly have heard a syllable from the other end. After half an hour or so, the crowd thinned, and a hotel waiter passed through carrying a tray of drinks, then disappeared. Carlos talked to his old friend; I exchanged some polite words with C——, and soon we left, the party obviously being over.

On our way to the car Carlos, a nonstop talker, said nothing, and he remained silent as we drove off. I had no idea what was wrong, and finally I asked him. He made a Spanish noise of disgust, and said, "Now you see what the fiesta brava has come to."

"No, I don't," I said. "I don't know what you're talking about."

"In my day a torero was a señor, not a businessman," Carlos said. "When I cut ears like that *muchacho* today, there was a real fiesta afterward, not a damned business conference. We'd go from the hotel to my house and the whole neighborhood would come in to celebrate. There was food and drink for everyone, and music and dancing. The people who came knew they were welcome and that I wasn't counting the number of drinks they took. They came to honor me and enjoy themselves, not to talk business. But to go up to that boy's rooms after he has had such a triumph and be offered one drink, like a priest, that is insulting. It is insulting to you, and to me, and to the fiesta. He is a talented boy, C——, but he must learn what it is to be a torero. Otherwise the businessmen will make him too rich too fast, and he will retire with a fat little Spanish wife before he is old enough to know what life is all about."

I argued that I didn't see why C—— should be expected to set up drinks for a mob of people he didn't even know, but Carlos was not interested in my arguments; he was offended in his soul. I knew more fully why later on, when I knew Carlos better. I came to realize that what had bothered him was not simply nostalgia for his own youth, as I had at first thought. It was instead his belief in the importance to a torero of character, his insistence that to be great in toreo one had to be one's own man. His anger at C—— was Carlos' objection to the acceleration of toreros' careers through massive publicity, to maximum exposure on two continents virtually at once made possible through jet-plane travel, and to the elimination of the long apprenticeship customary in the past. Carlos did not have the tiresome middle-aged view that the animals and the men of his youth were gold and those on the contemporary scene brass. He was too honest and had too vivid a memory for that. His version of the threat to the fiesta, expressed and implied over a long period in many contexts, was that toreo was likely to get entirely into the wrong hands, that the operators without any pretense to afición, lured by the profits possible from television and advertising, would take over every aspect of toreo, from the raising of toros to the selection, training, and shaping of young toreros. In short, he feared the influence of mass society, and he was more attuned than many aficionados to what that influence might turn out to be.

Toreo, after all, is not a free, uncircumscribed art like painting, but an art given form and meaning through ritual. Without the unvarying ritual of the tercios, the set and measured movements from cape to varas to banderillas to muleta to estocada, there can be no toreo. For ritual to exist, however, for the symbolic action of toreo to be registered upon the spectators in the tendidos, there must be a society, a community whose senses are refined to the language of that ritual. The threat to toreo then is not in the accusation of "decadence" since Belmonte's revolution, nor even from businessmen, but from the decline of the community itself. If the fragmentation of sensibility that seems to accompany mass society should extend to toreo, toreo could go the way of poetry and poetic drama in our time. It could become a cultist activity, cut off from the community for lack of communal response to the elements of the art: allusion, metaphor, symbol, symbolic action. Toreo is not so likely to go the way of poetry, because in its traditional form it remains a genuinely popular art (therefore a lesser art than poetry), and because it is canonical, and "the formation of a canon serves to safeguard a tradition."[2] The training of toreros, the observation of a set ritual in the plaza, both imposed by the animal and therefore inevitable, serve to preserve tradition in toreo, just as the existence of a canon preserves certain religious traditions. It is for these reasons, his necessary awareness of tradition and observation of a canon that the torero is a true artist, even though he may be without formal education or exposure to the other sides of culture that we assume in the conventional figure of the artist. And without being hairy-chested and macho about it, I would say that much of the vigor of toreo comes from the injection of energy by men who have not had a traditional and often deadening "broad" education. Certainly the ambiente has a tang that is missing from the company of painters and poets.

That the tang and savor of toreo is not to everyone's taste is abundantly clear. Every aficionado has been out to dinner and suffered through an idiot conversation with the woman in the green dress, who between forkfuls of beefsteak accuses him of cruelty to bulls, exhibitionism, sadism or worse, finishing him off with, "All I can say is it must be a very peculiar sport. You yourself just said the bull hasn't got a chance." The woman in the green dress made a fast bus-tour of Mexico which included a ticket

---

[2] E. R. Curtius, *European Literature and the Latin Middle Ages* (New York: Bollingen, 1953), p. 256.

to a novillada in Plaza México. She sat next to Carlos and me, and when a novillero, attempting to place his own banderillas, was caught and badly gored in the chest, her reaction was as noisy as it was peculiar. Bullfighting was barbarous, the Mexicans were cruel and uncivilized, and finally, it served the boy right if he was such a fool as to want to be a bullfighter. As for her, she was on the bull's side. Carlos merely said to me after the corrida that it was a strange point of view coming from a country that had invented and exploded atom bombs. "How many people do you kill on your highways every year?" he asked.

Arguments for the abolition of toreo had always seemed devious and off the mark; they centered on cruelty to animals, but they disguised an underlying unease about the place of violence and death in our whole society. No issue is more important, but it seemed unfortunate that hostility to toreo and moves to ban it should displace understanding of its therapeutic possibilities, quite apart from the abolitionists' self-deprivation of an entire range of experience. I have known men who felt that they were somehow upholding civilization through their lifelong study of one decade of the sixteenth century, but who would not hear of toreo without a scornful smirk on their faces. I had heard their standard comment dozens of times: "Bullfighting is all very well for Spain or Mexico and their cult of death, but it can have nothing to do with progressive, humane, forward-looking countries like America and Britain." When they attended a corrida, they saw a series of one-dimensional actions having no resonance, no relationship to their own lives and experience. They were only alarmed at blood, at the promise of violence in every suerte, and disturbed at the death of the toro. Later they would remind you of dark Aztec sacrifices, of the sugar skulls sold to children on All Souls' Day in Mexico, of the blood and corpses in the Murillos and Goyas at the Prado, of the baroque blood of the saints in Spanish churches, of the funeral processions passing flauntingly in the streets. Was this not the cult of death?

Carlos' answer was not devious. "Let me ask you," he said, "have you seen gas ovens in Mexico? Did you see men boiled into soap in Madrid? Have you seen any slave-labor camps in our countryside? Or missile sites for launching hydrogen weapons? Why not a German cult of death? Or Russian? Or American? We Mexicans and Spanish, we are amateurs of death compared to you—green novilleros. We do not cultivate death, and we have no cult of death. What we do, and what you refuse to do, is to recognize death. We have a way of life which recognizes that death is natural and that every man must die. But is this a cult of death, or a cult of life?" He agreed that the tough Catholicism of Spain had a great deal to do with instilling the attitude toward death which the abolitionists attacked, and that in Mexico, far as it was from the Catholicism of the Spanish missionaries, the attitude remained, enforced among the Indians particularly by conscious or subconscious memories of the prehistoric past.

The burden of his argument, however, was that toreo is an art in which violence is controlled, and death opposed, actually and symbolically, through tragic realization of its very existence. This is what it was all about; this is why men could respond to it in our time, even more fully than a century ago. Toreo affirmed life, not death, by its recognition of violence and death as a fact. Toreo was a way to sanity, not a brutalization of sensibility. Its language had to be learned, even as the language of a hermetic poet, a Mallarmé or a Valéry, had to be learned, but the language of toreo was more accessible to us because whether we wanted to admit it or not, it was in the modern air, a part of our lives as it had not been since the mediaeval plagues.

I thought of Ernst Juenger's character in *The Glass Bees* who writes, "My unlucky star had destined me to be born when there was much talk about morality and, at the same time, more murders than in any other period." One way or another, we Americans had become the great deniers. We denied the old by calling them "senior citizens," and we denied the poor by calling them "underprivileged" or "unfortunate." When a plane crashed consuming in flames every human being in it, we could not find the energy for indignation, and while men were tortured and killed in distant jungles in nominal defense of our kind of politics, we went on being kind to dogs and cats. It seemed ironically appropriate that the Christian notion of hell, eternal incineration, was a fate which we all had to live with in some corner of our minds, but we denied that too, or tried to, through jargon about bomb shelters, selected targets, civil defense, and retaliation. Our denials made us into victims, passive sufferers, like patients in a pesthouse waiting for death. Our literature gave us portraits of men in stasis, immobilized, dehumanized, unsexed, and suffering; our theater had produced some kind of ultimate in the form of a play which takes place in a public toilet and was called, logically, *The Toilet*.

In such a world of colossal vulgarity, inhuman passivity, and denial, toreo was an island of order and sanity, and the toreros I met and admired were true Starbucks—"here in this critical ocean to kill whales for my living, and not to be killed by them for theirs." I could only feel grateful to Spain for having evolved an art that remained classical in its essence, canonical and traditional, to set against the suicidal nihilism that we meet at every turn in our lives. I felt privileged to have been admitted into the world of toros, and to have associated with a handful of fine toreros. I always shall.

# POSTSCRIPT: ICE CREAM AT THE BULLFIGHT

$B$LOND GIRLS from the United States hawking American ice cream at a bullfight, and in Las Ventas, Madrid, once revered as the "cathedral" of bullfighting? It was blasphemy, and worse was to follow. After long abstinence, I was in Madrid for the six corridas of the annual autumn fair, which mark the end of the major bullfights of the year. It proved to be a mixed pleasure, not for lack of ability on the part of the *toreros* but because the bulls had been bred down and were overfed and deficient in the qualities rigorously selected by breeders in the past. The Spanish used to say, "*Sin toros, no hay toreros*" (Without bulls, you cannot have bullfighters).

Whether one regards bullfighting as being on a moral level with cock-fighting or French dwarf-throwing, as does the Animal Rights Party, or with the conviction that it is an art form unappreciated in the United States and Britain, it remains just to consider that bullfighting offers a far more accurate gauge of the state of Spanish society than graphs, statistics, or sociological studies can provide. With roots in prehistory, in religion, in both the aristocracy and the peasantry, bullfighting (*toreo*) cannot be equated with mere sport, as foreigners tend to think. Mediterranean folklore depicts the bull as symbol of power, fertility, and even godhood, but in no country other than Spain has the blood sacrifice of the bull retained its ancient, deeply rooted meaning and evolved into a ritual death to the animal involving mortal danger to the *torero*, whose every movement in the plaza derives from long tradition as well as individual style. At its rare best, bullfighting is elegant, formal, and efficient. It combines all the elements of tragedy, it is intensely real, and it can be beautiful. Like the other arts, it can be corrupted and often is. Serious but also joyful, the *corrida de toros* juxtaposes fatality and festivity to form a uniquely Spanish combination.

Francisco Franco's death in 1975, the restoration of the monarchy under Juan Carlos, and the adoption of a new constitution in 1978 led to distinct and profound changes in Spanish society, changes that all too soon were reflected in bullfighting. Unparalleled prosperity had its usual effect of depopulating the countryside, as people flocked to the cities to work in banks and offices: Madrid now boasts that it has more banks than any city in the world. Once passports became freely obtainable, for the first time in memory, many Spaniards could learn how other people lived and thought; Spain became in part Europeanized, in part Americanized. Prosperity is fickle, however, for with it came inflation, affecting every area in national life.

All this and more was in my mind as I took my place in the plaza, comparing the scene of forty and more years ago with the problematic present. By preference I sat high above the ring in the cheap seats, where until the recent past, the company was almost entirely male and working class, salty of speech and generous with wine, cigarettes, and chorizo. Such men had sometimes had a try at the bulls themselves in village festivals and knew at first hand what it is like to see the animal come through the gate into the ring like a locomotive. Years of studying the events in the plaza, if only through a drunken haze, had taught them to distinguish the modish cheat from the subtle, authentic, but sometimes dry work of the genuine artist. When the prosperous but less knowledgeable in the *barreras* (seats adjoining the ring) applauded the matador who flourished the *muleta* (small cape) *after* the horn had passed, my neighbors could sit in ominous silence or growl curses at the *sinverguenza* (shameless one). To a man, they were *toristas*, who would go out of their way to see *toros* that they could hope from blood lines and from recent performance would challenge the matador to exert all his professionalism, all his resources. The *torerista*, by contrast, followed *toreros*, as the young follow rock stars, tending not to discriminate the difficult, demanding bull from the bred-down, relatively easy animal favored by all but a precious few matadors, the rare, genuine artists.

The first three days of the autumn fair were passable but disappointing. Five-hundred-kilo animals, some fifty to a hundred kilos over their proper weight, were weak and often collapsed, depriving the *toreros'* work of either dignity or finesse. The animals were poorly matched, as tradition demanded they should be, while several bulls showed signs of horn clipping, a criminal practice designed to make the animal safer for the *torero* by altering the natural, precise use of its horns. As day succeeded day, it became painfully obvious that all was not well in the world of the bulls. The spectacle of indiscriminate breeding and profit from such animals led me to pay more attention to my present-day companions in the once-cheap seats than to the often boring ritual being enacted in the ring.

Gone were the horny-handed, knowledgeable proletariat of the past. Now my companions were well-dressed, soft-palmed business people of some sort, often with their legitimate wives, armed with Japanese binoculars, their thirst assuaged by Coca-Cola. Seated just above me, a man of affairs answered a mobile telephone, an effect at a bullfight as gauche as a nude leaping from a cake in church during mass. A few of the ancient, frog-voiced, male vendors of beer and whiskey were on hand, contrasting ludicrously with the pretty American ice cream sellers. Not only wives but groups of unaccompanied young girls made up perhaps half of the section, in contrast to the days when the only women present were mistresses and whores. The expensive *barreras* were now occupied by businessmen on expense accounts, for bullfighting had become chic among the newly prosperous, whose experience derived from occasional corridas on television. The passion and long experience of the art and spectacle were missing among such gentry.

On day four we were treated, if that is the word, not to the regulation six bulls but to ten, in a three-hour endurance contest. Four of the scheduled animals were rejected by the public and the president of the proceedings as unfit, although they were not much different from many of the bulls we saw on other days. No longer festive, the glum crowd filtered out into a moonless night, while several variously cynical of my friends gathered at the bar. Lingering too long, we found the great gates shut, but we knew the pressroom was open, and through it, the abattoir and the attendants' exit. In the abattoir, the butchers were still at work. Normally they completed their tasks and were away, but ten bulls to slaughter was not normal. They went about their indelicate surgery on the suspended tenth carcass, as the apprentices hosed down blood and excrement, each man covered in a black, cloaklike waterproof and black boots, silent and efficient under the dim, artificial light. Except for the sanitary hose-pipe, the scene was meant for William Hogarth or Francisco Goya. The butcher's work cannot be gentrified, as so many other phases of Spanish life have been.

Until recently, fighting bulls were bred on the extensive lands of the grand or lesser aristocracy, whose motive commonly was not profit but pride, an expression of a way of life and expertise. Not all breeders were rigidly honorable, for complaints about deliberate alteration in stock to produce a bull easy for the *torero* go back generations. Of late, however, abuses have multiplied, given the proliferation of corridas throughout Spain in the past ten years and the profits now to be gained from bulls: A standard string of seven bulls now brings the rancher, on average, 70 million pesetas. Cows that once would have gone straight to the butcher are now bred despite defects, leading to public disappointment and too often to a bogus "triumph" on the part of cynical *toreros,* who also may gain untold riches from the cornucopia of contracts on offer. Not only does the over-production of bulls and of corridas reflect the gentling of bullfighting, but by depriving bullfighting of a necessary element, it may well mean that pure, classical bullfighting will change from high to low, from near-tragedy to farce.

*Toreros* often come from the villages near the breeding ranches, learning their craft from childhood to young manhood, when, if they are talented and lucky, they might also become wealthy. Like any true art, bullfighting demands mastery of craft, intelligence, knowledge of tradition, and the spontaneity deriving from imagination. Unlike the other arts, bullfighting also depends on the craftsman's long experience of the animal, which trains his intuition of the bull he must face and properly kill. It is a rural rather than an urban pursuit, one rooted in both aristocratic and peasant sources; sadly, both sources in Spain become muddied as gentrification takes over. Formerly, bullfighting belonged to the *pueblo* (people, village, land), and even the most citified Spaniard formerly returned annually to his village to witness the celebration of its saint's day in a corrida and in homage to his rural roots. Too busy now in the city, he may no longer make the pilgrimage, but his attendance at the corrida in the city, however corrupted, becomes a surrogate, subliminal form of homage, which soccer cannot supply. Extremely high prices for tickets in the small, provincial plazas mean that the *pueblo* have virtually been eliminated from their own celebrations, their places taken by city people and tourists. Some ground for hope in the future of bullfighting nevertheless exists. Entrance into the European Community (EC) brought high prices, inflation, and demands in the European parliament for the abandonment of the abomination of bullfighting in Spain. In the face of a warm campaign in northern Europe and in Spain itself, the struggle was quietly abandoned; Spaniards who rarely or never went to the bulls were deeply offended at the insult to their tradition; did not the royal family itself frequently occupy the royal box in Las Ventas? The controversy has recently been renewed in the EC with the news that matadors are being paid £35 for each bull they kill in the plaza, thanks to a curious bureaucratic reading of arcane regulations.

If gentrification was held briefly at bay by loyalty to tradition, the good life nevertheless continued to spread. One no longer skis over prawn shells, cigarette ends, spit, and abandoned newspapers to make one's way to the tapas bar. Trash bins have been placed at strategic intervals, and the noxious old smells have vanished. Only the din of unwatched television and the shouted talk, assertion not conversation, remain. Many of the lovely old bars have been remodeled in plastic or have become boutiques, while U.S. fast-food chains purveying gastronomic disaster abound.

In Madrid just outside the Bank of Spain, the subway to the Paseo del Prado used to be inhabited by begging gypsies and ill-trained guitarists; now a lone busker expertly plays a harp taller than he is.

Just as a market economy and entrance into the EC has brought a measure, or the illusion, of prosperity to Spain, and with it a shift in manners and mores, so a rough underside of Spanish life has not been dislodged, nor has unemployment, currently standing at 22 percent. Spain remains, for better or for worse, a man's country. Long overdue, women's liberation in Spain is decades behind the women's movement in Britain, northern Europe, or the United States. Women's presence at the corridas, in the soldiery, and the police may be seen as a gesture of liberation, but it can also be seen as a coarsening of outlook. The abrupt changes in Spain after Franco's death affected sexual mores and speech as in no other country: For sale on the Gran Via, Madrid, is a magazine called *New C——s*, to cite only one example of the pornography that would put to shame the worst of Eighth Avenue in New York or Soho in London. Drugs are bought and sold, muggings, unknown before, are an everyday fact in the cities.

It is stupid and sentimental to wallow in recollections of a possibly better past, but it remains essential to try to assess modern fact against past fact, against the times when men had to work two full-time jobs in order to feed their families, when agricultural workers lived on bread, olives, and on feast days, dried fish. Spain dirty and hungry was not pleasant, but Spain well-fed and prosperous has lost savor and character as it joins the rest of the well-off world. Both that world and Spain, although unknowingly, will surely become impoverished and thinner if they continue to gentrify, to vulgarize, and thus to lose the unique art and spectacle of the *corrida de toros*.

# INDEX